**Intellectual disability: definition,
classification, and systems of supports**

Intellectual Disability

Intellectual Disability

Definition, Classification, and Systems of Supports

The AAIDD Ad Hoc Committee on
Terminology and Classification

11th Edition

American Association
on Intellectual and
Developmental Disabilities

Copyright © 2010 by the American Association on Intellectual and Developmental Disabilities

Published by
American Association on Intellectual and Developmental Disabilities
501 3rd Street, NW, Suite 200
Washington, DC 20001-2760

Printed in the United States of America

Library of Congress Cataloging-in-Publication Data

Intellectual disability : definition, classification, and systems of supports / The AAIDD Ad Hoc Committee on Terminology and Classification.—11th ed.
    p. cm.
 Includes bibliographical references and index.
 ISBN 978-1-935304-04-3 (alk. paper)
 1. Mental retardation—Classification. I. American Association on Intellectual and Developmental Disabilities.
 RC570.C515 2010
 616.85'88—dc22   2009040030

The AAIDD Ad Hoc Committee on Terminology and Classification

Robert L. Schalock, PhD, Chair
Professor Emeritus and Former Chair,
  Department of Psychology
Hastings College
Chewelah, WA

Sharon A. Borthwick-Duffy, PhD
Professor of Special Education, Graduate
  School of Education
University of California, Riverside
Riverside, CA

Valerie J. Bradley, MA
President
Human Services Research Institute
Cambridge MA

Wil H. E. Buntinx, PhD
Director, Buntinx Training &
  Consultancy
Research Assistant Professor, Governor
  Kremers Center
Maastricht University
Maastricht, the Netherlands

David L. Coulter, MD
Associate Professor of Neurology
Harvard Medical School
Institute on Community Inclusion
Children's Hospital
Boston, MA

Ellis M. Craig, PhD
Consultant Psychologist
Self-employed
Mountain City, TX

Sharon C. Gomez, FAAIDD
Quality Enhancement Officer
Evergreen Presbyterian Ministries, Inc.
Lake Charles, LA

Yves Lachapelle, PhD
Professor and Chairman
Self-Determination Support
  Technologies Research Chair
Department of Psychoeducation
Université du Québec à Trois Rivières
Trois Rivières, Québec, Canada

Ruth Luckasson, JD
Distinguished Professor, Regents'
  Professor, and Professor of Special
  Education
Chair, Department of Educational
  Specialties
University of New Mexico
Albuquerque, NM

Alya Reeve, MD
Associate Professor in Psychiatry &
  Neurology, Department of Psychiatry
Co-Investigator, Continuum of Care
  Project
University of New Mexico
Albuquerque, NM

The AAIDD Ad Hoc Committee on Terminology and Classification

continued

Karrie A. Shogren, PhD
Assistant Professor
University of Illinois at
    Urbana–Champaign
Champaign, IL

Martha E. Snell, PhD
Professor of Special Education,
    Coordinator of Special Education,
    Department of Curriculum,
    Instruction, and Special Education
Curry School of Education
University of Virginia
Charlottesville, VA

Scott Spreat, EdD
Vice President for Behavioral Health
Woods Services, Inc.
Langhorne, PA

Marc J. Tassé, PhD
Director, Nisonger Center
Ohio State University
Columbus, OH

James R. Thompson, PhD
Professor, Department of Special
    Education
Illinois State University
Normal, IL

Miguel A. Verdugo-Alonso, PhD
Professor, Director of INICO Research
    Center on Disabilities
Universidad de Salamanca
Salamanca, Spain

Michael L. Wehmeyer, PhD
Professor, Department of Special
    Education
Director, Kansas University Center on
    Developmental Disabilities
Senior Scientist and Associate Director,
    Beach Center on Disability
University of Kansas
Lawrence, KS

Mark H. Yeager, PhD, FAAIDD
Executive Director
TEAAM (Together Enhancing Autism
    Awareness in Mississippi)
Clinical Director
The Yeager Group
Mize, MS

Information as of August 2009

CONTENTS

TABLES

FIGURES

PREFACE

The construct of *intellectual disability* (ID) belongs within the general construct of disability that has evolved over the last 2 decades to emphasize an ecological perspective that focuses on the interaction of the person with his or her environment and the recognition that the systematic application of individualized supports can enhance human functioning. This evolution has been due primarily to an increased understanding of the process of disablement and its amelioration. Major factors in this increased understanding include the research on the social construction of illness and the extensive impact that societal attitudes, roles, and policies have on the ways that individuals experience health disorders (Aronowitz, 1998), the blurring of the historical distinction between biological and social causes of disability (Institute of Medicine, 1991), and the recognition of the multidimensionality of human functioning (Wehmeyer et al., 2008; World Health Organization, 2001). Because of these factors, the construct of disability has evolved from a person-centered trait or characteristic (often referred to as a *deficit*) to a human phenomenon with its genesis in organic and/or social factors. These organic and social factors give rise to functional limitations that reflect an inability or constraint in both personal functioning and performing roles and tasks expected of an individual within a social environment (De Ploy & Gilson, 2004; Hahn & Hegamin, 2001; Oliver, 1996; Rioux, 1997).

The importance of this evolutionary change is that ID is no longer considered entirely an absolute, invariant trait of the person. Rather, this social-ecological construct of ID exemplifies the interaction between the person and his or her environment, focuses on the role that individualized supports can play in enhancing human functioning, and allows for the pursuit and understanding of the principles inherent within the disability movement. These principles include self-worth, subjective well-being, pride, and engagement in political action (Powers, Dinerstein, & Holmes, 2005; Putnam, 2005).

Since its founding in 1876, the American Association on Intellectual and Developmental Disabilities (AAIDD; formerly American Association on Mental Retardation [AAMR]) has led the field of ID in understanding, defining, and classifying the construct that is currently referred to as intellectual disability. Throughout its previous 10 manuals, the Association has fulfilled its responsibility by formulating and disseminating information that reflected the then current understanding of the ID construct and guidelines to use in defining, diagnosing, and classifying individuals with ID. Based on the evolving understanding of the disability and ID construct, in the ninth edition of *Intellectual Disability: Definition, Classification, and Systems of Supports*, Luckasson et al. (1992) (a) expressed the changing understanding that ID (then referred to as mental retardation) is a state of functioning; (b) reformulated what ought to be classified (intensities of supports) as well as how to describe the systems of supports that people with ID require; (c) represented a paradigm shift, from a view of "mental retardation" as an absolute trait expressed solely by an individual to an expression of the interaction between the person with limited intellectual functioning and the environment; and (d) extended the concept of adaptive behavior another step, from a global description to specifying particular adaptive skills.

In the 10th edition of the *Manual*, Luckasson et al. (2002) retained the essential features of the 1992 system, including its functional orientation and supports emphasis; the three diagnostic criteria related to intellectual functioning, adaptive behavior and age of onset, and a strong commitment to a multidimensional classification system. In addition, the 2002 system incorporated (a) a standard deviation criterion to the intellectual and adaptive behavior components; (b) a fifth dimension of human functioning that involves participation, interactions, and social roles; (c) a tripartite model of adaptive behavior focused on conceptual, social, and practical skills; (d) a supports assessment and application model; (e) an assessment framework related to the three functions of diagnosis, classification, and planning individualized supports; (f) an expanded discussion of clinical judgment; and (g) a discussion of the relationship between the 2002 system and other classification systems such as *Diagnostic and Statistical Manual of Mental Disorders* (*DSM-IV*), *International Classification of Diseases* (*ICD-10*), and *International Classification of Functioning, Disability, and Health* (*ICF*).

This 11th edition of the *Manual* continues the organization's commitment to disseminating to the field of ID information and best practice guidelines regarding the diagnosis, classification, and planning of individualized supports to people with ID. The material found in this edition of the *Manual* builds on that presented in the 1992 and 2002 *Manuals* and reflects the AAIDD Terminology and Classification Committee's (hereafter referred to as the committee) belief that knowledge is cumulative and emerges from research-based information and an active dialog among all stakeholders.

Development of the *Manual* was based on two major activities. First, we read and discussed the numerous reviews and critiques of the 2002 *Manual*. These appeared in *The Psychological Record* (2003, *13*, 327–329), *International Journal of Disability, Development, and Education* (2004, *51*[1], 117–122), *Mental Retardation* (2003, *41*[2], 135–140), *Intelligence* (2003, *31*, 425–427), *Journal of Intellectual Disability Research* (2003, *47*[4/5], 400–402), *Journal of Intellectual and Developmental Disabilities* (2003, *28*[3], 310–311), and in the book *What Is MR: Ideas for an Evolving Disability* (Switzky & Greenspan, 2006a). Reviews of the 2002 *Manual* were generally positive, with some concerns expressed by the reviewers about the need to better operationalize a multidimensional classification system; simplify the supports model presented; discuss the ID construct in more detail with regard to people who have ID and higher IQ scores as well as individuals involved in the criminal justice system; clarify relevant measurement errors and their impact on the diagnostic and classification process; develop more valid measures of conceptual, social, and practical adaptive skills; and interpret more thoroughly the published research on diagnosis, classification, and planning individualized supports. We have taken these concerns seriously and have responded to them in both the *Manual* and in the series of articles mentioned next that have been published by the Committee.

The second committee activity has been to publish over the past 2 years a series of articles in *Intellectual and Developmental Disabilities* regarding terminology and definition of ID (Schalock, Luckasson, & Shogren, 2007), the ID construct and its relation to human functioning (Wehmeyer et al., 2008), conceptualizing supports and support needs (Thompson et al., 2009), the characteristics and needs of people with ID who have higher IQ scores (Snell & Luckasson, 2009), and public policy implications of the 11th edition (Shogren et al., 2009). The development and publication of these articles has allowed the committee to integrate current knowledge about the respective topic and share our thinking as we approached the writing of the 11th edition of the *Manual*. In reference to each article, we asked for input from readers prior to the *Manual*'s publication.

These two activities reflected our commitment to build on the previous AAIDD manuals and to integrate into this 11th edition current information and knowledge about the construct of ID and best practice guidelines regarding the diagnosis, classification, and planning of individualized supports for individuals with ID. To that end, readers will find in this *Manual* the following:

- A reaffirmation of the authoritative definition of intellectual disability, including the five assumptions that are essential to the application of the definition (chapter 1)

- A distinction between an operational definition of ID (chapter 1) and a constitutive definition that is consistent with an ecological model of human performance, the multidimensional framework for understanding ID, and the supports paradigm (chapter 2)

- An assessment framework that is focused on the role of assessment in diagnosis, classification, and developing systems of support (chapter 3)

- A detailed discussion of intellectual functioning and its assessment (chapter 4) and adaptive behavior and its assessment (chapter 5); these two chapters contain an update on the conceptualization and measurement of these two prongs of a diagnosis of ID, including best practices regarding cutoff scores, measurement error, and confidence intervals for the person's true score. Additionally, throughout these and related chapters, we stress the need to give equal consideration to IQ and adaptive behavior assessment in the diagnostic process.

- The role of etiological factors in the diagnosis of ID (chapter 6)

- A multidimensional approach to classification stressing that (a) individuals with ID can be grouped or classified for several purposes (such as for conducting research, providing service reimbursement/funding, planning services and supports, and communicating about selected characteristics); and (b) clinicians and other users of the *Manual* must be careful not to use classification information for inappropriate purposes (chapter 7)

- The role of clinical judgment in the diagnosis, classification, and developing systems of supports, including the role of clinical judgment in professional practices and a description of four clinical judgment strategies that when used enhance the validity and precision of the clinician's decision or recommendation (chapter 8)

- An updated approach to the conceptualization and assessment of individual support needs and the provision of supports (chapter 9), prevention as a form of support (chapter 10), and the components of community-based mental and physical health-related supports (chapter 11)
- A detailed discussion of persons with ID with higher IQ scores (chapter 12)
- Implications of the AAIDD System as presented in this 11th edition of the *Manual* for public policy (chapter 13), education (chapter 14), and support provider organizations (chapter 15)
- A glossary that provides current definitions of the major terms and concepts used in the *Manual*
- A complete bibliography of all references used in the development of the *Manual*. The thoroughness of these references reflects our commitment to formulating best practices on the basis of research-based information.

Throughout the *Manual*, the term intellectual disability is used. As discussed more fully in Schalock, Luckasson, & Shogren (2007), the term *ID* (a) reflects the changed construct of disability described by AAIDD (Buntinx, 2006; Luckasson et al., 2002; World Health Organization, 2001); (b) aligns better with current professional practices that focus on functional behaviors and contextual factors; (c) provides a logical basis for an individualized supports provision due to its basis in a social-ecological framework; (d) is less offensive to persons with the disability; and (e) is more consistent with international terminology, including journal titles, published research, and organization names. We also stipulate, consistent with the President's Committee for People With Intellectual Disabilities (2004), that the term *ID* covers the same population of individuals who were diagnosed previously with mental retardation in number, kind, level, type, and duration of the disability and the need of people with this disability for individualized services and supports; and every individual who is or was eligible for a diagnosis of mental retardation is eligible for a diagnosis of ID.

Robert L. Schalock, PhD
On behalf of the AAIDD Terminology and Classification Committee
June 2009

DEFINITION OF INTELLECTUAL DISABILITY

Intellectual disability is characterized by significant limitations both in intellectual functioning and in adaptive behavior as expressed in conceptual, social, and practical adaptive skills. This disability originates before age 18. The following five assumptions are essential to the application of this definition:

1. Limitations in present functioning must be considered within the context of community environments typical of the individual's age peers and culture.
2. Valid assessment considers cultural and linguistic diversity as well as differences in communication, sensory, motor, and behavioral factors.
3. Within an individual, limitations often coexist with strengths.
4. An important purpose of describing limitations is to develop a profile of needed supports.
5. With appropriate personalized supports over a sustained period, the life functioning of the person with intellectual disability generally will improve.

PART I

UNDERSTANDING INTELLECTUAL DISABILITY AND ITS ASSESSMENT

OVERVIEW

The term *intellectual disability* (ID) is used throughout this *Manual* to replace the previously used term *mental retardation*. The term ID is preferred because it (a) better reflects the changed construct of disability that is described more fully in chapter 2, (b) aligns better with current professional practices that focus on functional behaviors and contextual factors, (c) provides a logical basis for understanding supports provision due to its basis in a social-ecological framework, (d) is less offensive to persons with disabilities, and (e) is more consistent with international terminology.

The purpose of the following three chapters is to assist readers in understanding ID and its assessment. To that end, readers will find in these three chapters a discussion of the following:

- The historical approaches to defining ID
- The current definition of ID and five assumptions essential to the application of the definition
- The historical consistency of the three essential elements of ID: significant limitations in intellectual functioning, significant limitations in adaptive behavior, and early age of onset
- How the construct's boundaries (i.e., cutoff scores) have been operationalized historically
- A multidimensional model of human functioning (intellectual abilities, adaptive behavior, health, participation, and context)
- The contextual basis of individualized supports
- An assessment framework organized around three clinical functions: diagnosis, classification, and planning supports
- The assessment criteria required to achieve specific assessment purposes

CHAPTER 1

DEFINITION OF INTELLECTUAL DISABILITY

> **Intellectual disability is characterized by significant limitations both in intellectual functioning and in adaptive behavior as expressed in conceptual, social, and practical adaptive skills. This disability originates before age 18.**

OVERVIEW

Defining refers to precisely explaining the term and establishing the meaning and boundaries of the term. Significant consequences can result from the way a term is defined. As discussed by Gross and Hahn (2004), Luckasson and Reeve (2001), and Stowe, Turnbull, and Sublet (2006), a definition can make someone eligible or ineligible for services, subjected to something or not subjected to it (e.g., involuntary commitment), exempted from something or not exempted (e.g., from the death penalty), included or not included (as to protections against discrimination and equal opportunity), and/or entitled or not entitled (e.g., as to Social Security benefits or other financial benefits). Our purpose in this chapter is to review briefly the historical approaches to defining *intellectual disability* (ID), present the current definition of ID and the assumptions that are essential to the application of the definition, discuss the historical consistency in regard to the three criteria used to operationally define the construct, and summarize how the boundaries of the construct have been operationalized over the past 50 years.

HISTORICAL APPROACHES TO DEFINING INTELLECTUAL DISABILITY

Historically, four broad approaches (i.e., social, clinical, intellectual, and dual-criterion) have been used to define the construct now referred to as ID. Remnants of these four approaches are still evident in current discussions regarding who is (or should be) diagnosed as an individual with an ID (see, for example, Switzky & Greenspan, 2006a, 2006b).

Social Approach

Historically, persons were defined or identified as having ID because they failed to adapt socially to their environment. Because an emphasis on intelligence and the role of intelligent people in society was to come later, the oldest historical definitional approach focused on social behavior and the natural behavioral prototype (Doll, 1941; Goodey, 2006; Greenspan, 2006a, 2006b).

Clinical Approach

With the rise of the medical model, the definitional focus shifted to one's symptom complex and clinical syndrome. This approach did not negate the social criterion, but it gradually shifted toward a more medical model that included an increase in the relative role of organicity, heredity, and pathology and led to a call for segregation (De Kraai, 2002; Devlieger, Rusch, & Pfeiffer, 2003).

Intellectual Approach

With the emergence of intelligence as a viable construct and the rise of the mental testing movement, the approach changed to an emphasis on intellectual functioning as measured by an intelligence test and reflected in an IQ score. This emphasis led to the emergence of IQ-based statistical norms as a way to both define the group and classify individuals within it (Devlieger, 2003).

Dual-Criterion Approach

The first formal attempt to systematically use both intellectual functioning and adaptive behavior to define the class was found in the 1959 American Association on Mental Deficiency (AAMD) *Manual* (Heber, 1959), in which *mental retardation* was defined as referring to subaverage general intellectual functioning that originates during the developmental period and is associated with impairments in maturation, learning, and social adjustment. In the 1961 AAMD *Manual* (Heber, 1961), maturation, learning, and social adjustment were folded into a single, largely undefined new term, *adaptive behavior*, that has been used in all subsequent AAMR manuals. The dual-criterion approach also has included age of onset as an accompanying element.

CURRENT DEFINITION AND ASSUMPTIONS

The authoritative definition of ID is that of the AAIDD (previously the AAMR). The definition in the 2002 AAMR *Manual* (Luckasson et al., 2002, p. 1), which remains in effect in this 11th edition of the *Manual*, is shown here with a minor edit that substitutes the term ID for mental retardation.

> Intellectual disability is characterized by significant limitations both in intellectual functioning and in adaptive behavior as expressed in conceptual, social, and practical adaptive skills. This disability originates before age 18.

Assumptions are an explicit part of the definition because they clarify the context from which the definition arises and indicate how the definition must be applied. Thus, the definition of ID cannot stand alone. The following five assumptions, which are essential to the application of the definition of ID, are described more fully as follows:

Assumption 1: "Limitations in present functioning must be considered within the context of community environments typical of the individual's age peers and culture." This means that the standards against which the individual's functioning are compared are typical community-based environments, not environments that are isolated or segregated by ability. Typical community environments include homes, neighborhoods, schools, businesses, and other environments in which people of similar age ordinarily live, play, work, and interact.

Assumption 2: "Valid assessment considers cultural and linguistic diversity as well as differences in communication, sensory, motor, and behavioral factors." This means that in order for assessment to be meaningful, it must take into account the individual's diversity and unique responses. The individual's culture or ethnicity (including language spoken at home), nonverbal communication, and customs that might influence assessment results, must be considered in making a valid assessment.

Assumption 3: "Within an individual, limitations often coexist with strengths." This means that people with ID are complex human beings who likely have certain gifts as well as limitations. Like all people, they often do some things better than others. Individuals may have capabilities and strengths that are independent of their ID (e.g., strengths in social or physical capabilities, some adaptive skill areas, or one aspect of an adaptive skill in which they otherwise show an overall limitation).

Assumption 4: "An important purpose of describing limitations is to develop a profile of needed supports." This means that merely analyzing someone's limitations is not enough and that specifying limitations should be a team's first step in developing a description of the supports the individual needs in order to improve his or her functioning. Labeling someone with the term ID should lead to a benefit, such as a profile of needed supports.

Assumption 5: "With appropriate personalized supports over a sustained period, the life functioning of the person with ID generally will improve." This means that if appropriate personalized supports are provided to an individual with ID, improved functioning should result. A lack of improvement in functioning can serve as a basis for reevaluating the profile of needed supports. In rare circumstances, however, even appropriate supports may merely maintain functioning or stop or limit regression. The important point is that the old stereotype that people with ID never improve is incorrect. Improvement in functioning should be expected from appropriate supports, except in rare cases.

DEFINITIONAL CONSISTENCY

Although the term or name has changed over time (see, for example, Bach, 2007; I. Brown, 2007; Wright & Digby, 1996), an analysis of the United States–based definitions used over the last 50 or more years shows that the three essential elements of ID—limitations in intellectual functioning, behavioral limitations in adapting to environmental demands, and early age of onset—have not changed substantially (Schalock, Luckasson, & Shogren, 2007). A summary of this analysis is presented in Table 1.1 (history of definition) and Table 1.2 (age of onset criterion).

TABLE I.I

Historical Definitions of Mental Retardation as Formulated by the American Association on Mental Retardation (AAMR) and the American Psychiatric Association (APA)

American Association on Mental Retardation
1959 (Heber): Mental retardation refers to subaverage general intellectual functioning that originates during the developmental period and is associated with impairment in one or more of the following: (1) maturation, (2) learning, (3) social adjustment. (p. 3)
1961 (Heber): Mental retardation refers to subaverage general intellectual functioning that originates during the developmental period and is associated with impairment in adaptive behavior. (p. 3)
1973 (Grossman): Mental retardation refers to significantly subaverage general intellectual functioning existing concurrently with deficits in adaptive behavior, and manifested during the developmental period. (p. 1)
1983 (Grossman): Same as 1973. (p. 1)
1992 (Luckasson et al.): Mental retardation refers to substantial limitations in present functioning. It is characterized by significantly subaverage intellectual functioning, *existing concurrently with* related limitations in two or more of the following applicable adaptive skill areas: communication, self-care, home living, social skills, community use, self-direction, health and safety, functional academics, leisure, and work. Mental retardation manifests before age 18. (p. 1)
2002 (Luckasson et al.): Mental retardation is a disability characterized by significant limitations both in intellectual functioning and in adaptive behavior as expressed in conceptual, social, and practical adaptive skills. This disability originates before age 18. (p. 1)
American Psychiatric Association (*Diagnostic and Statistical Manuals*)
1968 (*DSM-II*): Mental retardation refers to subnormal general intellectual functioning that originates during the developmental period and is associated with impairment of either learning and social adjustment or maturation, or both. (These disorders were classified under "chronic brain syndrome with mental deficiency" and "mental deficiency" in *DSM-I* [American Psychiatric Association, 1952, p. 14].)
1980 (*DSM-III*): The essential features are: (1) significantly subaverage general intellectual functioning, (2) resulting in, or associated with, deficits or impairments in adaptive behavior, (3) with onset before the age of 18. (p. 36)
1987 (*DSM-III-R*): The essential features of this disorder are: (1) significantly subaverage general intellectual functioning, accompanied by (2) significant deficits or impairments in adaptive functioning, with (3) onset before age of 18. (p. 28)

TABLE 1.1 (*continued*)

1994 (*DSM-IV*): The essential feature of mental retardation is significantly subaverage general intellectual functioning (Criterion A) that is accompanied by significant limitations in adaptive functioning in at least two of the following skill areas: communication, self-care, home living, social/interpersonal skills, use of community resources, self-direction, functional academic skills, work, leisure, health, and safety (Criterion B). The onset must occur before age 18 years (Criterion C). Mental retardation has many different etiologies and may be seen as a final common pathway of various pathological processes that affect the functioning of the central nervous system. (p. 39)
2000 (*DSM-TR*): Same as 1994. (p. 41)

TABLE 1.2

Age of Onset Criterion

Tredgold (1908): A state of mental defect from birth, or from an early age, due to incomplete cerebral development. (p. 2)
Tredgold (1937): A state of incomplete mental development. (p. 4)
Doll (1941): A state of social incompetence, obtained at maturity, or likely to obtain at maturity, resulting from developmental arrest of constitutional origin. (p. 215)
Heber (1959, 1961): . . . which originates during the developmental period (i.e., birth through approximately 16 years). (p. 3)
Grossman (1973): . . . manifested during the developmental period (upper age limit at 18 years). (p. 11)
Grossman (1983): . . . manifested during the developmental period (period of time between conception and the 18th birthday). (p. 1)
Luckasson et al. (1992): Mental retardation manifests before age 18. (p. 1)
Luckasson et al. (2002): This disability originates before age 18. (p. 1)

Consistency is also reflected in related concepts and definitions not shown in Tables 1.1 and 1.2. For example, Scheerenberger (1983) reported that the major elements (intellectual deficits, problems coping with the demands of everyday life, and onset during the developmental period) common to the current definition were used by professionals in the United States as early as 1900. Similarly, the National Research Council (2002, pp. 1–5) reported that the first formal AAMR/AAIDD definition of the phenomenon in 1910 defined such persons as being feebleminded, with development arrested at an early age, or as evidenced by an inability to manage the demands of daily life or keep up with peers. Analogously, the Individuals With Disabilities Education Improvement Act of 2004 defines mental retardation as significantly subaverage general intellectual functioning existing concurrently with deficits in adaptive behavior and manifested during the developmental period that adversely affects a child's educational performance.

Construct's Boundaries

Table 1.3 summarizes how the boundaries (i.e., cutoff scores) have been operationalized in the AAMR/AAIDD manuals. Since 1959, two essential points are evident in these operationalizations. First, standard deviations have been used to establish the boundaries of ID. Second, the cutoff criterion, based on approximately two standard deviations from a population mean, pertained primarily to the IQ prong; however, as of the 2002 AAMR *Manual*, a corresponding cutoff criterion was established for the adaptive behavior prong.

Table 1.3
Cutoff Criteria Associated With Establishing the Boundaries of ID

Intellectual Functioning Cutoff Criteria
1959 (Heber): Less than one standard deviation below the population mean of the age group involved on measures of general intellectual functioning (p. 3)
1961 (Heber): Greater than one standard deviation below the population mean (p. 3)
1973 (Grossman): Two or more standard deviations below the population mean (p. 11)
1983 (Grossman): IQ of 70 or below on standardized measures of intelligence; upper limit is intended as a guideline and could be extended to 75 or more (p. 11)
1992 (Luckasson et al.): IQ standard score of approximately 70 to 75 or below, based on assessment that includes one or more individually administered general intelligence tests (p. 5)
2002 (Luckasson et al.): Approximately two standard deviations below the mean, considering the standard error of measurement for the specific assessment instruments used and the instruments' strengths and limitations (p. 58)

Adaptive Behavior Cutoff Criteria
2002 (Luckasson et al.): Performance that is at least two standard deviations below the mean of either (a) one of the following three types of adaptive behavior: conceptual, social, or practical or (b) an overall score on a standardized measure of conceptual, social, and practical skills (p. 76)

Tables 1.1, 1.2, and 1.3 show clearly how both the definition of ID and its operationalization have remained consistent over time. The minor changes that have occurred reflect three phenomena: (a) advances in understanding intellectual functioning and adaptive behavior; (b) advances in measurement theory and strategies that permit the use of statistical procedures to control for measurement error (standard error of measurement), practice effects, and normative changes over time; and (c) the essential role of clinical judgment in designing the evaluation, selecting the assessment instruments, and interpreting the results (Schalock & Luckasson, 2005; Schalock, Luckasson, & Shogren, 2007; see also chapter 8, this volume).

The historical consistency just summarized supports the trend in the field and the conclusion of the major organizations that regardless of the term used to name this disability, the same population has been described. This conclusion is the same as that drawn by the President's Committee for People With Intellectual Disabilities (2004), which stated,

> The PCPID [President's Committee for People With Intellectual Disabilities] considers the terms mental retardation and intellectual disabilities to be synonymous, covering the same population in number, kind, level, type and duration of the disability, and the need by individuals for specific services and supports. Thus, The American Association on Mental Retardation's definition for "mental retardation" serves as the definition for "intellectual disabilities." (p. 3)

This conclusion is critical because of the essential role that the term mental retardation/ID plays in public policy. For example, in the United States, a diagnosis of mental retardation/ID is commonly used to determine eligibility under state and federal disability programs such as Individuals With Disabilities Education Improvement Act of 2004, Social Security Disability Insurance, and Medicaid Home and Community Based Waiver. In addition, the term mental retardation/ID is typically still used in many states in relation to citizenship and legal status, civil and criminal justice, early care and education, training and employment, income support, health care, and housing and zoning (Schroeder, Gertz, & Velazquez, 2002).

SUMMARY

Defining refers to precisely explaining a term and establishing the term's meaning and boundaries. As defined in this *Manual*, ID is characterized by significant limitations both in intellectual functioning and in adaptive behavior as expressed in conceptual, social, and practical adaptive skills. This disability originates before age 18. As discussed earlier in the chapter, the following five assumptions are essential to the application of this definition: (1) limitations in present functioning must be considered within the context of community environments typical of the individual's age peers and culture; (2) valid assessment considers cultural and linguistic diversity as well as differences in communication, sensory, motor, and behavioral factors; (3) within an individual, limitations often coexist with strengths; (4) an important purpose of describing limitations is to develop a profile of needed supports; and (5) with appropriate personalized supports over a sustained period, the life functioning of the person with ID generally will improve.

The definition of ID found in this *Manual* is based on three criteria: significant limitations in both intellectual functioning and adaptive behavior as expressed in conceptual, social, and practical adaptive skills, and age of onset before age 18 years. Although the term or name has changed over time, these three criteria have not changed substantially over the last 50 years. Since 1959, the construct's boundaries in regard to intellectual functioning have been established on the basis of standard deviations from a population mean; since the 2002 *Manual*, this is also true for the adaptive behavior criterion. This historical consistency supports the trend in the field and the conclusion of the major organizations that regardless of the term (ID or mental retardation) used to name this disability, the same population has been described. More specifically, the term ID covers the same population of individuals who were diagnosed previously with mental retardation in number, kind, level, type, and duration of the disability and the need by people with this disability for individualized services and supports. Furthermore, every individual who is or was eligible for a diagnosis of mental retardation is eligible for a diagnosis of ID.

CHAPTER 2

MULTIDIMENSIONAL FRAMEWORK FOR UNDERSTANDING INTELLECTUAL DISABILITY

> A multidimensional framework for understanding intellectual disability depicts how human functioning and the manifestation of intellectual disability involve the dynamic, reciprocal engagement among intellectual ability, adaptive behavior, health, participation, context, and individualized supports.

OVERVIEW

There are two approaches one can use in defining a construct such as *intellectual disability* (ID). The first, which was the approach used in chapter 1, is focused on the operations with which the construct can be observed and measured (i.e., an operational definition of ID). As discussed in chapter 1, we use three criteria to operationally define ID: significant limitations both in intellectual functioning and in adaptive behavior as expressed in conceptual, social, and practical adaptive skills, and age of onset before age 18. This operational definition is essential in tasks related to diagnosis and classification.

The second approach, which is the focus of this chapter, is to define the construct in relation to other constructs (i.e., a *constitutive definition of ID*). This second approach helps to better understand the theoretical underpinnings of the construct of ID. In a related publication (Wehmeyer et al., 2008), we discussed the significant differences between the construct that underlies the term ID and the construct underlying the term *mental retardation*. The major difference is in regard to where the disability resides: the former construct (mental retardation) viewed the disability as a defect within the person, whereas the current construct (ID) views the disability as the fit between the person's capacities and the context in which the person is to function. The term mental retardation referred to a condition internal to the person (e.g., slowness of mind); ID refers to a state of functioning, not a condition. Both constructions, however, see the condition (as in mental retardation) or the state of functioning (as in ID) as best defined in terms of limitations in typical human functioning.

In this chapter, we use a constitutive definition of ID that defines ID in terms of limitations in human functioning, conceptualizes disability within an ecological and multidimensional perspective, and emphasizes the significant role that individualized supports play in improving human functioning. The three purposes of this chapter are to

(a) present the conceptual framework of human functioning used throughout the *Manual*, (b) describe in detail the five dimensions of human functioning, and (c) introduce readers to the concept of individualized supports as an effective way to enhance human functioning. As discussed throughout the chapter, a multidimensional framework for understanding ID results in a broader conceptualization of the phenomenon, an appreciation of the multidimensionality of behavior, and an emphasis on the person's need for individualized supports.

CONCEPTUAL FRAMEWORK OF HUMAN FUNCTIONING

A multidimensional model of human functioning was first proposed by AAIDD (formerly AAMR) in the 1992 *Manual* (Luckasson et al., 1992) and further refined in the 2002 *Manual* (Luckasson et al., 2002). A further refinement is depicted in Figure 2.1. As shown in the figure, the conceptual framework of human functioning has two major components: five dimensions (intellectual abilities, adaptive behavior, health, participation,

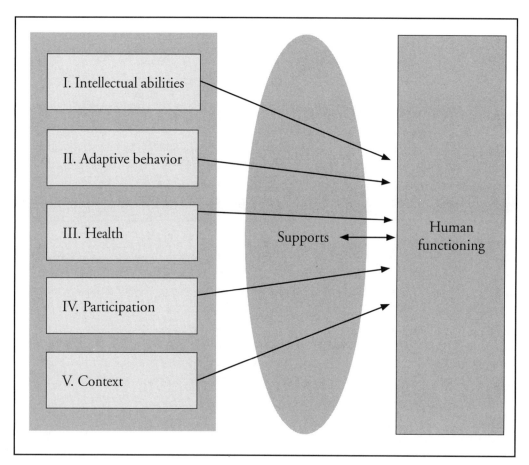

Figure 2.1. Conceptual framework of human functioning.

and context) and a depiction of the role that supports play in human functioning. This framework of human functioning recognizes that the manifestation of ID involves the dynamic, reciprocal engagement among intellectual ability, adaptive behavior, health, participation, context, and individualized supports.

The conceptual framework of human functioning depicted in Figure 2.1 is consistent with the International Classification of Functioning, Disability, and Health (ICF) model proposed by the World Health Organization (WHO; Buntinx, 2006; World Health Organization, 2001). According to this model, the term *human functioning* is an umbrella term for all life activities and encompasses body structures and functions, personal activities, and participation, which in turn are influenced by one's health and environmental or contextual factors.

Limitations in functioning are labeled a "disability" that can result from problem(s) in body structures and functions and personal activities. Furthermore, the ICF domains of *body functions* (impaired intellectual functioning) and of *activities* (limitations in adaptive behavior) refer to the diagnostic criteria specified in the operational definition of ID presented in chapter 1.

DIMENSION I: INTELLECTUAL ABILITIES

Intelligence is a general mental ability. It includes reasoning, planning, solving problems, thinking abstractly, comprehending complex ideas, learning quickly, and learning from experience (Gottfredson, 1997). As reflected in this definition, intelligence is not merely book learning, a narrow academic skill, or test-taking smarts. Rather, it reflects a broader and deeper capacity for comprehending our surroundings—catching on, making sense of things, or figuring out what to do. Thus, the concept of intelligence represents an attempt to clarify, organize, and explain the fact that individuals differ in their ability to understand complex ideas, to adapt effectively to their environments, to learn from experience, to engage in various forms of reasoning, and to overcome obstacles by thinking and communicating (Neisser et al., 1996). This understanding of intelligence was first adopted within the AAMR/AAIDD terminology and classification manuals by Grossman in 1983. It is also consistent with the ICF definition of *intellectual functions* as general mental functions required to understand and constructively integrate the various mental functions, including all cognitive functions and their development over the life span (World Health Organization, 2001, section b 117). Readers are referred to chapter 4 for a detailed discussion of intellectual functioning and its assessment.

DIMENSION II: ADAPTIVE BEHAVIOR

Adaptive behavior is the collection of conceptual, social, and practical skills that have been learned and are performed by people in their everyday lives. The concept of adaptive behavior (as expressed in conceptual, social, and practical adaptive skills) is a continuation of the historical attention given to adaptive behavior in the diagnosis of MR/ID

(Schalock, Luckasson, & Shogren, 2007). The concept of adaptive skills implies an array of competencies and provides the foundation to three key points: (a) the assessment of adaptive behavior is based on an individual's typical performance during daily routines and changing circumstances, not to maximum performance; (b) adaptive skill limitations often coexist with strengths in other adaptive skill areas; and (c) a person's strengths and limitations in adaptive skills should be documented within the context of ordinary community environments typical of the person's age peers and tied to the person's individualized needs for support. Readers are referred to chapter 5 for a detailed discussion of adaptive behavior and its assessment.

DIMENSION III: HEALTH

The World Health Organization (1999) defined *health* as a state of complete physical, mental, and social well-being. Health is a component of an integrated understanding of individual functioning because the health condition of an individual can affect his or her functioning directly or indirectly in each or all of the other four dimensions of human functioning. Health problems are disorders, diseases, or injuries and are classified in the *International Statistical Classification of Diseases and Related Health Problems—ICD-10* (World Health Organization, 1999).

For people with ID, the effects of health and mental health on functioning range from greatly facilitating to greatly inhibiting. Some individuals enjoy robust health with no significant activity limitations, which allows them to participate fully in social roles such as work, recreation, or leisure activities. On the other hand, some people have a variety of significant health limitations, such as epilepsy or cerebral palsy, that greatly impair body functioning in areas such as mobility and nutrition and that severely restrict personal activities and social participation. Similarly, some individuals may have activity and other limitations related to mental illness. Most individuals with ID are somewhere in between these extremes. Readers are referred to chapter 11 for a detailed discussion of mental and physical health-related supports.

DIMENSION IV: PARTICIPATION

Participation, which is the performance of people in actual activities in social life domains, is related to the functioning of the individual in society. Participation in everyday activities is important for an individual's learning and is a central feature of development-in-context perspectives of human growth and development (Bronfenbrenner, 1999; Dunst, Bruder, Trivette, & Hamby, 2006).

Participation refers to roles and interactions in the areas of home living, work, education, leisure, spiritual, and cultural activities. It also includes social roles that are valid activities considered normative for a specific age group. Participation is best reflected in the direct observation of engagement and the degree of involvement in everyday activities.

In the assessment of the level of one's participation, the individual's strengths and limitations in each of the following areas can be evaluated using direct observation of everyday activities:

- Participation in activities, events, and organizations
- Interactions with friends, family, peers, and neighbors
- Social roles in regard to home, school, community, work, leisure, and recreation

DIMENSION V: CONTEXT

Context describes the interrelated conditions within which people live their everyday lives. Context, as used in this *Manual* (see especially Figure 13.2), represents an ecological perspective that involves at least three different levels (Bronfenbrenner, 1979): (a) the immediate social setting including the person, family, and/or advocate(s) (microsystem); (b) the neighborhood, community, or organizations providing education or habilitation services or supports (mesosystem); and (c) the overarching patterns of culture, society, larger populations, country, or sociopolitical influences (macrosystem). These various environments are important to persons with ID because they frequently determine what the person is doing, where he or she is doing it, when the person is doing it, and with whom.

Contextual factors include environmental factors and personal factors that represent the complete background of an individual's life (see Guscia, Ekberg, Harries, & Kirby, 2006; World Health Organization, 2001, p. 10). They may have an impact on the individual and thus need to be considered in the evaluation of human functioning.

- *Environmental factors* make up the physical, social, and attitudinal environment in which people live and conduct their lives. Environmental factors interact with personal factors and thereby impact human functioning. For example, positive employee attitudes and accessibility ramps act as facilitators when contributing to an adaptive behavior such as working. On the other hand, barriers such as inaccessible buildings or negative attitudes hinder human functioning.
- *Personal factors* are characteristics of a person, such as gender, race, age, motivation, lifestyle, habits, upbringing, coping styles, social background, educational level, past and current life events, character style, and individual psychological assets. All or any of these characteristics may play a role in the manifestation of a disability. They are composed of features of the person that are not part of a health condition or health state.

The assessment of contextual factors requires a focus on the person's education, living, work, recreation/leisure, safety, material comfort, financial security, civic activities, and spiritual life. In the assessment of contextual factors, a person's strengths and limitations in each of the following areas can be made based on observation or interviews:

- Immediate surroundings (microsystem) factors, such as the family, advocate, or direct supporter
- Community and neighborhood (mesosystem) factors, such as community, home, residential services, surrounding area, support organizations
- Society (macrosystem) factors, such as culture, country, sociopolitical trends

SUPPORTS

Human functioning is typically enhanced through the use of individualized supports. As defined and discussed more fully in chapter 9, *supports* are "resources and strategies that aim to promote the development, education, interests, and personal well-being of a person and that enhance individual functioning."

Contextual Basis of Supports

Contextualism, or the context within which supports are given, is a critical concept in understanding the current use of supports, the supports paradigm, and the influence of external factors on one's functioning. Contextualism has three central themes (Luckasson et al., 2002, p. 149): (a) milieu, circumstances, environment, or perspective within which behavior occurs are important; (b) reality is ongoing and changing and involves the environment being transformed by its members, who are, in turn, transformed by the environment; and (c) the person is an active determiner of their development and functioning. These three themes are evident in the ecological and egalitarian bases of supports that are discussed more fully in chapters 9 through 15.

Ecological Basis of Supports

There is clear evidence that human functioning is facilitated by the congruence between individuals and their environments. Facilitating such congruence involves determining the profile and intensity of needed supports for a particular person and providing the supports necessary to enhance human functioning. This social-ecological model is consistent with the current concept of ID that views the disabling process as a relationship among pathology, impairments, and one's environment (Institute of Medicine, 1991; Luckasson et al., 1992, 2002; World Health Organization, 2001).

Egalitarian Basis of Supports

Egalitarianism is the belief in human equality, especially with respect to social, political, and economic rights. Since the 1960s, we have seen the emergence of the egalitarian movement from both a legal and service delivery perspective. Legally, we have seen that people with ID have the right to free and appropriate public education, community-based services, and freedom from discrimination solely on the basis of their disability. Programmatically, we have seen the egalitarian movement reflected in person-centered planning, self-advocacy and personal empowerment, and an emphasis on person-referenced outcomes. The net result of these legal and service-delivery trends has been to stress the role that appropriate supports play in enhancing human functioning.

SUMMARY

Intellectual disability refers to a particular state of functioning that begins in childhood, is multidimensional, and is affected positively by individualized supports. As discussed in this chapter, it includes the structure and expectations of the systems within which individuals function and interact: micro-, meso-, and macrosystems. Thus, a comprehensive and correct understanding of the ID construct requires a multidimensional and ecological approach that reflects the interaction of the individual and his or her environment.

To that end, in this chapter we have focused on the multidimensional nature of ID and human functioning as opposed to the trait or "defect of the mind" conception reflected in the previously used term, mental retardation. The advantages to understanding the multidimensional nature of ID are that it (a) recognizes the vast biological and social complexities associated with ID (Baumeister, 2006; Switzky & Greenspan, 2006a); (b) captures the essential characteristics of a person with this disability (Simeonsson, Granlund, & Bjorck-Akesson, 2006); (c) establishes an ecological (Person × Environment) framework for supports provision (Thompson et al., 2009); (d) provides a solid conceptual basis to differentiate between persons with ID and those with closely related developmental disabilities (Thompson & Wehmeyer, 2008); and (e) recognizes that the manifestation of ID involves the dynamic, reciprocal engagement among intellectual ability, adaptive behavior, health, participation, context, and individualized supports (Wehmeyer et al., 2008).

CHAPTER 3

ROLE OF ASSESSMENT IN DIAGNOSIS, CLASSIFICATION, AND SYSTEMS OF SUPPORTS

> **Assessment in the field of intellectual disability is conducted in order to diagnose a disability, classify by disability characteristics, and plan for individualized needed supports. In order to achieve specific assessment purposes, three criteria need to be met: (a) the assessment tools and process should match the purpose for assessment, (b) the assessment findings should be as valid as possible, and (c) the results should be both useful and purposefully applied.**

OVERVIEW

Assessment in the field of *intellectual disability* (ID) involves systematically collecting information for decision making and communication related to three assessment functions: diagnosis, classification, and planning individualized supports. Within each of these functions, professionals conduct assessments for a variety of specific purposes. For example, a diagnosis might determine an individual's eligibility for services or legal protection, or it might establish whether a person could be included in a research sample. Some assessment measures, such as intelligence tests or adaptive behavior measures, are useful for more than one purpose but generally not for all three assessment functions.

This chapter has two purposes: first, to describe a framework for assessing individuals with ID; and second, to review several criteria for high quality assessment. If assessment information is to benefit people with an ID, it is necessary that these criteria be met.

ASSESSMENT FRAMEWORK

In 2002, AAIDD proposed an assessment framework that was organized around the three functions of diagnosis, classification, and planning supports (Lukasson et al., 2002). An updated version of this framework is shown in Table 3.1. The intent of the framework is to illustrate that assessment tools and results may be useful for some purposes but not other purposes. For example, an earlier AAIDD *Manual* (Luckasson et al., 1992) was critical of the often used classification categories of mild, moderate, severe, and profound "levels of mental retardation" because these categories, based only on an intelligence test score, were too often used as profiles to make decisions about support needs. This stated concern was misinterpreted by some to mean that AAIDD was opposed to IQ classification for *any* purpose. Although classification by IQ subgroups might be appropriate for a research study in which measured intelligence is a relevant variable, it is not useful for decisions about residential or educational placement. Instead, such classification decisions should be based on more meaningful assessment information and planning procedures related to the purpose of developing support systems.

As shown in Table 3.1, assessment in the field of ID is conducted in order to diagnose a disability, classify by relevant characteristics, and plan for an individual's needed supports. As shown in the second column, each broad assessment function can be purposefully directed to take certain actions. The third column illustrates examples of assessment measures, tools, and methods that are needed to conduct assessments associated with different purposes. For diagnosis, certain assessment tools are required, while other assessment purposes typically necessitate different measures, tools, and assessment methods.

Assessing to Diagnose Intellectual Disability

Intellectual disability is diagnosed using assessment information obtained from standardized and individually administered instruments that assess intellectual functioning and adaptive behavior (along with the criterion that age of onset is documented). If criteria for a diagnosis of ID are met, the diagnosis may be applied to achieve several focused purposes, including, but not limited to, establishing the presence of the disability in an individual and confirming an individual's eligibility for services, benefits, and legal protections. Chapters 4 and 5 provide specific guidelines and recommendations for the assessment of intelligence and adaptive behavior, respectively.

Assessing to Classify

Information about individuals with ID (or the individuals themselves) can be grouped or classified for several purposes, such as conducting research, providing service reimbursement/funding, developing services and supports, and communicating about selected characteristics. As discussed in chapter 7, clinicians and other users of this *Manual* should select classification systems that are consistent with a specific purpose and must be careful not to use classification information for inappropriate purposes. For example, a clinician may classify adults with ID by their adaptive behavior levels if this information contributes to an agency's systematic way of determining caregiving reimbursement rates; but adaptive behavior levels should not guide programming content and work choice options. Multiple classification systems are available based on the assessment of adaptive behavior, intellectual functioning, educational requirements, and individual support needs. To prevent inappropriate grouping of individuals with ID, classification systems

TABLE 3.1
Framework for Assessment

Assessment function	Specific purpose	Examples of measures, tools, and assessment methods[a]
Diagnosis	Establish presence or absence of intellectual disability Establish eligibility for services Establish eligibility for benefits Establish eligibility for legal protections	• Intelligence tests • Adaptive behavior scales • Documented age of onset • Developmental measures • Social history and educational records
Classification	Classify for intensity of needed support(s) Classify for research purposes Classify by selected characteristics Classify for special education supports Classify for reimbursement/funding	• Support needs intensity scales • Levels of adaptive behavior • IQ ranges or levels • Environmental assessment • Etiology-risk factor systems • Mental health measures • Benefit categories
Planning and developing a systems of supports	Support to enhance human functioning Support to improve outcomes Support to help implement person's choices Support to assure human rights	• Person-centered planning • Self-appraisal • Ecological inventory • Developmental tests • Speech/language, motor, sensory assessment • Achievement tests • Support needs intensity scales • Functional behavioral assessment • Behavior support plan • Family centered support plan • IFSP, IEP, ITP[b] • Self-directed plan

[a] Column 2 purposes are not parallel to Column 3 examples.
[b] IFSP = Individualized Family Support Plan, IEP = Individualized Education Program, ITP = Individualized Transition Plan.

that lead to similar services, placements, or other outcomes for individuals in particular subcategories must be based on strong evidence that the classification system used will be beneficial to every person in the group.

Assessing for Planning and Developing Supports

Planning is undertaken by teams comprised of people with different types of expertise in order to meet an individual's needs in different life domains (e.g., education, behavior support, safety requirements, medical support), to improve specific outcomes, to help implement individual choices, and to assure human rights. As discussed more fully in chapters 9 and 14, the individual planning process focuses on a specific aspect of improving human functioning or enhancing personal outcomes. The planning process should integrate assessment information obtained from standardized and informal measures of individual support needs, person-centered planning, and other input from knowledgeable informants. When plans identify needed supports that are not currently available, the team should locate and obtain the supports by communicating with relevant agencies, using the assessment findings as evidence of need.

ASSESSMENT CRITERIA

In order to achieve specific assessment purposes, three criteria need to be met: (a) the assessment tools and process should match the purpose for assessment, (b) the assessment findings should be as valid as possible, and (c) the results should be both useful and purposefully applied.

Match Between Assessment Purpose and Process

Examiners or teams need to identify the assessment function (diagnosis, classification, or support planning), understand the specific purpose of the assessment, and then select the assessment tools and methods suited to achieve that purpose for a given individual. When there is a match between purpose and procedure, assessment information that is gathered is relevant to decision making.

Validity

Achieving the criterion of validity depends somewhat on the assessment purpose and measures chosen as well as on the accuracy with which the assessment is conducted. Accuracy of assessment for a given individual requires that those conducting the psychological and educational assessments do the following:

- Adhere to standards of their relevant professions regarding the assessment of intellectual functioning and adaptive behavior, such as those standards published by the American Educational Research Association (1999) and the American Psychological Association (1992, 1999, 2002).

- Take into account such factors as the individual's culture, language, and any physical or other disabilities that may affect the validity of the assessment.
- Obtain data from multiple sources. Relevant data should be obtained from service professionals, record review, interview, or observation.
- Use appropriate norms. The norms used to interpret information from the standardized instrument used to determine the presence or absence of ID must be current and must include members of the person's age and cultural/ethnic group.
- Use knowledgeable informants. When informant data are the basis of an assessment (such as in assessment with an adaptive behavior measure, an ecological inventory, or a functional behavioral assessment), the informant must be knowledgeable of the person being assessed and have observed and interacted with the person across different community environments over time.

Benefit

Assessment findings must be of some benefit to the individual being assessed or to the population of individuals with ID. Key components of this third criterion include (a) the assessment process is logical, legal (i.e., follows Institutional Review Board [IRB] procedures), sequential, and transparent; (b) key stakeholders are involved; and (c) the assessment information obtained is timely, relevant to the purpose, and clearly reported (Schalock & Luckasson, 2005). Particularly when assessment is directed toward support planning, its benefit or usefulness depends on assessment teams applying assessment data to make decisions about support, to implement action plans, and to devise ways to assess outcomes so decisions are evaluated and needed improvements made.

SUMMARY

Assessment provides data from which to make recommendations or decisions related to the diagnosis, classification, and/or supports planning for individuals with ID. In this chapter we described an assessment framework with three broad functions: diagnosis, classification, and planning and developing supports. Good decisions regarding assessment conducted for diagnosis, classification, and supports planning and development depend, in part, on the quality of the assessment tool, process, and results. Regardless of the broad function or the specific purpose for assessment, the assessment findings should meet three broad criteria: reflect a match between assessment purpose and process used, be valid, and have potential benefit to the individual or others with ID.

PART II

DIAGNOSIS AND CLASSIFICATION OF INTELLECTUAL DISABILITY

OVERVIEW

A diagnosis of *intellectual disability* (ID) involves meeting three criteria: (a) significant limitations in intellectual functioning, (b) significant limitations in adaptive behavior, and (c) age of onset before age 18. As discussed more fully in Schalock, Luckasson, and Shogren (2007), there has been considerable consistency in these three criteria—and their operational definitions—for the last 50 years. As discussed more fully in chapters 4 and 5, the operational definitions of the first and second criteria are as follows:

- *Intellectual functioning*: an IQ score that is approximately two standard deviations below the mean, considering the standard error of measurement for the specific assessment instruments used and the instruments' strengths and limitations
- *Adaptive behavior*: performance on a standardized measure of adaptive behavior that is normed on the general population including people with and without ID that is approximately two standard deviations below the mean of either (a) one of the following three types of adaptive behavior: conceptual, social, and practical or (b) an overall score on a standardized measure of conceptual, social, and practical skills

The third criterion, *age of onset*, refers to the age at which the disability began. The purpose of the age of onset criterion is to distinguish ID from other forms of disability that may occur later in life. Intellectual disability typically originates close to the time of birth—either during fetal development, the birth process, or soon after birth. Sometimes, however, especially when the etiology of the disability indicates progressive damage (such as malnutrition) or damage related to an acquired disease or injury (such as infection or traumatic brain injury), the condition may originate later. Thus, disability does not necessarily have to have been formally identified, but it must have originated during the developmental period. The early onset criterion is apparent in the earliest formulation of the definition of the disability. As shown in Table 1.2, there has been very little change in the age of onset criterion (generally before age 18) over the last 50 years.

One may analyze the age of onset from both a neurological perspective and a social policy perspective. Neurologically, the primary time of brain development and change is the prenatal, infancy, and childhood years, although considerable change occurs during the teen years and thereafter. Thus, from a neurological perspective, 18 is generous for manifestation. From a social policy perspective, one currently finds both ages 18 and 21 used as the upper limit. Although there is historical consistency in the use of age 18, the criterion of 21 is found in the Developmental Disabilities Act of 1990 (although it too originally used the age of 18; Thompson & Wehmeyer, 2008). Although this discrepancy can cause some confusion, it is our position that 18 is still the best upper limit due to the following: (a) extending to the age of 21 may change the number of people eligible for diagnosis and thus impact prevalence rates because the class would include individuals with other cognitive disabilities (e.g., traumatic brain injury [TBI] and mental illness); (b) extending to age 21 would not be helpful in accurately diagnosing individuals who have not been diagnosed before 18 because any examination would most likely refer to school records to determine how the student was functioning at that time; (c) retaining age 18 is consistent with diagnostic practices in many countries (e.g., throughout Europe and the Pacific Rim); and (d) maintaining the current criterion of "originates before age 18" leaves open the possibility that when an accurate diagnosis of ID was not made during the developmental period, a retrospective diagnosis may be necessary in some situations (see chapter 8).

In the following five chapters, we discuss in detail factors impacting diagnostic best practices. These are an understanding of (a) intellectual functioning and its assessment (chapter 4), (b) adaptive behavior and its assessment (chapter 5), (c) the role of etiological factors in the diagnosis of ID (chapter 6), (d) a multidimensional approach to classification (chapter 7), and (e) the role of clinical judgment in diagnosis, classification, and developing systems of supports (chapter 8). Throughout these five chapters, readers will also find a discussion of best practices guidelines regarding the diagnosis and classification of ID. Chief among these guidelines are the following:

- A diagnosis of ID is based on three criteria: significant limitations in intellectual functioning and adaptive behavior as expressed in conceptual, social, and practical skills, and age of onset before age 18.

- ID is diagnosed using assessment information obtained from standardized and individually administered instruments that assess intellectual functioning and adaptive behavior.

- A valid diagnosis of ID is based on multiple data points that not only include giving equal consideration to significant limitations in adaptive behavior and intellectual functioning but also require evaluating the pattern of test scores and factors that affect the standard error of measurement for the standardized assessment instruments used.

- If the diagnostic criteria are met, the diagnosis may be applied to achieve several focused purposes, including, but not limited to, establishing the presence of the disability in an individual and confirming an individual's eligibility for services, benefits, and legal protections.

- Information about individuals with ID (or individuals themselves) can be grouped or classified for several purposes, such as providing service reimbursement/funding, developing individualized services and supports, conducting research, and/or communicating about selected characteristics.

- Clinicians and other users of this manual should select among multidimensional classification systems, consistent with a specific purpose. Additionally, one must be careful not to use classification information for inappropriate purposes.

- To prevent unsuitable grouping of individuals with ID, classification system(s) that lead to similar services, placements, or other outcomes for individuals in particular subcategories, must be based on strong evidence that the classification system(s) employed will be beneficial to every person in the group.

- Clinical judgment is essential, and a higher level of clinical judgment is frequently required in complex diagnostic and classification situations in which the complexity of the person's functioning precludes standardized assessment alone, legal restrictions significantly reduce opportunities to observe and assess the person, historical information is missing and cannot be obtained, or there are serious questions about the validity of the data. *Clinical judgment* is defined as a special type of judgment rooted in a high level of clinical expertise and experience and judgment that emerges directly from extensive training, experience with the person, and extensive data. The purpose of clinical judgment and the use of clinical judgment strategies is to enhance the quality, validity, and precision of the clinician's decision or recommendation in a particular case.

- A retrospective diagnosis should be based on multiple data points that not only involve giving equal consideration to adaptive behavior and intelligence but also require evaluating the pattern of test scores and factors that affect scores obtained from the assessment instruments used as the time of the assessment(s). If indicated, it might also be necessary to develop a contemporary assessment in order to show similarities and changes in functioning over the life span.

- If there is inconsistency in data sets or obtained information, clinicians need to explore the possible reasons for these differences, including mistakes, poorly trained examiner(s), improper selection of tests, administration of the same test too close in time, administering different editions of the same test and not using the most recent version, and/or not acknowledging the effects of personal characteristics and environmental factors that can affect test results.

CHAPTER 4

INTELLECTUAL FUNCTIONING AND ITS ASSESSMENT

> For purposes of diagnosis, intellectual functioning is currently best conceptualized and captured by a general factor of intelligence. Intelligence is a general mental ability. It includes reasoning, planning, solving problems, thinking abstractly, comprehending complex ideas, learning quickly, and learning from experience. The "significant limitations in intellectual functioning" criterion for a diagnosis of intellectual disability is an IQ score that is approximately two standard deviations below the mean, considering the standard error of measurement for the specific instruments used and the instruments' strengths and limitations.

OVERVIEW

The multidimensional model of human functioning presented in Figure 2.1 includes intellectual abilities as one of the five dimensions of human functioning. Intellectual functioning, which is a broader term than either intellectual abilities or intelligence, reflects the fact that what is considered intelligent behavior is dependent upon other dimensions of human functioning: the adaptive behavior that one exhibits, the person's mental and physical health status, the opportunity to participate in major life activities, and the context within which people live their everyday lives. Thus, as discussed throughout this chapter, commonly used measures/indices of intelligence need to be interpreted within a broader context than a single IQ score.

Although the primary focus in this chapter is on intelligence and its assessment, it is important that readers of this manual should note the following implications of intelligence on the multidimensionality of ID:

- Limitations in intelligence should be considered in light of four other dimensions of human functioning: adaptive behavior, health, participation, and context.
- The measurement of intelligence may have different relevance, depending on whether it is considered for purposes of diagnosis or classification.
- Although far from perfect, intellectual functioning is currently best represented by IQ scores when they are obtained from appropriate, standardized and individually administered assessment instruments.

The assessment of intellectual functioning is essential to making a diagnosis of ID, as virtually all historical definitions of ID (formerly mental retardation) make reference to significantly subaverage intellectual functioning as one of the diagnostic criteria. Our three purposes in this chapter are to present discussions of (a) the definition and nature of intelligence, (b) the operational definition of significant limitations in intellectual functioning, and (c) challenging issues and related guidelines regarding the measurement of intelligence and the interpretation of IQ scores.

DEFINITION AND NATURE OF INTELLIGENCE

Individuals vary in their ability to understand complexities and reason, adapt to the environment, and use thought to solve problems (Neisser et al., 1996). Although reasoning, adaptation, comprehension, and thinking are somewhat descriptive of intelligence, the construct itself has successfully eluded a definition that is acceptable to everyone. Over the past century, three broad conceptual frameworks have been used in an attempt to better define the construct of intelligence: intelligence as a single (i.e., unifactorial) trait; intelligence as a multitrait, hierarchical phenomenon; or intelligence as a multidimensional construct.

Intelligence as a Single Trait

Because so many of the available measures of cognitive ability were highly correlated, Spearman (1927) concluded that the relationship among these various cognitive ability measures could be described as a single factor of general intelligence (i.e., g). Most of the more commonly used individual tests of intelligence, such as the Wechsler family of scales and the Stanford-Binet Intelligence Scale, 4th edition (SBIS-4; Thorndike, Hagen, & Sattler, 1986a), provide metrics of this g factor. Although Thurstone (1938) was initially unable to replicate the results of Spearman's work, he later acknowledged that there was an error in his factor analytic calculations. When this miscalculation was corrected, Thurstone also obtained Spearman's general factor of intelligence (see Carroll, 1997). In general, this general factor framework is currently the most widely accepted conceptualization of intelligence (Gottfredson, 1997).

Multitrait Hierarchical Phenomenon

Some theorists conceptualize intelligence as a hierarchical structure, with g at the apex, supported by various more specialized cognitive abilities. Carroll (1993) reviewed hundreds of intelligence test factor analysis studies published between the 1920s and the 1990s. His analysis yielded a three strata hierarchical model, with the g factor at the apex of a pyramidal structure. In Carroll's model, there were approximately 60 discrete narrow abilities at the base of the pyramid. These narrow cognitive abilities were highly correlated and were further factor analyzed into the 10 broader abilities that formed the second stratum of the hierarchy. Finally, these 10 broader abilities were submitted to factor analysis, which yielded a single factor of *g*.

Multiple Intelligences

Critics (e.g., Ceci, 1990; H. Gardner, 1983; Gould, 1978) of the above two conceptual frameworks noted that the reliance on a single metric of intelligence ignores a number of important areas of mental ability. Gardner argued that most tests of intelligence assess only linguistics, logic, and some aspects of spatial intelligence; other forms and types of intelligence are largely ignored. He went on to note that the paper and pencil format of the typical intelligence test further narrows the focus of intelligence testing to those things that lend themselves to paper and pencil testing.

Recent theories of multiple intelligence have proposed anywhere from two to eight types of intelligence (see Cattell, 1963; Das, Naglieri, & Kirby, 1994; H. Gardner, 1983; Greenspan, 1981). A brief summary of the main theories of multiple intelligences follows.

Cattell (1963) and Horn and Cattell (1966) identified two main factors explaining intellectual ability: *crystallized intelligence* (*gc*) and *fluid intelligence* (*gf*). Crystallized intelligence was defined as those more global activities, such as knowledge and information, that were gained by the individual through life experiences and education. Fluid intelligence was explained in reference to abilities in reasoning and memory. Furthermore, Cattell defined *gc* as a stable trait, whereas *gf* may, in fact, decrease with age.

H. Gardner (1983, 1993) posited a theoretical model of multiple intelligences. Initially, his model consisted of seven different intelligences, each tapping distinctive problem-solving and information-processing capabilities and each with its own distinctive developmental trajectory. The original seven intelligences in Gardner's model were linguistic, logical-mathematical, spatial, musical, bodily kinesthetic, interpersonal, and intrapersonal. In 1998, H. Gardner added an eighth independent ability, naturalistic intelligence, to his model. Of Gardner's eight types of intelligence, he claimed that only three (linguistic, logical-mathematical, and spatial) are assessed by contemporary intelligence tests. Gardner (see Chen & Gardner, 1997) advocated for the use of nonstandardized means of assessing the multiple intelligences; he viewed the process as an ongoing one in which personalized assessments in a variety of contexts should be used. The significant criticism remains valid and pertinent that Gardner's multiple intelligences model lacks an empirical base and psychometric validation.

Das et al. (1994) and Naglieri and Das (1997) proposed a four factor model of cognitive processes that underlie intelligence: planning, attention, simultaneous processing, and successive processing. Referred to as the *PASS model*, its origins may be found in the early work of the Russian neurologist Luria. The *planning* process includes self-regulation, analysis and evaluation of situations, and the use of knowledge to solve problems. The *attentional* process involves the regulation of activity, focusing on specific stimuli while inhibiting responses to other less relevant stimuli. *Simultaneous* processing involves the understanding of groupings of stimuli or the identification of commonalities of a grouping of stimuli. *Successive* processing involves the process of grouping a number of stimuli into a linear series that makes sense.

Sternberg (1988) and Sternberg and Detterman (1986) proposed a three factor model of intelligence that they called the triarchic theory of human intelligence. According to Sternberg (1988), the three fundamental aspects of intelligence are *analytical, creative,* and *practical.* Analytic abilities involve the capacity to analyze and be critical of ideas. Creativity is defined as a person's ability to generate novel ideas that offer a significant contribution, and practical intelligence is an individual's ability to convert ideas into practical application and to convince others of their utility. This sort of distinction between academic and practical intelligence has been offered by a number of theorists (cf. Neisser, 1976). Sternberg has also faced the challenge of developing a metric with which to assess each of his proposed aspects of intelligence; to date no such instrument exists.

Greenspan's (1981) model of multiple intelligences, which has some overlap with Sternberg's triarchic model as well as the current definition of adaptive behavior presented in chapter 5 of this manual, has evolved over time. The tripartite model of intelligence proposed by Greenspan and his colleagues (Greenspan, 1997, 2006b; Greenspan & Love, 1997; Greenspan, Switzky, & Granfield, 1996) defined *intelligence* as being composed of conceptual, practical, and social intelligence. *Conceptual intelligence* is essentially equivalent to the single factor of *g*, although Greenspan (1996, 1997) vehemently opposed the position of using only *g* or a unitary IQ score as representing an individual's intellectual abilities. *Practical intelligence* involves the performance of everyday skills that are typically measured by adaptive behavior scales, with *social intelligence* being defined as an individual's social and interpersonal abilities (e.g., moral judgment, empathy, social skills). Gullibility and credulity have been added as critical elements of social intelligence (Greenspan & Granfield, 1992; Greenspan, Loughlin, & Black, 2001).

In summary, many of the aforementioned theories of multiple intelligences have not been validated via standardized and quantifiable measures. H. Gardner's multiple intelligences, with the exception of some useful application in educational settings, continues to remain theoretical. Sternberg failed in his attempts to develop a measure capable of reliably measuring his triarchical model of intelligence. The Greenspan and Sternberg models face the common challenge of operationalizing tasks to quantify the constructs of their tripartite models, particularly in the area of social intelligence.

A single dimension of intelligence continues to garner the most support within the scientific community (Carroll, 1997; Gottfredson, 1997; Hernstein & Murray, 1994). Thus, until such measures of multiple intelligences can be assessed reliably and validly, it is the position of AAIDD that intellectual functioning (as defined at the beginning of this chapter) is best conceptualized and captured by a general factor of intelligence (*g*).

SIGNIFICANT LIMITATIONS IN INTELLECTUAL FUNCTIONING: OPERATIONAL DEFINITION

In this *Manual*, and consistent with the 2002 *Manual* (Luckasson et al., 2002), the intellectual functioning criterion for a diagnosis of ID is approximately two standard deviations below the mean, considering the standard error of measurement for the specific assessment instruments used and the strengths and limitations of the instruments. In reference to this operational definition of significant limitations, consider the following guidance:

- The intent of this definition is not to specify a hard and fast cutoff point/score for meeting the significant limitations in intellectual functioning criterion of ID. Rather, one needs to use clinical judgment in interpreting the obtained score in reference to the test's standard error of measurement, the assessment instrument's strengths and limitations, and other factors such as practice effects, fatigue effects, and age of norms used (see following section). In addition, significant limitations in intellectual functioning is only one of the three criteria used to establish a diagnosis of ID.

- The use of "approximately" reflects the role of clinical judgment in weighing the factors that contribute to the validity and precision of a decision. The term also addresses statistical error and uncertainty inherent in any assessment of human behavior. In that regard, the decision-making process cannot be viewed as only a statistical calculation.

CHALLENGING ISSUES AND RELATED GUIDELINES REGARDING THE MEASUREMENT OF INTELLIGENCE AND THE INTERPRETATION OF IQ SCORES

Just as defining intelligence has proven to be a challenging task, measuring or quantifying intelligence is equally difficult. It is important to note that IQ scores derived from an intelligence test are now developed on the basis of a deviation (from the mean) score and not on the older conception of mental age. Thus, in reference to the significant limitations in intellectual functioning criterion for a diagnosis of ID, a valid diagnosis of ID is based on how far the person's score deviates from the mean on the respective standardized assessment instrument and *not* on the ratio of mental age to chronological age.

There are a number of challenges and psychometric issues related to the measurement of intelligence and the interpretation of IQ scores. Although one potentially can take comfort from the fact that intelligence tests generally have good reliability and have demonstrated validity for some purposes, the typical intelligence test is not without psychometric challenges. In that regard, in this section of the chapter, we discuss 10 challenges and related guidelines regarding the measurement of intelligence and the interpretation of IQ scores: measurement error, test fairness, the Flynn Effect, comparability of scores from different tests, practice effect, the utility of scores at the extreme ends of a distribution, determining a cutoff score, evaluating the role that an IQ score plays in making a diagnosis, assessor credentials, and test selection.

Measurement Error

The results of any psychometric assessment must be evaluated in terms of the accuracy of the instrument used and such is the case with the assessment of intelligence. An IQ score is subject to variability as a function of a number of potential sources of error, including variations in test performance, examiner's behavior, cooperation of test taker, and other personal and environmental factors. Thus, variation in scores may or may not represent the individual's actual or true level of intellectual functioning. The term *standard error of measurement*, which varies by test, subgroup, and age group, is used to quantify this variability and provide a stated statistical confidence interval within which the person's true score falls.

For well-standardized measures of general intellectual functioning, the standard error of measurement is approximately 3 to 5 points. As reported in the respective test's standardization manual, the test's standard error of measurement can be used to establish a statistical confidence interval around the obtained score. From the properties of the normal curve, a range of confidence can be established with parameters of at least one standard error of measurement (i.e., scores of about 66 to 74, 66% probability) or parameters of two standard error of measurement (i.e., scores of about 62 to 78, 95% probability).

Understanding and addressing the test's standard error of measurement is a critical consideration that must be part of any decision concerning a diagnosis of ID that is based, in part, on significant limitations in intellectual functioning. Both AAIDD and the American Psychiatric Association (2000) support the best practice of reporting an IQ score with an associated confidence interval. Both systems rely on the reported standard error of measurement that is derived from the standard deviation of the test and a measure of the test's reliability. Currently, the prevailing best practice standard in test construction, reporting, and interpretation is to use internal consistency measures of reliability (along with the test's standard deviation) to estimate a standard error of measurement. Reporting an IQ score with an associated confidence interval is a critical consideration underlying the appropriate use of intelligence tests and best practices; such reporting must be a part of any decision concerning the diagnosis of ID.

Test Fairness

There are at least two areas in which test fairness may be of particular concern. The first is when tests requiring a verbal response are employed with individuals who have severely limited verbal abilities. In these situations, the test score may underestimate their level of intellectual functioning. The second area involves individuals of diverse ethnicity or culture, who may achieve markedly different results. Readers are referred to chapters 3 and 8 for a discussion of guidelines regarding test selection and test fairness.

The Flynn Effect

Flynn's research (1984, 1987, 2006, 2007) as well as that of others (e.g., Kanaya, Scullin, & Ceci, 2003; Scullin, 2006) found that IQ scores have been increasing from one generation to the next in the United States as well as in all other developed countries for which IQ data are available. This increase in IQ scores over time was called the *Flynn Effect* by Hernstein and Murray (1994). The Flynn Effect refers to the observation (Flynn, 1984) that every restandardization sample for a major intelligence test (e.g., SBIS-4 and Wechsler) from 1932 through 1978 resulted in a mean IQ that tended to increase over time. Flynn (1987) reported that this effect was also observed in samples from other countries. Although the cause of this effect is unknown, Neisser et al. (1996) suggested that potential factors might well be improved nutrition, cultural changes, testing experience, changes in schooling, and changes in child-rearing practices.

The Flynn Effect raises potential challenges for the diagnosis of ID (Kanaya et al., 2003). Because Flynn (1984) reported that mean IQ increases about 0.33 points per year, some investigators (e.g., Flynn, 2006) have suggested that any obtained IQ score should be adjusted 0.33 points for each year the test was administered after the standardization was completed. For example, if the Wechsler Adult Intelligence Scale (WAIS-III; 1997) was used to assess an individual's IQ in July 2005, the population mean on the WAIS-III was set at 100 when it was originally normed in 1995 (published in 1997). However, based on Flynn's data, the population mean on the Full-Scale IQ raises roughly 0.33 points per year; thus the population mean on the WAIS-III Full-Scale IQ corrected for the Flynn Effect would be 103 in 2005 (9 years × 0.33 = 2.9). Hence, using the significant limitations of approximately two standard deviations below the mean, the Full-Scale IQ cutoff would be approximately 73 (plus or minus the standard error of measurement).

There are also data suggesting that the Flynn Effect may not be a purely linear function of time and that the impact of the effect may asymptote or even reverse. Teasdale and Owens (2005), for example, reported on a large sample of Danish males in which the Flynn Effect peaked and subsequently reversed. In a Norwegian sample, Sundet, Barlaug, and Torjussen (2004) reported a slowing and eventual cessation of the Flynn Effect over time. These data would seem to suggest that while the Flynn Effect is evident, how one corrects for it is still a challenging issue.

As discussed in the *User's Guide* (Schalock et al., 2007) that accompanies the 10th edition of this *Manual*, best practices require recognition of a potential Flynn Effect when older editions of an intelligence test (with corresponding older norms) are used in the assessment or interpretation of an IQ score. As suggested in the *User's Guide* (Schalock et al., 2007, pp. 20, 21):

> The main recommendation resulting from this work [regarding the Flynn Effect] is that all intellectual assessment must use a reliable and appropriate individually administered intelligence test. In cases of tests with multiple versions, the most recent version with the most current norms should be used at all times. In cases where a test with aging norms is used, a correction for the age of the norms is warranted.

Comparability of Scores From Different Tests

Not all scores obtained on intelligence tests given to the same person will be identical. Specifically, IQ scores are not expected to be the same across tests, editions of the same test, or time periods (Evans, 1991). A number of studies have revealed significantly different results from appropriately selected tests. For example, Quereshi and Seitz (1994) reported that the Wechsler Preschool and Primary Scale of Intelligence-Revised (WPPSI), Wechsler Intelligence Scale for Children-Revised (WISC-R), and the Wechsler Preschool and Primary Scale of Intelligence-Revised (WPPSI-R) did not yield the same results when used on young children. Highest IQ scores were obtained on the WPPSI and lowest on the WPPSI-R. The SBIS-4 yielded significantly higher scores (by over 14 points) than did the WISC-R for students with lower IQ scores but yielded significantly lower scores for students with higher IQ scores. The two tests yielded similar scores for students with IQ scores between 70 and 90 (Prewett & Matavich, 1992). Scores on the WISC-III were significantly correlated with scores on the SBIS-4 with a population of students with mild mental retardation, but the average IQ on the WISC-III was 8 points lower (Lukens & Hurrell, 1996). Nelson and Dacey (1999) reported that in a sample of adults who had mild to moderate mental retardation an SBIS will yield a significantly lower score than a Wechsler test. Their results were consistent with earlier work published in the Stanford Binet Technical Manual (Thorndike, Hagen, & Sattler, 1986b).

Users of this *Manual* need to be aware of—and sensitive to—potential differences in scores obtained from two different tests. Sources of variation can result from (a) group versus individually administered tests; (b) the purposes for which the test was administered (e.g., administered initially to measure academic achievement but later used to derive an IQ score); (c) the properties of the test (e.g., using two tests with very disparate standard errors of measurement); (d) nonstandardized administration of the assessment instrument(s); (e) test content across different scales and between different age levels on the same scale; (f) scores obtained on verbal versus nonverbal tests; (g) differences in the standardization samples; (h) changes between different editions of the same scale/test; (i) use of an alternative scale as an individual's chronological age increases; and/or (j) variations in the person's abilities or performance.

Practice Effect

The *practice effect* refers to gains in IQ scores on tests of intelligence that result from a person being retested on the same instrument. Kaufman (1994) noted that practice effect can occur when the same individual is retested on a similar instrument. For example, the WAIS-III *Manual* presents data showing the artificial increase in IQ scores when the same instrument is readministered within a short time interval. The WAIS-III *Manual* also reports the average increase between administrations with intervals of 2 to 12 weeks (Wechsler, 1997). For this reason, established clinical practice is to avoid administering the same intelligence test within the same year to the same individual because it will often lead to an overestimate of the examinee's true intelligence.

Extreme Scores

It is generally recognized that a psychometric instrument performs best when used with persons who score within two to three standard deviations of the mean. The diagnosis of ID, however, can involve the assessment of performance at the extreme tail of the IQ distribution (e.g., four to five standard deviations below the mean). Although the *Manual*s for the WISC-IV (Wechsler et al., 2004), WAIS-IV (Wechsler, 2008), and SSIB-4 (Thorndike et al., 1986b) indicate that these instruments can be used to classify ID, all caution about using the respective scale to assess extreme populations, noting that extrapolation was needed to create norm group data for persons who achieve very low scores (such as 25 or below).

We note, in reference to highlighting the fragility of tests for use with individuals who achieve extreme scores, that based on the properties of the normal distribution, the WISC-III standardization sample of 2,200 children would be expected to include only about 50 individuals whose IQ scores fall below 70 across all age groups. If one examines the number of individuals in the normative sample broken down by age strata (5-year-olds, 6-year-olds, etc.) and upon which IQ scores are derived, there may be fewer than three individuals below the cutoff score of 70. Despite these cautions, Sattler (1988) noted the utility of both the Wechsler scales and the SBIS-4 in making the diagnosis of ID. He did, however, mention that neither instrument was designed for use with persons whose test performance yields extremely low or high scores. Although standard practices certainly involve the use of these scales to help in the diagnosis of ID, it must be recognized that extreme scores are more subject to measurement error and are, perhaps, less trustworthy than scores closer to the mean of the test.

This reliance on the interpretation of extreme scores might be of a greater concern if ID were diagnosed solely on the basis of IQ score—which it is not. The three criteria are significant limitations in intellectual functioning, significant limitations in adaptive behavior, and age of onset before age 18. By having the two significant limitations criteria (i.e., significant limitations in intellectual functioning and adaptive behavior, which are given equal consideration) for diagnosing an individual as having ID, there are additional safeguards against falsely identifying an individual as having ID. There are those who would argue that the considerable correlation between IQ scores and adaptive behavior among persons who have ID, in effect, creates a redundant process to ensure better diagnosis. No such safeguards exist, however, for a false negative, a serious problem that demands the field's attention. The problems faced by people who have ID but do not receive the diagnosis of ID can be significant. These individuals are vulnerable to the denial of essential supports and exclusion from eligibility for important protections (see chapter 12).

Determining a Cutoff Score

The significant limitations in intellectual functioning criterion for a diagnosis of ID is an IQ score of approximately two standard deviations below the mean, considering the standard error of measurement for the specific instruments used and the instruments' strengths and limitations. It is clear from this significant limitations criterion used in this *Manual* that AAIDD (just as the American Psychiatric Association, 2000) *does not* intend for a fixed cutoff point to be established for making the diagnosis of ID. Both systems (AAIDD and APA) require clinical judgment regarding how to interpret possible measurement error. Although a fixed cutoff for diagnosing an individual as having ID is not intended, and cannot be justified psychometrically, it has become operational in some states (Greenspan & Switzky, 2006). It must be stressed that the diagnosis of ID is intended to reflect a clinical judgment rather than an actuarial determination. A fixed point cutoff score for ID is not psychometrically justifiable. The choice of an intelligence test will be driven by clinical judgment of the most appropriate instrument. The IQ scores obtained from different intelligence tests themselves are not necessarily equivalent. Given that the diagnostic process involves drawing a line of inclusion/exclusion, it is important to use a range as reflected in the test's standard error of measurement.

Evaluating the Role That an IQ Score Plays in Making a Diagnosis

An IQ score should be reported with confidence intervals rather than a single score. Thus, in evaluating the role that an IQ score plays in making a diagnosis of ID, clinicians should (a) determine what the standard error of measurement is for the particular assessment instrument used, realizing that the standard of measurement is test-specific and is used to establish a statistical confidence interval within which the person's true score falls; (b) interpret the obtained score in reference to the test's standard error of measurement, the assessment instruments' strengths and limitations, and other factors (such as practice effect, fatigue effects, and age or norms used) that determine the size of the error involved in estimating the person's true score; (c) determine whether the assessment process was consistent with the first two assumptions of the definition of ID (see p. 1); (d) use an assessment process based on research-based knowledge, professional ethics, and professional standards (see chapter 8); and (e) assure that within reporting, standard error of measurement is properly addressed.

As discussed in reference to the operational definition of significant limitations in intellectual functioning, the intent of using approximately two standard deviations below the mean is to reflect the role of clinical judgment in weighing the factors that contribute to the validity and precision of a diagnostic decision. The term *approximately* also addresses statistical error and uncertainty inherent in any assessment of human behavior. In that regard, the diagnostic decision-making process cannot be viewed as only a statistical calculation.

Assessor Credentials

The assessment of intellectual functioning is a task that requires specialized professional training. Assessment data should be reported by an examiner experienced with people who have ID; who is qualified in terms of professional and state regulations; and who has met the publisher's guidelines for conducting a thorough, valid psychological evaluation of the individual's intellectual functioning. It is also important for the evaluator to be familiar with the five assumptions essential to the application of the AAIDD definition of ID presented on page 1 of this *Manual*.

Test Selection

For evaluating whether or not a person meets the significant limitations in intellectual functioning criterion for a diagnosis of ID, one should employ an individually administered, standardized instrument that yields a measure of general intellectual functioning. Further, the selection of a specific standardized measure with which to assess intelligence should be based on several individual factors, such as the individual's social, linguistic, and cultural background. Short forms of screening tests are not recommended, and it is critically important to use tests with relatively recent norms. Although the Wechsler and SBIS scales are perhaps the most widely used and accepted measures to assess intelligence, there are clearly circumstances in which neither will be appropriate. This may be because the individual being assessed has cognitive deficits that fall below the floor of the test; has sensory or motor limitations that preclude certain forms of test presentation/response; or is influenced by a variety of cultural, social, ethnic, and language based factors. When this is the case, it may be necessary to select among alternative instruments rather than rely on the more traditional intelligence tests. For example, it may be appropriate to use a test such as the C-TONI (Hamill, Pearson, & Wiederholt, 1997) for individuals who do not speak, and some individuals with greater levels of intellectual impairment may be better assessed with scales such as the Slosson Intelligence Test (Slosson, 1983). When faced with the task of assessing an individual who appears to have profound intellectual impairment, some clinicians rely on the Bayley Scales of Infant Development (Bayley, 1993). This is not an intelligence test but rather a test of the developmental progress of infants. The test correlates moderately well (over 0.70) with the full scale IQ from the WPPSI.

SUMMARY

Intelligence is a general mental capacity that involves several different abilities. Until more robust instruments based upon one or more of the multifactorial theories of intellectual functioning are developed and demonstrated to be psychometrically sound, we will continue to rely on a global (general factor) IQ as a measure of intellectual functioning. *Subaverage intellectual functioning*, defined as approximately two or more standard deviations below the mean of an individually administered, standardized instrument, is a necessary but insufficient criterion to establish a diagnosis of ID. A valid diagnosis of ID requires that the person meets three criteria: significant limitations in intellectual functioning, significant limitations in adaptive behavior, and age of onset before age 18. As discussed in this chapter, the assessment of intellectual functioning must be based on sound procedures and may, at times, require information from multiple sources. Testing should be conducted on an individual basis and be carried out in strict guidance of accepted professional practice.

The three purposes of this chapter have been to discuss the definition and nature of intelligence, the assessment of intelligence, and a number of challenging issues and related guidelines regarding the measurement of intelligence and the interpretation of IQ scores. As mentioned repeatedly in the chapter, significant limitations in intellectual functioning is only one of the three criteria required for a diagnosis of ID. The second criterion, significant limitations in adaptive behavior, is discussed in the following chapter.

Chapter 5

Adaptive Behavior and Its Assessment

> **Adaptive behavior is the collection of conceptual, social, and practical skills that have been learned and are performed by people in their everyday lives.**
> <u>**For the diagnosis of intellectual disability**</u>**, significant limitations in adaptive behavior should be established through the use of standardized measures normed on the general population, including people with disabilities and people without disabilities. On these standardized measures, significant limitations in adaptive behavior are operationally defined as performance that is approximately two standard deviations below the mean of either (a) one of the following three types of adaptive behavior: conceptual, social, or practical or (b) an overall score on a standardized measure of conceptual, social, and practical skills. The assessment instrument's standard error of measurement must be considered when interpreting the individual's obtained scores.**

Overview

The inclusion of the concept of adaptive behavior in the diagnosis of persons with *intellectual disability* (ID) has a long history. Nihira (1999), for example, cited early leaders, such as Itard, Seguin, Voison, and Howe, who referred to signs of ID that included the absence of social competency, a need for skill training, an inability to meet social norms, and difficulty with fending for one's self. Although adaptive behavior did not play a formal role in the diagnosis of ID during the first half of the 20th century, the construct's importance to understanding ID was not completely abandoned. Doll, for example, introduced the Vineland Social Maturity Scale in 1936, an instrument that included 117 items focused on practical skills used in everyday situations.

When the intelligence test, resulting in an IQ score, was introduced in the early 1900s, it was embraced as an efficient and objective means to distinguish individuals with ID from the general population (Scheerenberger, 1983). The intelligence test not only produced a highly reliable score, but because it was normed on the general population, it yielded an unambiguous indicator of how much a person deviated from others. However, dissatisfaction with the IQ score as the sole indicator of ID emerged over time. Among the greatest concerns about intelligence testing was that IQ scores only provided a narrow measure of intellectual functioning related to academic tasks (i.e., linguistic, conceptual, and mathematical abilities and skills), thus ignoring important aspects of intellectual functioning that included social and practical skills. Also, the perception that IQ scores contributed to misdiagnosing children from poor and minority backgrounds shook people's confidence in using the IQ as the sole diagnostic measure (Reschly, Myers, & Hartel, 2002; Scheerenberger, 1983).

As a result of this dissatisfaction, adaptive behavior reemerged in 1959 as one of the three criteria used to diagnose ID. According to Heber in the AAIDD 1959 *Manual on Terminology and Classification*, "measured intelligence cannot be used as the sole criteria of mental retardation [the term in use then] since intelligence test performances do not always correspond to level of deficiency in total adaptation" (pp. 55–56). *Adaptive behavior* was defined by Heber (1959) as

> the effectiveness with which the individual copes with the nature and social demands of his environment. It has two major facets: the degree to which the individual is able to function and maintain himself independently, and the degree to which he meets satisfactorily the culturally-imposed demands of personal and social responsibility. (p. 61)

Grossman (1973, 1983) reaffirmed the importance of adaptive behavior in the diagnosis of ID. Grossman's (1983) definition of adaptive behavior was "the effectiveness or degree with which individuals meet the standards of personal independence and social responsibility expected for his age and cultural group" (p. 1). The importance of adaptive behavior in the diagnosis of ID has been reaffirmed in each of the successive AAIDD *Terminology and Classification Manuals* (Luckasson et al., 1992, 2002).

Both Heber and Grossman recognized the multidimensionality of adaptive behavior and the influence of culture on the assessment of the construct. Heber conceptualized adaptive behavior as consisting of three primary factors: maturation, learning, and social adjustment. These three domains continue to be part of the most current conceptualization of adaptive behavior but are reframed as practical, conceptual, and social skills.

The consensus, based on considerable published research on the factor structure of adaptive behavior (e.g., Harrison & Oakland, 2003; McGrew, Bruininks, & Johnson, 1996; Thompson, McGrew, & Bruininks, 1999), is that adaptive behavior is multidimensional and includes the following:

- *Conceptual skills*: language; reading and writing; and money, time, and number concepts
- *Social skills*: interpersonal skills, social responsibility, self-esteem, gullibility, naïveté (i.e., wariness), follows rules/obeys laws, avoids being victimized, and social problem solving
- *Practical skills*: activities of daily living (personal care), occupational skills, use of money, safety, health care, travel/transportation, schedules/routines, and use of the telephone

In this chapter we discuss the role that adaptive behavior and its assessment plays in the diagnosis of ID. The seven sections of the chapter are (a) key factors to keep in mind when reading the chapter, (b) the assessment of adaptive behavior, (c) the use of standard error of measurement in score interpretation, (d) adaptive behavior versus problem behavior, (e) special considerations in the assessment of adaptive behavior, (f) guidelines for selecting an adaptive behavior instrument, and (g) future considerations. Throughout the chapter, adaptive behavior is defined as the collection of conceptual, social, and practical skills that have been learned and are performed by people in their everyday lives. Material included in the chapter regarding assessment guidelines and the technical adequacy of adaptive behavior assessment instruments is based on the published work of Finlay and Lyons (2002), Greenspan (1999, 2006a), Harrison and Raineri (2008), and Reschly et al. (2002).

KEY FACTORS TO KEEP IN MIND WHEN READING THIS CHAPTER

In this chapter we discuss in more detail the following 10 key factors about adaptive behavior and its assessment that are relevant to a diagnosis of ID:

1. There are three criteria for a diagnosis of ID: significant limitations in intellectual functioning, significant limitations in adaptive behavior, and age of onset before age 18. Adaptive behavior and intellectual functioning should be given equal consideration.
2. Adaptive behavior is a multidomain construct. The domains that have emerged from a long history of factor-analytic studies are consistent with a conceptual model of adaptive behavior that has three general areas of adaptive skills: conceptual, social, and practical.
3. Adaptive behavior as defined in this *Manual* is the collection of conceptual, social, and practical skills that have been learned and are performed by people in their everyday lives.
4. The concept of adaptive skills implies an array of competencies and provides a foundation for three key points: (a) the assessment of adaptive behavior is based on the person's typical (not maximum) performance, (b) adaptive skill limitations often coexist with strengths, and (c) the person's strengths and limitations in adaptive skills should be documented within the context of community and cultural environments typical of the person's age peers and tied to the person's need for individualized supports.
5. Although no existing measure of adaptive behavior completely measures all adaptive behavior skills, most provide domain scores that represent the three domains used in this *Manual*: conceptual, social, and practical. A comprehensive assessment of adaptive behavior will likely include a systematic review of the individual's family history, medical history, school records, employment records (if an adult), other relevant records and information, as well as clinical interviews with a person or persons who know the individual well.

6. For a person with ID, adaptive behavior limitations are generalized across the domains of conceptual, social, and practical skills. However, because subscale scores on adaptive behavior measures are moderately correlated, a generalized deficit is assumed even if the score on only one domain meets the operational criterion of being approximately two standard deviations below the mean. A total score of two standard deviations below the mean from an instrument that measures conceptual, social, and practical skills will also meet the operational definition of a significant limitation in adaptive behavior.

7. It is important to recognize that personal characteristics and environmental factors can present challenges to the assessment of adaptive behavior. These include (a) personal characteristics, such as concurrent sensory, motor, or mental disabilities; fatigue or illness; high anxiety levels; and the person's motivational history of interaction in assessment situations and (b) environmental factors, such as absence of participation in community settings.

8. Problem or maladaptive behavior is not a characteristic or domain of adaptive behavior, although it often influences the acquisition and performance of adaptive skills. The presence of problem behavior(s) is not considered to be a limitation in adaptive behavior, although it may be important in the interpretation of adaptive behavior scores for diagnosis. The distinction between adaptive behavior and problem behavior is discussed later in this chapter.

9. Adaptive behavior must be examined in the context of developmental periods of infancy and early childhood, childhood and early adolescence, late adolescence, and adulthood. A continuing theme is the importance of the developmental relevance of specific skills within the three adaptive areas.

10. It is sometimes necessary to assess the previous functioning of the individual in those situations where a diagnosis of ID becomes relevant. A retrospective diagnosis may be required, for example, when clinicians are involved in determining eligibility for adult rehabilitation services, evaluating individuals for Social Security disability, or evaluating individuals involved in legal processes, such as guardianship petitions, competence determinations, or sentencing eligibility questions. If adaptive behavior assessments are used and reported in the records reviewed, clinicians should weigh the extent to which (a) multiple informants were used and multiple contexts sampled; (b) that limitations in present functioning were considered within the context of community environments typical of the individual's age peers and culture; (c) important social behavioral skills, such as gullibility and naïveté, were assessed; (d) behaviors that are currently viewed as developmentally and socially relevant were included; and (e) adaptive behavior was assessed in reference to typical and actual functioning in the community. The use of previously administered adaptive behavior scales in a retrospective diagnosis should address these five assessment standards.

ASSESSMENT OF ADAPTIVE BEHAVIOR

Use Standardized Measures

Significant limitations in adaptive behavior are established through the use of standardized measures and, like intellectual functioning, significant *limitations in adaptive behavior* are operationally defined as performance that is approximately two standard deviations below the population average on one of the three adaptive skills domains of conceptual, social, or practical. In evaluating the role that an adaptive behavior score—as assessed on a standardized measure—plays in making a diagnosis of ID, clinicians should (a) determine the standard error of measurement (see following section) for the particular assessment instrument used, realizing that the standard error of measurement is test-specific and is used to establish a statistical confidence interval within which the person's true score falls and (b) assure that within reporting, standard error of measurement is properly addressed.

Focus on Typical Performance

The assessment of adaptive behavior focuses on the individual's typical performance and not their best or assumed ability or maximum performance. Thus, what the person typically does, rather than what the individual can do or could do, is assessed when evaluating the individual's adaptive behavior. This is a critical distinction between the assessment of adaptive behavior and the assessment of intellectual functioning, where best or maximal performance is assessed. Individuals with an ID typically demonstrate both strengths and limitations in adaptive behavior. Thus, in the process of diagnosing ID, significant limitations in conceptual, social, or practical adaptive skills is not outweighed by the potential strengths in some adaptive skills.

Use Knowledgeable Respondents

Using standardized adaptive behavior measures to determine significant limitations in adaptive behavior usually involves obtaining information regarding the individual's adaptive behavior from a person or persons who know the individual well. Generally, individuals who act as respondents should be very familiar with the person and have known him/her for some time and have had the opportunity to observe the person function across community settings and times. Very often, these respondents are parents, older siblings, other family members, teachers, employers, and friends. Parents are often the best respondents available because they have known the individual the longest and observed attainment of developmental milestones, maturation, and the achievement of adaptive behavior skills. Because adaptive behavior assessment relies on third party respondents, it is important for clinicians to assess the reliability of any respondent providing adaptive behavior information. Obtaining information from multiple respondents and other relevant sources (e.g., school records, employment history, previous evaluations) is essential to providing corroborating information that provides a comprehensive picture of the individual's functioning.

When Standardized Assessments Cannot Be Used

If a standardized assessment measure cannot be used (e.g., if the assessment cannot be reliably administered per the test's recommended administrative procedures or if there are no reliable respondents to provide adaptive behavior information regarding the assessed person), other sources of adaptive behavior information can be used. In these infrequent cases, other information-gathering methods can be employed, such as direct observation (see chapter 8 for guidelines); review of school records, medical records, and previous psychological evaluations; or interviews with individuals who know the person and have had the opportunity to observe the person in the community but may not be able to provide a comprehensive report regarding the individual's adaptive behavior in order to complete a standardized adaptive behavior scale. In reference to any method used, when a standardized adaptive behavior assessment instrument cannot be used, the following guidelines should be followed:

- Use multiple types and sources of information to obtain convergence of information regarding the individual's limitations in comparison to same-age peers.

- Use reasonable caution when weighing qualitative information obtained from respondents, especially in the presence of conflicting information.

- Interpret results obtained from direct observations of adaptive skills with caution because these may not be reflective of the individual's typical behavior and may be a narrow measure of actual adaptive behavior. For example, having the person screw in a light bulb does not fully capture all aspects of the adaptive behavior of identifying when it is time to change a burnt light bulb, what wattage is needed for the replacement bulb, knowing how to get a replacement bulb, and safely accessing an electrical outlet and replacing the light bulb.

- Use clinical judgment (see chapter 8) to guide the evaluation of the reliability of information provided by respondents as well as possible sources of bias (positive or negative).

- Analyze critically all types of information for accuracy and pertinence. One should also consider the comparison group when determining significant limitations. For example, in some special education programs, a grade of *C* denotes something very different in achievement level than a *C* grade given in a general education classroom.

USE OF STANDARD ERROR OF MEASUREMENT IN SCORE INTERPRETATION

The established procedure in psychological measurement, in which standardized measures are used, is to report results using a statistical confidence interval around the obtained score(s). As discussed in chapter 4, the standard error of measurement, which varies by test, subgroup, and age group, is used to estimate this statistical confidence interval.

For example, the use of plus/minus one standard error of measurement yields a statistical confidence interval (around the obtained score) within which the person's true score will fall 66% of the time; whereas the use of plus/minus two standard error of measurement yields a statistical confidence internal (around the obtained score) in which the person's true score will fall 95% of the time. Thus, an obtained standard score on an adaptive behavior scale should be considered as an approximation that has either a 66% or 95% likelihood of accuracy, depending on the confidence interval used.

ADAPTIVE BEHAVIOR VERSUS PROBLEM BEHAVIOR

Adaptive behavior is conceptually different from maladaptive or problem behavior, even though many adaptive behavior scales contain assessments of problem behavior, maladaptive behavior, or emotional competence (Thompson et al., 1999). Correlational relationships between domains of adaptive and maladaptive behavior are generally low, $r <$ 0.25, with a tendency to be higher in samples of persons with more severe forms of ID (Harrison, 1987). There is general agreement that the presence of clinically significant levels of problem behavior found on adaptive behavior scales does not meet the criterion of significant limitations in adaptive functioning (Greenspan, 1999; Borthwick-Duffy, 2007). Therefore, behaviors that interfere with a person's daily activities, or with the activities of those around him or her, should be considered problem behavior rather than the absence of adaptive behavior. It should also be recognized, however, that the function of inappropriate or maladaptive behavior may be to communicate an individual's needs and, in some cases, may even be considered adaptive. For example, research on the function of behavior problems in persons with severe disabilities (Durand & Crimmins, 1988; Durand & Kishi, 1987) demonstrates that such behavior may be an adaptation judged by others to be undesirable but often represents a response to environmental conditions and, in some cases, a lack of alternative communication skills. In the vast majority of cases, this would not apply to persons with higher levels of intelligence whose diagnosis is in question.

SPECIAL CONSIDERATIONS IN THE ASSESSMENT OF ADAPTIVE BEHAVIOR

Selection of Adaptive Behavior Measures

For the purpose of making a diagnosis or ruling out ID, a comprehensive standardized measure of adaptive behavior should be used in making the determination of the individual's current adaptive behavior functioning in relation to the general population. The selected measure should provide robust standard scores across the three domains of adaptive behavior: conceptual, social, and practical adaptive skills. The preferred adaptive behavior instrument should have current norms developed on a representative sample of the general population. The individual's adaptive behavior should be evaluated using multiple respondents and multiple sources of converging data. Relevant archival data may include medical evaluations, school records, prior psychoeducational evaluations, Social Security Administration records, employment history, and family history.

Technical Adequacy

General issues in the assessment of adaptive behavior derive in large part from those issues that relate to psychological measurement in general (American Educational Research Association, American Psychological Association, and National Council of Measurement in Education, 1999). Therefore, the demonstration of validity, reliability, stability of measures, generalization, prediction, and appropriateness of use are essential technical standards guiding the assessment of adaptive behavior. Although some available scales have been used for many years, longevity alone does not validate a test's results for diagnostic purposes. Many of the available adaptive behavior scales fall short of appropriate standards for norming (Kamphaus, 1987) and clarity of the construct of adaptive behavior (Evans, 1991). On the other hand, several measures have been developed and tested in recent years that do meet the criteria of a good diagnostic assessment instrument. Independent of these scales, a technologically sound adaptive behavior assessment instrument should meet the eight technical standards listed in Table 5.1. New instruments should be evaluated against these eight standards as well.

TABLE 5.1

Technical Standards for Adaptive Behavior Assessment Instruments

- Focus on identifying significant limitations in adaptive behavior for the diagnosis of ID.

- Assess specific dimensions that have emerged from factor analytic studies of adaptive behavior that have indicated that the three primary areas of adaptive behavior are conceptual, social, and practical skills.

- Include measures of some aspects of adaptive behavior that are not currently measured by existing standardized instruments. These aspects include naïveté, gullibility (i.e., wariness), and technology-based skills.

- Contain items that maximally differentiate between individuals with and without ID

- Use item response theory to reliably measure individual levels of performance across the continuum of adaptive skills and ages, with special attention to providing precise information around the cutoff point for determining significant limitations in adaptive behavior.

- Allow the interviewer to probe further those items whose scoring is influenced by the opportunity to perform the behavior or by cultural factors that influence the behavior's expression.

TABLE 5.1 (*continued*)

- Use an interviewer who is a professional (e.g., psychologist, case manager, social worker), one who has training in assessment and direct work experience with people with ID, and one who has had previous assessment experience.

- Use respondents who know the individual being assessed very well and have had the opportunity to observe the person on a daily or weekly basis in a variety of community settings and over an extended period of time. Respondents should be adults and may be selected from family members, friends, teachers, coworkers, employers, direct-support staff, case managers, or other adults who meet the above criteria.

Appropriateness of Measure for the Individual

Not only must professionals select instruments that are technically adequate, they must also be cautious to select ones designed for the particular individual or group (Harrison & Raineri, 2008). The potential user must employ adaptive behavior assessment instruments that are normed within community environments on individuals who are of the same age grouping as the individual being evaluated. Scales normed primarily on persons in segregated settings, including schools, work, or living arrangements, may have validity limited to those contexts that is useful for programming but are not acceptable for diagnostic purposes.

Multimethod Approaches to Measurement

Although every effort must be made to select an instrument that is appropriate to the person being assessed, clinicians must recognize that adaptive behavior instruments are imperfect measures of personal competence that distinguish persons with and without ID as they face the everyday demands of life. For example, credulity and gullibility can provide key information for a diagnosis of ID. Greenspan (1981, 1999, 2006a; Greenspan, Loughlin, & Black, 2001) has long argued that the victimization of people with ID, observed in social and economic exploitation, is a central problem in diagnosing ID. Because there are currently no standardized measures that assess adaptive skills related to credulity and gullibility, these characteristics must be considered in the clinical judgment of adaptive behavior limitations.

Use of Self-Ratings

Self-ratings of individuals—especially those individuals with higher tested IQ scores—may contain a certain degree of bias and should be interpreted with caution when determining an individual's level of adaptive behavior. The following cautions are warranted if self-ratings are used in establishing a diagnosis of ID: (a) persons with higher IQ scores are more likely to mask their deficits and attempt to look more able and typical than they actually are (Edgerton, 1967); (b) "mental retardation" has been a particularly stigmatizing and pejorative label that leads most individuals with this label to fight hard not to be identified as "MR"; (c) ID is a social status that is closely tied to how a person is perceived by peers, family members, and others in the community; and (d) persons with ID typically have a strong acquiescence bias (Finlay & Lyons, 2002) or a bias to please that might lead to erroneous patterns of responding. Based on these considerations, the authors of this *Manual* caution against relying heavily only on the information obtained from the individual himself or herself when assessing adaptive behavior for the purpose of establishing a diagnosis of ID.

Individual's Physical Condition and Mental Health

Individuals who exhibit specific sensory, motor, or communicative limitations present special difficulties for accurate assessment. As a consequence, the evaluation of adaptive skills for an individual who may have vision, hearing, or motor impairments frequently becomes a complex process (Meacham, Kline, Stovall, & Sands, 1987). For example, the assessment of individuals with hearing impairments generally requires a nonverbal instrument, whereas the assessment of persons with visual impairments requires measures that do not include object manipulation or cards or pictures. An individual with severe motor limitations may have quite limited voluntary responses and, therefore, may need to respond via an eye scan or blink. Some individuals may exhibit multiple disabilities, thus compounding the task for the assessment specialist. In addition, some may simply lack test-taking skills. As a consequence, they may refuse to stay seated for the duration of an assessment session or may exhibit a high rate of stereotyped or self-stimulatory behavior. Individuals who rely on nonverbal communication may have difficulty making the requisite responses indicated for a given test. Additional problems may include fatigue, low levels of frustration, motivation, noncompliance, limited comprehension of instructions, drowsiness due to medication, and test anxiety (Evans, 1991; Pollingue, 1987). Finally, and significantly, a general principle is that the test results should not be unduly affected by limitations in receptive or expressive language capabilities. Such limitations may cause the test to be a measure of the problem rather than a valid assessment of adaptive skills.

Identifying Factors That Influence Adaptive Behavior Scores

For purposes of diagnosis, it is also important to identify factors that typically affect the learning or performing of adaptive skills. Some of the more important factors are discussed below.

Opportunities. Opportunities to participate in community life must be considered in decisions about significant limitations in adaptive behavior. A person whose opportunities to learn adaptive skills has been restricted in comparison to same-age peers may have acquisition deficits unrelated to ID. For example, a person with ID who has a lower IQ and who has not been provided opportunities to make purchases is likely to lack the adaptive skills needed for shopping.

Relevant context/environments. Adaptive behavior needs to be evaluated in relation to contexts typical of the individual's age peers. However, in some cases, typical behavior is observed in "atypical" environments. This disconnect must be taken into account in the clinical interpretation of scores. A second issue is that in some contexts raters will have no direct information about the individual's typical performance of a specific behavior or a behavior that occurs in another setting. For example, the Adaptive Behavior Assessment System-II (Harrison & Oakland, 2003) allows the respondent the option to "guess" a rating for a specific behavior that might not have been observed directly by the respondent. Thus, the respondent is providing an estimate of the assessed individual's typical behavior based on their knowledge of the person. The reliability of ratings that are not based on personal observation of typical behavior must be evaluated cautiously. In fact, Harrison and Oakland (2003) recommend a cautious interpretation of any domain in which the respondent "guessed" on more than three items.

Sociocultural considerations. Clinicians considering a diagnosis of ID must take into account the cultural context of the individual. The key challenges are to describe important sociocultural differences and, subsequently, "to evaluate the individual's status in light of expectations and opportunities for the development of various competencies" (Reschly, 1987, p. 53). Behavioral expectations may differ across cultural groups, along with education and training in adaptive skills. Assessments, therefore, must consider relevant ethnic or cultural factors and expectations (Tassé & Craig, 1999). This issue, which some believe is not relevant for basic behaviors contained on adaptive behavior scales (e.g., persons in all ethnic or socioeconomic groups are expected to perform daily living skills with increasing independence as they get older), has received increasing attention. Because it would be impossible to obtain many standardization samples to represent all cultural variations in the United States, this may need to be dealt with in the clinical interpretation of scores rather than the actual scoring procedure. The authors of this *Manual* also strongly discourage any score corrections that are not part of test procedures that attempt to correct for any cultural or socioeconomic factors that are thought to impact the individual's scores on a standardized adaptive behavior scale. Until firmly supported by empirical evidence, we strongly caution against practices such as those recommended by Denkowski and Denkowski (2008).

GUIDELINES FOR SELECTING AN ADAPTIVE BEHAVIOR SCALE FOR THE PURPOSE OF DIAGNOSING ID

Table 5.2 summarizes current best practice guidelines for selecting the best adaptive behavior measure for a particular individual or group. These guidelines should be used in conjunction with those guidelines discussed in the two previous sections on "Assessment

---

TABLE 5.2

Guidelines for Selecting an Adaptive Behavior Assessment Instrument

- Select an instrument that is a comprehensive measure of conceptual, social, and practical adaptive behavior skills and is applicable to the population in question. In that regard, one should (a) read the *User's Manual*; (b) review all components of the instrument; (c) consult with colleagues who may have familiarity with the instrument; and (d) search the literature for research on its usage, particularly as related to validation of its use for the particular setting, population, and purpose in question.

- For the purpose of making or ruling out a diagnosis of ID, the instrument must be normed on the general population, including individuals with and without disabilities. The selected instrument's norms should be current.

- Determine, based on the publisher's specifications and state and professional regulations, who is properly trained to administer the instrument (e.g., instruments that require direct interaction with the client require greater expertise than rating scales completed by others, such as teachers or parents).

- Determine that the assessment instrument has acceptable reliability and established validity for its intended purpose. In this regard, one should read reviews of the instrument in manuals such as the *Mental Measurements Yearbook* or *Test Critiques*.

- Determine whether scoring software has been "error-trapped" to prevent the entering of impossible answers or to control for circumstances such as missing data that may yield errors.

---

of Adaptive Behavior" and "Special Considerations in the Assessment of Adaptive Behavior."

FUTURE CONSIDERATIONS

Currently, adaptive behavior is defined and measured on the basis of the individual's typical present functioning. The person's performance is then compared to the norm of the general population that contains the individual's same-age peers. In that regard, there is some concern that the construct of adaptive behavior may violate some of the postulates of the normal distribution. It is relatively well accepted in the area of intelligence testing that there is a small but stable proportion of the population that falls more than two standard deviations above the population mean (in the genius range). It is, however, more difficult to ascertain a comparable size group of the general population that is greater than two standard deviations above the population mean on standardized measures of adaptive behavior. It is harder to imagine 2% of the population as geniuses when it comes to adaptive behavior. It is possible that one day we will move away from a normative evaluation and explore other methods of assessment strategies to define significant limitations in adaptive behavior.

There is a growing need for research at the intersection of ID determination and forensic science, especially in relation to the measurement of adaptive behavior of individuals living in prisons and for whom it is challenging to assess their typical present adaptive functioning to meet societal demands in the community. Many professionals rely on a retrospective assessment approach to measure the adaptive behavior of these individuals. In addition, it may be relevant one day to broaden the realm of skills measured on adaptive behavior scales to continually evolve with societal expectations. Any changes in how we define, measure, or interpret adaptive behavior should be driven by empirical findings and sound research.

SUMMARY

Our purpose in this chapter was to familiarize readers with current knowledge regarding the factor structure of adaptive behavior and key issues involved in the valid assessment of adaptive behavior. As discussed in the chapter, adaptive behavior is defined as the collection of conceptual, social, and practical skills that have been learned and performed by people in their everyday lives. For the diagnosis of ID, significant limitations in adaptive behavior should be established through the use of standardized measures normed on the general population, including people with disabilities and people without disabilities. On these standardized measures, significant limitations in adaptive behavior is approximately two standard deviations below the mean of either (a) one of the following three types of adaptive behavior: conceptual, social, or practical or (b) an overall score on a standardized measure of conceptual, social, and practical skills.

There are three criteria for a diagnosis of ID: significant limitations in intellectual functioning, significant limitations in adaptive behavior, and age of onset before age 18. Since 1959, these three criteria have been given equal consideration in the diagnostic process. Due to the equal consideration of adaptive behavior and intellectual functioning indices in the diagnosis of ID, it is critical that clinicians be familiar with—and employ—the guidelines discussed in this chapter regarding the assessment of adaptive behavior, the use of standard error of measurement in score interpretation, understanding the distinction between adaptive behavior versus problem behavior, important special considerations in the assessment of adaptive behavior, the technical standards regarding adaptive behavior assessment instruments, and the suggested guidelines for selecting an adaptive behavior instrument. As with the assessment of intellectual functioning, clinical judgment is involved in the interpretation of information regarding the assessment of adaptive behavior and the formulation of a valid diagnosis. Readers are referred to chapter 8 for a detailed discussion of clinical judgment strategies that enhance the validity and precision of the clinician's decision or recommendation.

...HE DIAGNOSIS OF
...Y

...nstruct composed of four categories
...vioral, and educational) that interact
...verall functioning. Diagnostic assess-
...consists of a description of all of the
...lar individual and that contribute to
...potential diagnosis of intellectual dis-
...may be useful, but caution is needed
...ircumstances.

...EW

...nature of the etiology of *intellectual dis-*
...d classified based on biomedical, social,
b..........., and educational risk factors. The five sections of the chapter cover (a) the importance of etiology, (b) the multifactorial nature of etiology, (c) etiologic assessment, (d) etiologic diagnosis and classification, and (e) etiology and performance. These five sections incorporate genetic research advances and research about behaviors that are associated with specific etiologies. Additionally, the system for etiologic diagnosis and classification presented in the chapter is consistent with the multidimensional approach to ID presented in this *Manual* and facilitates the design and implementation of strategies for prevention and support (see chapter 10).

IMPORTANCE OF ETIOLOGY

Consideration of the etiology of ID is important for several reasons. Chief among these are the following:

1. The etiology may be associated with other health-related problems that may influence physical and psychological functioning.

2. The etiology may be treatable, which could permit appropriate treatment to minimize or prevent ID.
3. Accurate information is needed for the design and evaluation of programs to prevent specific etiologies of ID.
4. Comparison of individuals for research, administrative, or clinical purposes may depend on formation of maximally homogeneous groups composed of individuals with the same or similar etiologies.
5. The etiology may be associated with a specific behavioral phenotype that allows anticipation of actual, potential, or future functional support needs.
6. Information about the etiology facilitates genetic counseling and promotes family choice and decision making, including preconception counseling.
7. Individuals and families can be referred to other persons and families with the same etiologic diagnosis for information and support.
8. Knowing the etiology facilitates self-knowledge and life planning for the individual.
9. Understanding the etiology may clarify clinical issues for service providers.
10. Clarification of biomedical, social, behavioral, and educational risk factors that contribute to the etiology offers opportunities for prevention of the disability.

Performing a diagnostic evaluation to determine the etiology may be questioned by some providers. They may argue that the cost of testing is excessive and that the results will not change the individual's treatment. If the parents do not plan to have any more children, they may argue that testing for an inherited disorder is pointless. When the individual with ID is an adult, the parents may no longer have any interest in finding the etiology. Adult service providers may feel that the etiology is irrelevant to the development of the individual's plan of supports and services. These objections can be answered by considering the reasons for establishing the etiology listed earlier, and the cost of diagnostic testing can often be justified in specific situations. For example, knowing that an adult with cognitive decline has Down syndrome should alert the provider to look for hypothyroidism or depression. Knowing that a child with cognitive decline has Angelman syndrome should alert the provider to look for subclinical seizures. Knowing that an individual with new neurological findings has tuberous sclerosis should alert the provider to look for the characteristic brain tumor associated with this diagnosis. Knowing that an adult man has fragile X syndrome should alert the provider to offer genetic testing to the man's sisters who may be carriers and could have affected sons. Knowing that a child has a particular condition allows the family to search the Internet and to contact other families affected by this diagnosis, thereby learning more about it than their health care provider may know. These examples illustrate why testing to establish the etiologic diagnosis may be important for many individuals with ID.

MULTIFACTORIAL NATURE OF ETIOLOGY

In this chapter we build on the approach to etiology described in previous AAMR *Manuals* (Luckasson et al., 1992, 2002). Etiology is conceptualized as a multifactorial construct composed of four categories of risk factors (biomedical, social, behavioral, and educational) that interact across time, including across the life of the individual and across generations from parent to child. This construct replaces prior approaches that divided the etiology of ID into two broad types: ID of biological origin and ID due to psychosocial disadvantage (Grossman, 1983). The two-group approach (biological and cultural-familial) was defended on the basis of developmental theory (Hodapp, Burack, & Zigler, 1990). Different developmental pathways were associated with ID due to identified biological disorders compared to ID for which no organic etiology is apparent (due to cultural-familial factors or psychosocial disadvantage). These researchers recommended a biological or genetic classification of etiology, in which there is either a demonstrated biological cause or there is not. This approach is consistent with the approach presented in this chapter. In fact, the risk factor approach can be seen as a fine-tuning of the developmental (two-group) approach. What was called "ID of biological origin" can be seen as involving individuals for whom biomedical risk factors predominate, while "ID of cultural-familial origin" can be seen as involving individuals for whom social, behavioral, or educational risk factors predominate.

The two-group distinction is often blurred in real life, however. The multiple risk factor approach correctly notes that biomedical risk factors may be present in persons with ID of cultural-familial origin, and social, behavioral, and educational risk factors may be present in persons with ID of biological origin. For example, individuals with the same biomedical genetic etiology often vary widely in functioning, presumably as the result of other modifying risk factors. The multiple risk factor approach to etiology thus is the logical extension of previous work in this area and provides a more comprehensive explanation of the many interacting causes of impaired functioning in persons with ID (Chapman, Scott, & Stanton-Chapman, 2008).

There has been an explosion of new genetic information in the past decade (cf. Butler & Meaney, 2005). This explosion has led some to consider the etiology of ID primarily in genetic terms. The recommendations of the American College of Human Genetics for the etiologic evaluation of ID (Curry, Stevenson, Aughton, & Byrne, 1997) emphasized genetic testing, as did the recommendations of the Committee on Genetics of the American Academy of Pediatrics (Moeschl & Shevell, 2006). The Child Neurology Society's practice parameter on the evaluation of children with global developmental delay (Shevell et al., 2003) also emphasized biomedical causes and included evidence-based recommendations for genetic testing. Although in a recent textbook on ID, Harris (2006) mentions AAIDD's multifactorial risk factor approach presented in the 2002 *Manual* (Luckasson et al.), the author discusses in depth primarily genetic and other biomedical causes.

Clearly, genetics cannot explain the cause of ID in every case. Individuals may be born with perfectly normal DNA and still develop ID due to a birth injury, malnutrition, child abuse, or extreme social deprivation. Understanding the cause of ID in these cases requires consideration of other biomedical, behavioral, and social risk factors. The guidelines reviewed above all note that even the most extensive and up-to-date genetic and biomedical testing will identify an etiology in less than half of all cases. Indeed, even if one could measure the entire genome in patients with ID (which should become feasible within the next 10 years), the results would not explain the cause when ID is due primarily to social or behavioral risk factors. On the other hand, at least one or more of the risk factors shown in Table 6.1 will be found in every case of ID. Thus a multifactorial approach to etiology (which incorporates all of the above genetic and biomedical testing,

TABLE 6.1

Risk Factors for Intellectual Disability

Timing	Biomedical	Social	Behavioral	Educational
Prenatal	1. Chromosomal disorders 2. Single-gene disorders 3. Syndromes 4. Metabolic disorders 5. Cerebral dysgenesis 6. Maternal illnesses 7. Parental age	1. Poverty 2. Maternal malnutrition 3. Domestic violence 4. Lack of access to prenatal care	1. Parental drug use 2. Parental alcohol use 3. Parental smoking 4. Parental immaturity	1. Parental cognitive disability without supports 2. Lack of preparation for parenthood
Perinatal	1. Prematurity 2. Birth injury 3. Neonatal disorders	1. Lack of access to prenatal care	1. Parental rejection of caretaking 2. Parental abandonment of child	1. Lack of medical referral for intervention services at discharge
Postnatal	1. Traumatic brain injury 2. Malnutrition 3. Meningoencephalitis 4. Seizure disorders 5. Degenerative disorders	1. Impaired child-caregiver interaction 2. Lack of adequate stimulation 3. Family poverty 4. Chronic illness in the family 5. Institutionalization	1. Child abuse and neglect 2. Domestic violence 3. Inadequate safety measures 4. Social deprivation 5. Difficult child behaviors	1. Impaired parenting 2. Delayed diagnosis 3. Inadequate early intervention services 4. Inadequate special education services 5. Inadequate family support

as well as consideration of all of the other potential risk factors that might be operative) provides the most thorough way to evaluate the etiology of ID in a particular case.

The multifactorial approach to etiology presented in this chapter expands the list of causal factors in two directions: types of factors and timing of factors. The first direction expands the types or categories of factors into four groupings:

1. *Biomedical*: biologic processes, such as genetic disorders or nutrition
2. *Social*: social and family interaction, such as stimulation and adult responsiveness
3. *Behavioral*: potentially causal behaviors, such as dangerous (injurious) activities or maternal substance abuse
4. *Educational*: availability of educational supports that promote mental development and the development of adaptive skills

The second direction concerns the timing of the occurrence of causal factors according to whether these factors affect the parents of the person with ID, the person with ID, or both. This aspect of causation is termed *intergenerational* to describe the influence of factors present during one generation on the outcome in the next generation. The modern concept of intergenerational effects must be distinguished from the historical concept that ID was related to "weak genes" due to psychosocial, cultural, or familial factors (Scheerenberger, 1983). This modern concept recognizes that reversible environmental factors in the lives of some families may be related to the etiology of ID and stresses that the understanding of these factors should lead to enhanced individual and family supports. Because of the relationship to prevention and supports, these intergenerational effects are considered further in chapter 10 (see Table 10.1 in particular).

Table 6.1 lists risk factors for ID by category and by the time of occurrence of the risk factor in the life of the individual. Unlike classification systems based primarily on biomedical conditions (such as the *ICD-10* [World Health Organization, 1993]), the classification system outlined in Table 6.1 represents a multifactorial approach to the etiology of ID. It incorporates biomedical risk factors but places them in context by including other risk factors that may be of equal or greater importance in determining the individual's level of functioning. The list of risk factors in Table 6.1 is not exclusive and can be expanded as new risk factors are discovered. Research should result in continual revision and updating of these specific risk factors, but the basic structure of the table should be relevant for the foreseeable future.

Because ID is characterized by impaired functioning, its etiology is whatever caused this impairment in functioning. A biomedical risk factor may be present but by itself may not cause ID (as, for example, when a patient with a genetic disorder has average intelligence). Any risk factor causes ID only when it results in impaired functioning sufficient to meet the criteria for a diagnosis of ID as described in this *Manual*. Table 6.1 emphasizes that the impairment of functioning that is present when an individual meets the three criteria for a diagnosis of ID usually reflects the presence of several risk factors that interact over time. Thus, the search for the etiology of ID in a particular individual must consist of a search for all of the risk factors that might have resulted in impaired functioning for that person. This search involves obtaining as much historical medical information as possible, performing psychological and physical examinations, and pursuing sufficient laboratory investigations to consider reasonable possibilities.

ETIOLOGIC ASSESSMENT

Medical History

Diagnostic assessment begins with a complete history and physical examination to uncover all of the potential risk factors that may be present in each of the four categories shown in Table 6.1. The medical history begins at conception and includes detailed information about the prenatal, perinatal, and postnatal periods. Information needed about the prenatal period includes maternal age; parity and health (including maternal infections such as hepatitis, HIV, rubella, cytomegalovirus, group B streptococcus, etc.); the adequacy of maternal nutrition; the amount and quality of prenatal care (including results of prenatal screening, ultrasound examinations, and amniocentesis if performed); maternal use of drugs, alcohol, and other substances; maternal exposure to potential toxins or teratogens (such as lead or radiation); and occurrence of any significant maternal injuries during the pregnancy. Information needed about the perinatal period includes growth status at birth (gestational age at birth, birthweight, length, and head circumference); labor and delivery experiences (including onset, duration, route of delivery, presence of fetal distress prior to delivery, Apgar scores after birth, need for resuscitation); and the occurrence of any neonatal disorders after birth (such as seizures, infections, respiratory distress, brain hemorrhage, and metabolic disorders). Information needed about the postnatal period includes the history of any significant head injuries, infections, seizures, toxic and metabolic disorders (such as lead poisoning), significant malnutrition or growth impairment, and any indication of loss of previously acquired developmental skills that could indicate the presence of a progressive or degenerative disorder or a disorder on the autism spectrum.

A detailed family history is necessary to identify potential genetic etiologies (Curry et al., 1997). A detailed three-generation pedigree is recommended that includes information about the health status, medical and psychological disorders, and level of functioning of all known relatives. In particular, relatives who were affected by conditions that may be associated with ID (such as autism) or who were diagnosed with ID should be noted. Additional records concerning these individuals may be requested to provide further details. The occurrence of ID in other family members does not necessarily imply a genetic mechanism however. Multiple individuals in a family may be affected by fetal alcohol syndrome, for example, or ID in a relative may be due to childhood infections or head trauma. Results of genetic testing performed previously on any relatives should be sought and examined for completeness because testing performed more than 5 to 10 years earlier may have missed conditions diagnosable with current methods.

Psychosocial Evaluation

The psychosocial evaluation includes detailed information about the individual, family, school or work setting, and community or cultural milieu. Information about the psychosocial environment is needed to evaluate possible social, behavioral, and educational risk factors that may have contributed to the occurrence of ID. When an intergenerational perspective is used, information is needed about the parents' social, educational, and psychological history. Information is also needed about the structure, stability, and functioning of the immediate and extended family of the person with ID. Information about the roles and expectations of the person with ID and relatives within the extended community or culture may also be useful. The sociocultural milieu in which the individual develops is important because it may influence the psychosocial environment, including the local community; the country of origin; and specific ethnic, cultural, or religious factors that may affect environmental experiences and interactions.

The developmental history of the individual with ID includes early milestones, such as the age when the person started walking or talking. The age at entry into the educational system, the adequacy of the educational experience, and the duration of formal education should also be noted. The occurrence of other mental disorders, such as attention deficit/hyperactivity disorder, specific learning disability, or anxiety disorder should be noted because this may provide clues to a behavioral phenotype associated with a specific etiology.

Evaluation of the psychosocial environment may not yield any relevant information about causal factors in a particular individual. Even when the etiology appears straightforward, however, psychosocial factors may prove to be contributory. Reflecting the multiple risk factor approach to causation, known biomedical factors may be affected by social, behavioral, or educational factors. The ultimate etiology of ID in such cases reflects the interaction of all of these factors. For example, whether or not an individual with fetal alcohol syndrome develops ID may be influenced by environmental influences in early childhood, and the individual's level of functioning will likely reflect the adequacy of educational interventions.

Physical Examination

The physical examination serves several distinct purposes. The usual purpose is to assist in the diagnosis of a medical problem, such as pneumonia or back pain, for which the individual has sought attention and that may require specific medical treatment. The purpose considered in this chapter is to assist in the identification of the etiology of ID. A single physical examination may serve both purposes, but the conceptual distinction between them needs to be retained.

The physical examination may provide evidence of an obvious etiology, such as Down syndrome. More often, however, it will provide only supportive evidence for an etiology suspected from other data (such as spastic diplegia associated with a history of premature birth), or it will not provide any useful information about etiology at all. For most individuals whose etiology of ID is obscure or unknown, the physical examination may well be normal or noncontributory. Thus, one cannot expect to discover the etiology solely from the physical examination in most cases. Physical examination is necessary, but it is only one component in the diagnostic assessment and in many cases will not be the most important component.

Information needed from the physical examination includes measurements of growth (height, weight, and head circumference), which should be plotted against age on graphs that are appropriate for the individual's status. Additional measurement of specific body structures (such as the distance between the eyes or the arm span) also may be useful (Jones, 2005). Detailed examination of the head, eyes, ears, nose, throat, glands, heart, blood vessels, lungs, abdomen, genitalia, spine, extremities, and skin should be conducted. Any major or minor malformations should be noted (Jones, 2005). A detailed neurologic examination should include evaluation for any focal or generalized deficits (Campbell, 2005). Specific neurologic findings will rarely indicate the etiology directly, but certain findings (such as hypotonia, tremor, or ataxia) could be important clues to the etiology. In some instances, examination of parents, siblings, or other relatives may be helpful.

Laboratory Investigation

All of the data derived from the history and physical examination is then evaluated to determine whether additional laboratory testing is indicated. Table 6.2 provides a guide to the evaluation of these data. In some cases the diagnosis may be fairly obvious (e.g., when the child meets all of the clinical criteria for fetal alcohol syndrome). In most cases, however, the available data are sufficient only to provide clues or ideas about the etiology that warrant further investigation. When the etiology is not obvious, it is often helpful to list the most likely possibilities. This list, which is often referred to as *the differential diagnosis of the problem*, can be considered as a series of hypotheses regarding possible etiologies. For example, the clinical finding of microcephaly (small head) may suggest several hypotheses, such as cerebral malformation or birth injury. Clinicians can then identify a strategy for testing each hypothesis to increase or decrease the probability of it being correct. In the example of microcephaly, a hypothesis of cerebral malformation might be tested by looking for other malformations, performing neuroimaging (CT or MRI scanning of the brain) or pursuing genetic testing for a chromosome disorder. A hypothesis of birth injury might be tested by examining birth records and determining whether the head circumference was normal at birth. This example is not intended to be a complete analysis of the possible causes of microcephaly. It is described here only to illustrate the process of generating and testing hypotheses regarding possible etiologies.

The purpose of evaluating several competing hypotheses is to optimize the probability of making the correct diagnosis. In some cases, the evaluation of these hypotheses will consist of obtaining additional historical information or more extensive physical examination. In many cases, however, the evaluation will necessitate the performance of properly selected laboratory tests and procedures. Table 6.2 suggests some laboratory tests

TABLE 6.2

Hypotheses and Strategies for Assessing Etiologic Risk Factors

Onset	Hypothesis	Social
Prenatal	Chromosomal or single gene disorder	Extended physical examination Referral to clinical geneticist Chromosomal and DNA analyses
	Syndrome disorder	Extended family history and examination of relatives Extended physical examination Referral to clinical geneticist
	Inborn error of metabolism	Newborn screening using tandem mass spectrometry Analysis of amino acids in blood, urine, and/or cerebrospinal fluid Analysis of organic acids in urine Blood levels of lactate, pyruvate, very long chain fatty acids, free and total carnitine, and acylcarnitines Arterial ammonia and gases Assays of specific enzymes in cultured skin fibroblasts Biopsies of specific tissue for light and electron microscopy and biochemical analysis
	Cerebral dysgenesis	Neuroimaging (CT or MRI)
	Social, behavioral, and environmental risk factors	Intrauterine and postnatal growth Placental pathology Detailed social history of parents Medical history and examination of mother Toxicological screening of mother at prenatal visits and of child at birth Referral to clinical geneticist
Perinatal	Intrapartum and neonatal disorders	Review of maternal records (prenatal care, labor, and delivery) Review of birth and neonatal records

TABLE 6.2 (*continued*)

Onset	Hypothesis	Social
Postnatal	Head injury	Detailed medical history Brain X-rays and neuroimaging
	Brain infection	Detailed medical history Cerebrospinal fluid analysis
	Demyelinating disorders	Neuroimaging Cerebrospinal fluid analysis
	Degenerative disorders	Neuroimaging Specific DNA studies for genetic disorders Assays of specific enzymes in blood or cultured skin fibroblasts Biopsies of specific tissue for light and electron microscopy and biochemical analysis Referral to clinical geneticist or neurologist
	Seizure disorders	Electroencephalography Referral to clinical neurologist
	Toxic-metabolic disorders	See "Inborn errors of metabolism" above Toxicological studies Lead and heavy metal assays
	Malnutrition	Body measurements Detailed nutritional history Family history of nutrition
	Environmental and social disadvantage	Detailed social history History of abuse or neglect Psychological evaluation Observation in new environment
	Educational inadequacy	Early referral and intervention records Review of educational records

and procedures that might be helpful in evaluating the hypotheses listed in the table. This table should not be considered complete or prescriptive because the evaluation must be tailored to the facts in an individual case. The clinician is responsible for identifying the appropriate hypotheses, devising strategies for testing them, and evaluating the results of whatever tests and procedures are performed.

Reasonably current guidelines have been published to assist clinicians in selecting appropriate laboratory tests (Moeschler & Shevell, 2006; Shevell et al., 2003). These guidelines are generally valid but need to be updated in light of subsequent research. Two areas of investigation deserve special comment. Chromosomal microarray technology (comparative genomic hybridization) is continually improving, and patients who were studied even a few years ago may need to be studied again using the newer techniques. Eventually (probably within the next 10 years), the technology will be available to sequence the entire human genome as a routine clinical test in a particular case. Genetic technology is already ahead of clinical knowledge (i.e., we can test for things we do not yet completely understand), so clinicians should be careful when assessing all of this information.

Several computerized databases exist that provide a list of possible etiologies when all of the available clinical data for a particular individual are entered. These proprietary databases are updated continually and are generally utilized by clinical geneticists. The National Library of Medicine maintains an online database that is open to the public called "Online Mendelian Inheritance in Man" that contains up-to-date genetic information about many disorders that can cause ID. Indeed, the pace of genetic research is such that any guidelines will be outdated by the time they are published, and referral to a clinical geneticist is often the best way to ensure an up-to-date evaluation of genetic etiologies.

Intellectual disability begins before age 18, but individuals with ID may first present a need for services during adulthood. If the diagnosis of ID was not made previously, it may be difficult to gather all of the relevant information needed to make the diagnosis in an adult (see chapter 8 for guidelines regarding a retrospective diagnosis). This is also true for assessment of the etiology in such cases. Much of the information described here, such as details of the pregnancy, birth history, early developmental milestones, and family functioning during childhood, as well as details of the family history or pedigree, may simply be unavailable. Similar problems often arise when individuals present a need for services following immigration from another country. The physical examination becomes more important as the clinician looks for clues about the etiology. The list of possible hypotheses or differential diagnosis becomes longer and more tentative when the available data are limited. Laboratory tests and procedures are often needed to examine these hypotheses. In the end many risk factors may be more suspected than confirmed, and a degree of uncertainty or imprecision about the etiologic diagnosis may be expected.

ETIOLOGIC DIAGNOSIS AND CLASSIFICATION

The formulation of an etiologic diagnosis follows from the multifactorial model shown in Table 6.1. All of the information derived from the history, examinations, and laboratory testing is evaluated carefully. These data are then organized into risk factor categories (biomedical, social, behavioral, and educational), and a judgment is made as to whether the risk factors were present before (prenatal), during (perinatal), or after (postnatal) the individual's birth. All relevant risk factors are identified, including those that are thought to be most important (such as trisomy 21 or Down syndrome) as well as those that are thought to be less important (such as social deprivation or lack of timely educational intervention). The presence of interactions between risk factors are then evaluated and described. Etiologic diagnosis and classification thus consists of a comprehensive list of all of the risk factors and interactions among risk factors for which the available data provide sufficient evidence. In some cases this list may be fairly short and tentative, while in other cases it may be long and confirmed. Most cases will fall somewhere in the middle. Nonetheless, at least one reasonably plausible risk factor will usually be present in every case if sufficient diligence is applied. This multifactorial, etiologic diagnostic, and classification system for determining the etiology thereby eliminates the category of ID of unknown cause.

An example of what such an etiologic diagnosis might look like for a child with fetal alcohol syndrome (as well as other issues) would likely include the following risk factors:

- Biomedical risk factors might include the presence of fetal alcohol syndrome and congenital heart disease.
- Social risk factors might include family poverty, homelessness, and inadequate parenting skills.
- Behavioral risk factors might include parental substance abuse and abuse or neglect of the child.
- Educational risk factors might include lack of adequate early intervention services.
- Interactions among risk factors might include maternal poverty and substance abuse causing lack of prenatal care and fetal alcohol syndrome, and homelessness causing lack of adequate early intervention services.

This example is considered further in chapter 10 (see Table 10.2). The intent of this multifactorial approach to etiology is to describe all of the risk factors that contribute to the individual's present functioning. This approach then allows providers to identify strategies for supporting the individual and the family so that these risk factors might be prevented or ameliorated.

ETIOLOGY AND PERFORMANCE

Genotype and Phenotype

The *genotype* (or genome) consists of all of the information contained within the individual's DNA. The *phenotype* refers to the actual observed properties of the individual, including physical, developmental, mental, behavioral, social, and other attributes. An individual's phenotype is determined by three factors: the genotype or genomic data, *epigenetic processes*, and *environmental factors*. Epigenetic processes refer to mechanisms that influence how the genetic information in the genotype is actually expressed. Epigenetic processes do not change the individual's underlying DNA, but they do modulate the effect of individual or multiple genes. For example, an individual may be born with one normal copy and one abnormal copy of the UBE3A gene located at 22q15. The maternal copy is the one that is usually expressed, due to an epigenetic process called *imprinting*. If the maternal copy is the abnormal one, the person will likely have Angelman syndrome. Environmental factors refer to any nongenetic influences (such as nutrition, emotional stimulation, education, physical exercise, or medical treatment) that affect overall functioning. Thus, individuals with the same genotype may differ significantly in their phenotype because of these epigenetic and environmental factors. Nonetheless, certain patterns may emerge in which individuals with a particular genotype will have reasonably predictable phenotypic attributes. The study of these genotype-phenotype correlations is an extremely active area of research that involves many aspects of biology and medicine. In this chapter we are particularly concerned with the genotype-phenotype correlations that are observed in individuals with ID.

The multifactorial system for describing the etiology of ID is particularly compatible with this emphasis on genotype-phenotype correlation. Intellectual disability represents an observable problem in functioning and thus is part of the individual's phenotype. This phenotypic problem in functioning reflects the interaction of the individual's genotype (which can be described as a biomedical risk factor) with epigenetic processes (which may well be due to biomedical risk factors as well) and with environmental influences (which can be described as social, behavioral, and educational risk factors). The genotype alone is not sufficient to predict the phenotype, so one must also identify and classify these additional risk factors using the multifactorial system described earlier.

Variation and Predictability

Using an etiological label such as Down syndrome has desirable and undesirable effects. For example, identifying an individual as having Down syndrome tells us a great deal about that person's actual, potential, and future support needs. Many babies with this condition have serious heart problems that require immediate medical and surgical attention. Individuals with Down syndrome may have nutritional and hormonal issues, so growth needs to be monitored closely using growth charts designed specifically for this condition. The prudent physician will search for other biomedical conditions that can be associated with Down syndrome, such as an unstable neck that may require surgical management. Once a diagnosis of Down syndrome is made, the child's educational risks will be apparent, and the educational system will need to assess and identify any needs for educational supports. These will likely change as the individual grows up, so potential support needs can be anticipated. Psychological difficulties may occur (especially as the person ages), so these will need to be anticipated, diagnosed promptly, and treated before they become disabling.

These benefits of an etiological diagnosis must be balanced with a sensitive and humane understanding of the person as an individual. Etiology is not destiny, and an individual with Down syndrome may or may not have any or all of the conditions commonly associated with the diagnosis. This reflects the inherent variability contained within a population of individuals with the same genotype and the extent to which genotypic expression is influenced by epigenetic and environmental factors. Each person must be seen as a unique individual with actual and potential strengths as well as needs for support. The benefit of being able to predict this profile of needed supports, based on an etiological diagnosis, needs to be balanced against the risk of unfair expectations that the person has aspects of the etiology that may or may not be present.

Phenotypic information about risks or expectations for actual and potential functioning may, therefore, be part of the etiological diagnosis, as was shown with the diagnosis of Down syndrome. Similar behavioral information is available for a number of other genetic conditions, such as Angelman syndrome, Williams syndrome, and Prader-Willi syndrome. This information is often referred to as the *behavioral phenotype* of the condition (Dykens, Hodapp, & Finucane, 2000). Researchers have identified behavioral phenotypes for a small number of genetic etiologies, using careful studies and analyses of the behaviors of individuals with each etiologic diagnosis. Table 6.3 provides examples of some of the more well-described behavioral phenotypes. The Web site of the Society for the Study of Behavioral Phenotypes lists 37 additional conditions for which behavioral data are available (as of January 1, 2009). Continuing research will certainly expand this list in coming years. Once again, one must be careful not to automatically equate a specific genotype with a described behavioral phenotype such as that shown in Table 6.3. Genotypic expression is modified by many other factors, which should be identified as part of the individual's multifactorial etiologic diagnosis described earlier.

TABLE 6.3
Behavioral Phenotypes of Selected Genetic Disorders

Etiologic diagnosis	Behavioral manifestations that are often present
Down syndrome	1. Better performance on visuospatial tasks than on verbal or auditory tasks 2. Adaptive behavior strength relative to intelligence 3. Pleasant and sociable personality 4. Depression common in adulthood

TABLE 6.3 (*continued*)

Etiologic diagnosis	Behavioral manifestations that are often present
Williams syndrome	1. Strengths in language, auditory memory, and facial recognition 2. Limitations in visuospatial functioning, perceptual-motor planning, and fine motor skills 3. Strength in theory of mind (interpersonal intelligence) 4. Friendliness with impaired social intelligence 5. Anxiety disorders common at all ages
Fragile X syndrome	1. Verbal skills better than visuospatial skills 2. Relative strengths in daily living and self-care skills 3. Frequent association with inattention, hyperactivity, and autistic-like behaviors 4. Anxiety disorders common at all ages
Prader-Willi syndrome	1. Impaired satiety, food-seeking behavior, and obesity 2. Strength in visual processing and solving jigsaw puzzles 3. Obsessive-compulsive disorders and impulse control disorders common at all ages 4. Occasional psychosis in adults
Velocardiofacial syndrome	1. Verbal skills better than nonverbal skills 2. Inattention and hyperactivity common in children 3. Schizophrenia and mood disorders more common in older adolescents and adults
Rubinstein-Taybi syndrome	1. Inattention and impulsivity common in children 2. Friendliness and interest in music 3. Occasional association with mood disorders, tics, and obsessive-compulsive disorders
Smith-Magenis syndrome	1. Delayed speech acquisition 2. Relative weakness in sequential processing 3. Sleep disorders common 4. Frequent stereotyped and self-injurious behaviors 5. Impulse control disorders common in children
Angelman syndrome	1. Bouts of inappropriate laughter are characteristic in younger persons 2. Generally happy disposition at all ages 3. Hyperactivity and sleep disorders in younger persons

Once an etiologic diagnosis is made, information can be sought as to whether a behavioral phenotype has been described. Because research studies on behavioral phenotypes may be flawed by methodological issues, such as small sample size, retrospective design, or inadequate analysis, this information needs to be scrutinized for its validity and reliability.

If a behavioral phenotype is known, this information may be useful for all of the team members, including teachers, therapists, counselors, and family members. Team members must understand that for a given individual, some, all, or none of the behaviors may be expressed and that the extent of expression may depend on the context of time and place. This information may be useful in planning the nature and extent of needed treatment and supports (see chapter 10). Although medication may be indicated for some behaviors (such as attention deficit/hyperactivity disorder or anxiety), prescription of medication is not the sole purpose of identifying the behavioral phenotype.

Summary

In this chapter we described the multifactorial nature of the etiology of ID and presented a classification system based on the identification and specification of all of the biomedical, social, behavioral, and educational risk factors, as well as their interactions, that are present in the life of the individual with ID. We also discussed the diagnostic assessment process that incorporates new research advances as well as research about behaviors that are associated with specific etiologies. The relationship between genotype and phenotype was described, and the particular relevance of the AAIDD multifactorial classification system for understanding this relationship was emphasized.

CHAPTER 7

MULTIDIMENSIONAL APPROACH TO CLASSIFICATION

> The primary purposes of classification in the field of intellectual disability are grouping for funding, research, provision of services and supports, and communication about selected characteristics of persons and their environments. As the field moves increasingly to an ecological focus, a supports paradigm, and the inclusion of persons with intellectual disability into the mainstream of life, a number of current policies and practices have emerged that require a broader approach to classification than that used previously. This chapter covers such a broader, multidimensional approach to classification.

OVERVIEW

The primary purposes of classification in the field of *intellectual disability* (ID) are grouping for funding, research, provision of services and supports, and communication about selected characteristics of persons and their environments. In addition, classification is used today for more than its historic purpose of grouping on the basis of IQ range bands or adaptive behavior limitation scores. Clinicians are currently being asked classification questions, such as, Is the person diagnosed with ID competent to be a witness, stand trial, consent to sexual activity, parent a child, avoid having a guardian appointed, and/or retain custody of a child? These classification questions require both thinking differently about the purposes of classification and approaching classification more broadly.

All classification systems have as their fundamental purpose the provision of an organized schema for the categorization of various kinds of observations. Such organization is essential for the advancement of any science in the acquisition and incorporation of knowledge and the provision of best practices. Thus, professionals in the field of ID need to be familiar with and often must use a variety of diagnostic, classification, and eligibility systems on a regular basis to communicate effectively with other professionals. In that regard, it is important that they be familiar with emerging trends in multidimensional classification systems that incorporate new knowledge and accommodate changing concepts and philosophies.

Our primary purpose in this chapter is to discuss the need to align a multidimensional approach to classification with the movement within the field of ID to an ecological focus, a supports paradigm, and the inclusion of persons with ID into the mainstream of life. To that end, the chapter's four sections (a) summarize current approaches to classifying persons with ID, (b) provide the rationale for a multidimensional classification system, (c) outline the parameters of a multidimensional classification system, and (d) discuss the advantages to the proposed multidimensional classification system.

CURRENT APPROACHES TO CLASSIFYING PERSONS WITH INTELLECTUAL DISABILITY

Many organizations have published or are using diagnostic/classification systems relevant to persons with ID. Chief among these are the following:

- The World Health Organization (WHO), which has published the *International Classification of Diseases* (World Health Organization, 1977, 1993, 2008) and the *International Classification of Functioning, Disability, and Health* (World Health Organization, 2001)
- The American Psychiatric Association, which has published the *Diagnostic and Statistical Manual of Mental Disorders* (4th ed., text rev.) (2000)
- The United States Social Security Administration (SSA), which publishes funding eligibility criteria for all disabilities (Social Security Administration, 2008)
- The Developmental Disabilities Administration, whose eligibility criteria are frequently incorporated into state and federal program eligibility criteria (Development Disabilities Assistance and Bill of Rights Act of 2000)
- The Centers for Medicaid and Medicare Services, whose state-specific Medicaid eligibility criteria are based largely on *ICD* or SSA classifications (Centers for Medicaid and Medicare Services, 2005)

Across these organizations one finds two published classification systems that are commonly used today: (a) The *ICD-9* and *ICD-10* (World Health Organization, 1977,1993), and (b) the multiaxial classification system published by the American Psychiatric Association (2000). Because of their pervasive use both nationally and internationally, each is described briefly.

ICD-9 and *ICD-10* Classification Systems

The diagnosis and classification of ID has historically (and even now in some instances) focused on IQ scores. Although there has been a shift in the field away from this unitary focus, it remains the key element in several current classification systems. For example, the *ICD-9*-CM (Hart, Hopkins, & Ford, 2005; World Health Organization, 1977) system is still currently used in the United States. In this system, a person with ID is classified primarily on the basis of IQ ranges. Virtually all United States governmental and most insurance benefit plans, as well as many service delivery systems, require use of these codes. This system is widely viewed as outdated because of its limited number of codes (about 17,000) and lack of flexibility for expansion (National Center for Health Statistics, 2008).

Most of the rest of the world has been using a revised *ICD* system (*ICD-10*) for a number of years (World Health Organization, 1993). This system has more than 155,000 codes for procedures and diagnoses. It is planned that the United States will begin using a further revised *ICD-10*-CM in 2011 (National Center for Health Statistics, 2008). Interestingly, work has already begun on a revision, the *ICD-11* (World Health Organization, 2008).

The *ICD-10* (World Health Organization, 1993) replaces the previous *ICD-9* numeric coding scheme with an alphanumeric one. This expands the coding structure and permits future revisions without disrupting the coding system. For example, all the endocrine, nutritional, and metabolic diseases are E codes (e.g., Code E70.0—classical phenylketonuria), whereas mental and behavioral disorders (where "mental retardation" or ID is included) are F codes.

The *ICD-10* (World Health Organization, 1993) is essentially a tabular classification list built around 21 chapters covering a wide area from infectious and parasitic diseases to factors influencing health status and contact with health services. Each classification item is labeled with a four-character alphanumeric code. The *ICD-10* description of mental retardation (i.e., ID) is as follows:

> A condition of arrested or incomplete development of the mind, which is especially characterized by impairment of skills that contribute to the overall level of intelligence, i.e., cognitive, language, motor, and social abilities. Retardation can occur with or without any other mental or physical condition. Degrees of mental retardation are conventionally estimated by standardized intelligence tests. These can be supplemented by scales assessing social adaptation in a given environment. These measures provide an approximate indication of the degree of mental retardation. The diagnosis will also depend on the overall assessment of intellectual functioning by a skilled diagnostician. Intellectual abilities and social adaptation may change over time, and, however poor, may improve as a result of training and rehabilitation. Diagnosis should be based on the current levels of functioning. (pp. 369–370)

Although the *ICD-10* description represents a slight improvement over the *ICD-9*-CM in terms of breadth (more than just IQ), it still has significant limitations related to language that continues to be stigmatizing; its emphasis on classification based on IQ scores alone, with adaptive behavior assessment presented as an optional supplement; its emphasis on mental age scores, although their use in current practice is quite limited; and the functional expectations that are described for persons with ID that are quite minimal, especially for individuals in the moderate and severe categories.

APA Multiaxial System

The *Diagnostic and Statistical Manuals of Mental Disorders* (*DSM*) have been a component of the *ICD* systems since 1952. The *DSM-IV* (American Psychiatric Association,

2000) system is the one currently in use, although work has begun on a *DSM-V* version, expected to be finalized in 2012 (American Psychiatric Association, 2008).

The *DSM-IV* multiaxial system comprises five domains that provide information about an individual. Axis I includes all the clinical mental disorders except for personality disorders and "mental retardation," which are included on Axis II. Axis III is used for reporting medical conditions, using the *ICD* codes. Axis IV is used for describing psychosocial or environmental problems that may influence the diagnosis and treatment of an individual due to resulting stress (e.g., housing problems). A judgment of an individual's overall level of functioning is reported on Axis V. This is based on an assessment using the Global Assessment of Functioning (GAF) scale that addresses psychological, social, and occupational functioning.

Although the coding system is identical, the treatment of "mental retardation" (i.e., ID) in *DSM-IV* is significantly different from that of the *ICD-9* or *ICD-10* systems. The most notable exception is the clear adoption in *DSM-IV* of the 1992 and 2002 AAMR/ AAIDD diagnostic criteria (i.e., significantly subaverage intellectual functioning, limitations in adaptive skills, and age of onset prior to age 18 years). Recommendations regarding IQ cutoff scores are comparable, and the equal importance of adaptive functioning as a diagnostic criterion is emphasized. A major distinction, however, is the retention in the *DSM-IV* of a severity classification based on IQ ranges. The IQ ranges and accompanying descriptions or labels (mild, moderate, severe, and profound) are based on standard deviation ranges (from two to five or more) below the theoretical average IQ score of 100.

RATIONALE FOR A MULTIDIMENSIONAL CLASSIFICATION SYSTEM

The approach taken to classification in this *Manual* is a departure from that found in the two previous *Manuals* (1992 and 2002) in that we present a multidimensional classification system based on the Conceptual Framework of Human Functioning (Figure 2.1) and its associated dimensions (intellectual abilities, adaptive behavior, health, participation, and context) and emphasis on individualized supports. We propose that this conceptual framework (Figure 2.1) can be used for answering three questions related to the development and use of a classification system (Simeonsson et al., 2006): Does the classification contribute to a systematic, hierarchical way of organizing knowledge? Is the classification based on a coherent theoretical framework? Does the classification system contribute to the efficient organization of knowledge for application to practice?

The proposed multidimensional approach to classification recognizes that to focus on only one dimension of human functioning to the exclusion of the other dimensions no longer reflects current best practices. Furthermore, such a multidimensional approach to classification has other advantages over a unidimensional (e.g., IQ score) approach to classification in that it creates an organizing system for incorporating new knowledge, is consistent with a logical conceptual framework, identifies key factors that influence human functioning, and contributes positively to the portrayal of individuals or groups (Luckasson & Reeve, 2001).

As noted earlier, the four primary purposes of classification in the field of ID are grouping for service reimbursement or funding, research, provision of services/supports, and communication about selected characteristics of persons and their environments. As the field of ID moves increasingly to an ecological focus and a supports paradigm, a number of current policies and practices have emerged that require a broader approach to classification than that used previously. Chief among these trends—as they relate to the four purposes of a classification system—are grouping for reimbursement/funding, research, services/supports, and communication.

Grouping for Reimbursement/Funding

Increasingly, funding/resource allocation formulas are based on some combination and weighting of levels of assessed support need, level of adaptive behavior, challenging behaviors, health status, and contextual factors such as residential arrangement and geographical location. Thus, a multidimensional classification system will both promote and help establish the parameters for planning and resource allocation.

Research

Increasingly, there is a focus on personal outcomes related to two aspects of human functioning: level of personal competence and the individual's quality of life (see chapter 13). Multivariate research methods can be used to determine the contributions made to these personal outcomes by each of the five dimensions of the conceptual framework shown in Figure 2.1 (intellectual abilities, adaptive behavior, health, participation, and context). Thus, a multidimensional classification system can contribute to meaningful predictions for individuals and groups and allows for the determination of significant outcome predictors.

Services/Supports

Individualized services and supports are increasingly being based on the pattern and intensity of needed supports. There is an increasing focus on health-related services and prevention as a form of support (see chapters 10 and 11). This focus builds on the interaction or ecological understanding of ID and its causes and amelioration. Thus, a multidimensional classification system that identifies health and other etiological factors is consistent with both the supports paradigm and the ecological understanding of ID and its multidimensional nature.

Communication

A multidimensional classification system permits communication about many of the factors that influence human functioning. Such a system can result in coding into groups based on relevant characteristics of each dimension (intellectual functioning, adaptive behavior, health, participation, and context) and the pattern and intensity of the person's needed supports. A by-product is the use of a conceptual framework that employs consistent nomenclature and thus facilitates data collection, storage, and retrieval.

PARAMETERS OF A MULTIDIMENSIONAL CLASSIFICATION SYSTEM

The proposed multidimensional classification system expands the scope of potential classification to respond to changes in the field of ID related to its ecological focus, the supports paradigm, and the inclusion of persons with ID into the mainstream of life. The conceptual framework for this expansion is based on two factors. The first is the multidimensional model of human functioning presented in Figure 2.1. This ecological model depicts human functioning as being influenced by five dimensions (intellectual abilities, adaptive behavior, health, participation, and context) and the provision of individualized supports. The second factor is the alignment of this classification system with the five dimensions found in the *International Classification of Functioning, Disability, and Health* (Buntinx, 2006; Luckasson et al., 2002; World Health Organization, 2001).

Dimension I: Intellectual Abilities

Dimension I in a multidimensional classification system would continue the classification based on ranges of intellectual ability, in line with the *DSM/ICD* criteria, although excluding reference to mental age scores. This dimension corresponds to the *ICF* body functions and structures factor (World Health Organization, 2001).

Dimension II: Adaptive Behavior

Dimension II would continue the classification based on assessed levels of adaptive behavior. This classification component would build on a proposal in the 1959 *Terminology and Classification Manual* (Heber, 1959) that levels of adaptive behavior could be based primarily on descriptions of typical skills or limitations. Subsequently, we have seen more current application of this notion based on such adaptive behavior scales as the AAMR Adaptive Behavior Scale-School and Community Version (Nihira, Leland, & Lambert, 1993), the Adaptive Behavior Assessment System-II (Harrison & Oakland, 2003), the Comprehensive Test of Adaptive Behavior-Revised (Adams, 1999), the Inventory for Client and Agency Planning (ICAP; Bruininks, Hill, Weatherman, & Woodcock, 1986), and the Vineland Adaptive Behavior Scales (Sparrow, Cicchetti, & Balla, 2005). This dimension corresponds to the activities factor in the *ICF* model.

Dimension III: Health

Dimension III focuses on health in a broad perspective, including physical health, etiology, mental health, and positive health practices. Both *ICD* and *DSM* would be key classification schemes, with further development needed to measure positive health practices and those differential levels of mental and physical health-related supports discussed in chapter 11. The determination of medical necessity and related conditions in the Medicaid program could be addressed here. This dimension corresponds to the health condition and body functions and structures factors in the *ICF* (World Health Organization, 2001).

Dimension IV: Participation

Dimension IV focuses on the performance of people in society. *Participation* refers to roles and interactions in the areas of home living, work, education, leisure, spiritual, and cultural activities. This component of the multidimensional classification system could include classifying on the basis of the individual's involvement in his/her environment (e.g., degree of community integration). Various adaptive behavior scales contain relevant measures, as does the *DSM* GAF scale (American Psychiatric Association, 2000). This dimension corresponds to the participation factor in *ICF* (World Health Organization, 2001).

Dimension V: Context

Context focuses on the interrelated conditions within which people live their everyday lives. Because contextual factors include environmental and personal factors that represent the complete background of an individual's life, both environmental (external) and personal (internal) factors need to be measured (Fougeyrollas, Cloutier, Bergeron, & St. Michel, 1998). Axis IV of the *DSM* (psychosocial and environmental problems) is an example of a measure in this area, especially for environmental factors. This dimension corresponds to the contextual factor in *ICF* (World Health Organization, 2001). It is widely recognized that additional work on the measurement of contextual factors and how they form the basic elements of a classification system is needed (Dunst et al., 2006; Guscia et al., 2006).

Classification Based on Intensity of Support Needs

A multidimensional classification system must also allow for the classification of persons based on the pattern and intensity of their support needs. As we will see in chapter 9, support intensity scales assess the extraordinary support that a person with ID needs in order to participate in the activities of daily life. The focus of support assessment is on the pattern and intensity of supports that enable participation in home and community life, along with exceptional medical and behavioral support needs.

In 1992, AAMR (Luckasson et al., 1992) proposed this component of a multidimensional classification system, in which classification would be based on the intensity of supports needed by individuals with ID. This movement beyond a traditional IQ-based approach to classification reflected the shift to a functional definition of ID and an approach that emphasized the importance of individualized supports to human functioning. Subsequently, the AAMR published the Supports Intensity Scale (Thompson et al., 2004) that provides normative data on support needs in a variety of areas of functioning.

The percentile measures and standard scores obtained from this instrument can readily be used for classification purposes.

ADVANTAGES OF THE PROPOSED MULTIDIMENSIONAL CLASSIFICATION SYSTEM

The field of ID is changing in how a classification system is conceptualized and used. The changes relate specifically to the multiple purposes for which a classification system is used and the need to align a functional classification system to an ecological perspective and a supports paradigm. The proposed multidimensional classification system is consistent with these changes in purpose and formulation. Although future research and application efforts will evaluate the utility of the proposed multidimensional classification system, it is readily apparent that the system will impact the field positively in three respects in that it (a) extends the functional uses of a classification system, (b) overcomes many of the misuses of classification, and (c) establishes the parameters for best practices in classification.

Extends Functional Uses

There are a variety of functional uses of classification systems. Communication is a key one. Diagnostic criteria and a classification system comprise a language of the field. National and international agreement on definitional criteria and classification of conditions under the umbrella of ID is essential for effective communication.

A second functional use is to increase reliability. The probability of interrater agreement is increased when there are clear-cut criteria for specific diagnoses and subcategories of a diagnostic category. Such accuracy is essential in research, but is equally important in determining service eligibility.

Classification can also give added meaning to a phenomenon by identifying both subtle differences and similarities among subtypes of a disorder. This added meaning addresses tendencies to overgeneralize about a condition or diagnosis. On the other hand, classification can enhance predictability about the likely course of development for individuals with specific diagnoses. A multidimensional classification system facilitates the identification of co-occurring conditions, as well as the array of characteristics of a given individual.

Service and support systems for individuals with ID benefit greatly from the use of an appropriate classification system. Establishing eligibility for services and benefits and the classification system used need to assure that only those for whom the service or benefit was intended are actually deemed eligible. This often involves not only the diagnostic process but further classification as well (e.g., certain Medicaid programs require participants to have more significant levels of adaptive behavior limitations).

The organization of services also draws on classification systems. For example, grouping of individuals for some purposes (e.g., residential or vocational) may be most effective if based on level of support needs. Also, some specialized services may be highly dependent on diagnosis and classification (e.g., dual diagnosis or autism programs).

Objective service funding is a relatively new area that reflects the need for a multidimensional classification system. Many national and international entities are increasingly basing funding on actual support needs rather than less relevant dimensions such as IQ or even number of individuals served. However, the chosen system of classification must explicitly address relevant support needs in order to accomplish this important goal.

Misuses of Classification

Although classification can have many positive benefits, there have long been concerns about the potential misuse of a classification system. The primary concern has been over the stigmatizing labels to which classification categories often evolve. In fact, many of AAIDD's earlier classification systems were changed over time in an attempt to escape from the pejorative connotations of previously acceptable clinical terms (e.g., *feeble-minded*, *moron*, *imbecile*, *idiot*). Even more neutral classification categories, such as the mild through profound continuum for IQ, have been criticized. Although an argument can be made that continually changing classification labels will not be of benefit to the field in the long run, the source of disrespect for persons with ID needs to be continually addressed.

Current classification systems contribute to the problem by frequent references to scores or classifications that compare adults to children (e.g., mental age, social age, and age equivalent scores). For example, the *ICD* systems (World Health Organization, 1977, 1993) explicitly include mental age ranges for adults for the mild through profound categories based on IQ. The common reporting of such age equivalent scores likely contributes to the stigmatizing character of the disability. An argument can be made that the use of such age scores should cease or be used only in a much more limited way, such as in curricula necessary for developmentally sequenced stages of learning.

Although the organization of services was listed earlier as a benefit of classification, inappropriate use of classification may actually lead to unsupported groupings. For example, there may be an incorrect assumption of severe cognitive limitations in people with physical and mobility impairments if an adaptive behavior level classification is used. Although grouping people with similar functional levels may be useful in certain settings (e.g., residential), it may be entirely inappropriate in others (e.g., social).

This raises an essential question regarding classification: What are the benefits of generalization versus individualization? The field has been undergoing a transformation in recent decades in which greater emphasis has been placed on individualized support systems. Thus, the grouping inherent in classification has led some professionals to advocate the abolition of classification. Required diagnostic approaches could still be used according to this approach, but further classification is deemed unnecessary and potentially harmful.

A final common misuse of classification concerns misleading assumptions regarding precision of scores. Examples include an IQ score of 75 versus a score of 69 leading to qualitatively different eligibility decisions or determining eligibility or diagnosis on the basis of a single score or assessment. Although the statistical reliability of most scales, especially intellectual, is well established before the test is published, it is still important, as discussed in chapters 4, 5, and 8, that professionals carefully consider the possible statistical error in any score, the variability in scores across different tests, and the importance of the testee's physical limitations, motivation, and cultural background.

Establishes Parameters of Best Practices

Fulfilling one's professional responsibilities is one of the highest goals of a member of a profession. Being well trained in the current best practices of one's profession is essential to maintaining professional standards and abiding by a code of professional ethics. In the field of ID, this need is as appropriate to the classification function as it is to functions related to diagnosis and developing individualized supports. To that end, the authors of this *Manual* summarize in Table 7.1 the current best practices in classification.

TABLE 7.1

Best Practices in Classification

- Only nominal classification (i.e., classifying the person solely on the basis of the diagnosis) may be sufficient for some purposes.

- Use of ordinal classification (i.e., classifying the severity of the disability along a continuum) should have specific purposes and meaningful outcomes.

- Nonstigmatizing classification categories should be used if possible.

- Potentially stigmatizing classification categories must be justifiable for a specific critical purpose or with specific audiences or professional groups. However, they should be used only if communication is facilitated that could not be facilitated in any other way.

- Age-referenced scores (e.g., mental or developmental age) should be used cautiously, if at all, and only then for meaningful and educational communication.

- Statistically oriented classifications (e.g., standard scores and percentiles) are sometimes difficult to communicate to the lay public, families, and staff. Thus, meaningful translations must often be used.

- Information regarding precision of measurements (e.g., standard error of measurement for a test and history of test scores) needs to be considered in relation to risks associated with making an incorrect diagnosis (e.g., false positive or false negative).

- A multidimensional classification system can provide the most comprehensive and useful information about an individual.

SUMMARY

Classification is used today for more than its historic purpose of grouping on the basis of IQ range bands or adaptive behavior limitation scores. Clinicians are increasingly being asked classification questions regarding the inclusion of persons with ID into the mainstream of daily community life. These classification questions require that individuals in the field of ID think differently about the purposes of classification and approach classification more broadly. Additionally, as the field moves increasingly to an ecological focus and a supports paradigm, a number of current policies and practices have emerged that also require a broader approach to classification than that used previously.

In this chapter we have suggested that the parameters of a broader, multidimensional classification system should include those dimensions and factors that affect human functioning: intellectual abilities, adaptive behavior, health, participation, context, and individualized supports. These parameters are based on the multidimensional conceptual model of human functioning (Figure 2.1) and the five factors composing the *ICF* model of human functioning and disability (World Health Organization, 2001, p. 18).

Our major purposes in this chapter have been to summarize the current approaches to classifying persons with ID, provide the rationale for a multidimensional classification system, outline the parameters of a multidimensional classification system, and discuss the advantages to such a system. Among the recommendations of Simeonsson et al. (2006) was the incorporation of the AAIDD classification system into a revised system based on current knowledge about the multiple factors that impact human functioning and the integration of this information into the *ICF* model of human functioning. The multidimensional classification system presented in this chapter accomplishes this and also meets the three criteria proposed by Simeonsson et al. (2006): it provides a hierarchical organization of knowledge, it is based on a coherent framework, and it is a system that contributes to efficient application.

CHAPTER 8

ROLE OF CLINICAL JUDGMENT IN DIAGNOSIS, CLASSIFICATION, AND DEVELOPMENT OF SYSTEMS OF SUPPORTS

Clinical judgment is a key component—along with best practices in intellectual disability, professional standards, and professional ethics—of professional responsibility in the field of intellectual disability. Clinical judgment is different from either ethical or professional judgment based on one's professional ethics or standards. Clinical judgment is a special type of judgment rooted in a high level of clinical expertise and experience. It emerges directly from extensive data and is based on training, experiences, and specific knowledge of the person and his or her environment.

OVERVIEW

Members of a variety of professions, such as psychologists, physicians, diagnosticians, expert educators, special education teachers, and social workers, are frequently involved in the diagnosis, classification, and provision of individualized supports to persons with *intellectual disability* (ID). These individuals are members of their primary profession and may also be members of the unique interdisciplinary group of ID professionals (Drew & Turnbull, 1987).

A profession generally has special high status, exacting standards, requirements of personal character, and obligations to others that enable it to be identified as a profession. Entry into a profession usually requires the successful completion of a lengthy education and socialization process. A profession often assumes the responsibility to monitor the behavior of its members and requires its members to abide by a code of ethics (e.g., American Psychological Association, 2002). As a result, society has high expectations that a member of a profession will exercise a higher level of professional responsibility and judgment in making decisions than an ordinary person would. This trust demands that the members of a profession understand and think systematically, deeply, and seriously about the nature of high stakes decision making in working with individuals with ID and their families.

Fulfilling one's professional responsibilities is among the highest, if not *the* highest, goal of a member of a profession. Being well trained in the current practices of one's profession, maintaining professional standards, and abiding by the code of ethics are all necessary, but not sufficient, in meeting one's professional responsibilities. This is because professionals working in the field of ID frequently encounter situations involving diagnosis, classification, and supports planning that require extensive data obtained from multiple sources, specialized training in assessment and test interpretation, familiarity with public policy and public laws, direct experience with those with whom the professional is working, and specific knowledge of the person and their environment. Additionally, this responsibility typically becomes more apparent where there is a difficult or complex case and when standard professional practices are insufficient. Over the last decade, the term clinical judgment has come to be used to refer to the special type of judgment that is required in such cases both to fulfill one's professional responsibility and to enhance the quality, validity, and precision of the professional's decision or recommendation in that case.

This chapter is focused on clinical judgment and the role that it plays in diagnosis, classification, and developing individualized supports for persons with ID. Our three purposes in this chapter are to (a) define clinical judgment, including its purpose and use; (b) discuss the role of clinical judgment in professional responsibility related to diagnosis, classification, and systems of supports; and (c) outline the parameters of four clinical judgment strategies that are the basis of clinical judgment and that, when used, enhance the validity and precision of the clinician's decision or recommendation. Throughout the chapter we stress the importance of avoiding thinking errors and using critical thinking skills.

CLINICAL JUDGMENT: DEFINITION, PURPOSE, AND USE

Definition

As defined by Luckasson et al. (2002) and Schalock and Luckasson (2005), clinical judgment is a special type of judgment rooted in a high level of clinical expertise and experience; it emerges directly from extensive data. It is based on the clinician's explicit training, direct experience with those with whom he or she is working, and specific knowledge of the person and the person's environment. Clinical judgment is characterized by its being (a) *systematic* (i.e., organized, sequential, and logical), (b) *formal* (i.e., explicit and reasoned), and (c) *transparent* (i.e., apparent and communicated clearly).

Clinical judgment is a key component—along with best practices in ID, professional standards, and professional ethics—of professional responsibility in the field of ID. Clinical judgment is different from either ethical or professional judgment based on one's professional ethics or standards. Ethical judgment is generally concerned with judgments of value and obligation focusing on justice (treating all people equitably), beneficence (doing good), and autonomy (respecting the authority of every person to control actions that primarily affect him or herself). Professional judgment is a process that follows general professional guidelines or standards by which a member of that profession collects, organizes, and weighs information. In distinction, clinical judgment is a special type of judgment rooted in a high level of clinical expertise and experience. It emerges directly from extensive data and is based on training, experiences, and specific knowledge of the person and his or her environment.

Purpose

The overall purpose of clinical judgment is to enhance the quality, validity, and precision of the clinician's decision in a particular case. In addition, the use of clinical judgment strategies leads to more transparent analyses and increasingly logical and principled decisions and recommendations. Clinical judgment should not be thought of as a justification for abbreviated evaluation, a vehicle for stereotypes or prejudice, a substitute for insufficiently explored questions, an excuse for incomplete or missing data, or a way to solve political problems.

Use

Clinical judgment is used in the field of ID for actions related to diagnosis, classification, and/or developing individualized supports. In our judgment, members of a variety of professions, such as psychologists, physicians, diagnosticians, expert educators, special education teachers, and social workers, use clinical judgment in one or more in these three actions. Throughout the chapter this group is referred to as *clinician in ID* if they (a) have relevant training, (b) engage in clinical activities (diagnosis, classification, planning supports), and (c) use professionally accepted best practices, such as those described in this *Manual*.

The specific functions performed by the clinician will be affected by his or her professional roles and responsibilities. For example, some state statutes stipulate that only a licensed clinical psychologist can make a diagnosis of ID; others require a diagnosis by an educational diagnostician. Under the Individuals With Disabilities Education Improvement Act of 2004 (IDEIA), for example, diagnostic flexibility is a team process. Actions related to classification (e.g., grouping for services, communication about selected characteristics, or the person's competency) are frequently prescribed by state and federal statutes, and the planning and the evaluation of individualized supports are frequently conducted through either a transdisciplinary or multidisciplinary team.

Furthermore, the amount of emphasis on clinical judgment exercised will also vary depending on what is expected of the professional within an organization or by his or her professional practice standards. For example, a special education teacher is expected to use cumulative data to evaluate the effectiveness of a particular education or support strategy; the clinical psychologist might be expected to contribute information about the level of assessed support needs in developing the person's individualized plan; the physician is expected to make a diagnosis of fetal alcohol syndrome; or the geneticist is expected to make a diagnosis of Trisomy 21.

ROLE OF CLINICAL JUDGMENT

Figure 8.1 shows the role of clinical judgment in situations involving diagnosis, classification, and/or developing individualized supports for persons with ID. As shown in the figure, clinical judgment is parallel with best practices in ID, professional standards, and professional ethics. These four components are involved in addressing diagnosis, classification, and systems of supports situations, and they are basic to making a valid and precise decision or recommendation. Collectively, these four components, and the yet-to-be-discussed clinical judgment strategies, are basic to demonstrating one's professional responsibility in ID.

Best Practices in ID

In the preceding seven chapters in this *Manual,* we have presented current best practices in the field of ID. These best practices involve understanding (a) the definition of ID and its basis within an ecological, multidimensional framework (chapters 1 and 2); (b) the role of assessment in diagnosis, classification, and developing systems of supports (chapter 3); (c) intellectual functioning and adaptive behavior and their assessment (chapters

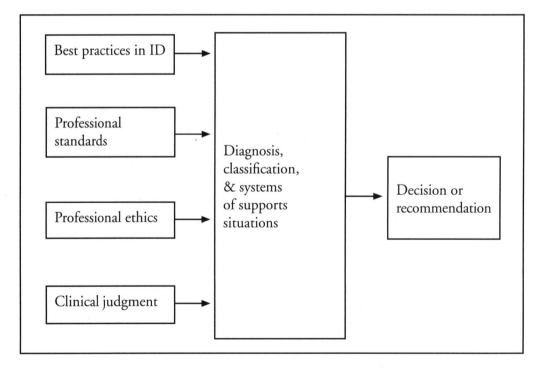

Figure 8.1. Clinical judgment as a component of professional responsibility.

4 and 5); (d) the role of etiological factors in the diagnosis of ID (chapter 6); and (e) a multidimensional approach to classification (chapter 7). The following two sections of the *Manual* summarize our current understanding and use of systems of supports for persons with ID (part III), and the implications of the 11th edition of this *Manual* for public policy, education, and support providers (part IV). Collectively, these 15 chapters spell out in detail current professional best practices in the field of ID.

Professional Standards

Each profession publishes professional standards that provide the basis for evaluating practices and personnel preparation and are used typically for accreditation or quality control. Additionally, professional standards are used as a measure against which to compare individual performance and/or as criteria to review professional behavior and enforce rules of conduct. As discussed more fully in Schalock and Luckasson (2005), a number of professional standards relate directly to diagnosis, classification, and systems of supports situations. Chief among these are recognizing boundaries of competence, using current information and objective judgment, maintaining wholesome client and professional relationships, minimizing conflict of interest, recognizing individual differences, obtaining consent, and respecting human rights and privacy.

Professional Ethics

Our reading of a number of organization documents regarding professional ethics (see, for example, American Psychological Association, 2002; Schalock & Luckasson, 2005, Table 1.1) indicates that most ethical guidelines can be integrated into the following three ethical principles: justice (treating all people equitable), beneficence (doing good), and autonomy (respecting the authority of every person to control actions that primarily affect himself or herself). Although each profession may define these principles in a slightly different manner, collectively these three principles encompass well the purpose of a profession having a set of ethical principles, which is to describe a system of moral behavior and the rules of conduct recognized in respect to a particular class of human actions or a particular group.

In summary, clinical judgment, which we define as a special type of judgment rooted in a high level of clinical expertise and emerges directly from extensive training, experience with the person, and extensive data, is a parallel component of professional responsibility, along with best practices in ID, professional standards, and professional ethics. As clinicians in ID address diagnosis, classification, and systems of supports situations, they also need to use the four clinical judgment strategies discussed next. These strategies, when combined with current best practices in ID, professional standards, and professional ethics, enhance the quality, validity, and precision of the decision or recommendation and also reflect the clinician's professional responsibility in ID.

Clinical Judgment Strategies: Overview and Purpose

Overview

The four clinical judgment strategies summarized in Table 8.1 reflect further revision of those originally published by Schalock and Luckasson (2005). This revised set is based on feedback from the field, critiques from practicing professionals, and published reviews of the Schalock and Luckasson (2005) text. As noted in Table 8.1, each strategy has an associated result. The sequential nature of the strategies is intended to impact the clinician's approach to the question at hand (Strategy 1), conduct or access a thorough history (Strategy 2), conduct or access broad based assessments (Strategy 3), and synthesize the obtained information in order to test hypotheses and determine the relative weight and possible combination of information as a basis for a professional decision or recommendation that answers the question at hand and does so within the framework of professional responsibility (Strategy 4).

Table 8.1
Clinical Judgment Strategies

1. Clarify and state precisely the question set before you and determine whether the question relates to diagnosis, classification, or systems of supports • Result: identifies needed activities and aligns data-collection efforts to the critical question(s) at hand
2. Conduct or access a thorough history • Result: understand personal and environmental factors that affect disability, including personal and family history, possible etiology, educational history, and course of disability
3. Conduct or access broad-based assessments • Result: provides a full picture of an individual's functioning
4. Synthesize the obtained information • Results: provides data and information for (a) generating and testing hypotheses; (b) considering the relative weight and possible combination of information as a basis for decisions and recommendations; and (c) improving the quality, validity, and precision of data-based decision making and recommendations

Purpose

Clinical judgment strategies are used to enhance the quality, validity, and precision of the clinician's decision or recommendation in a particular case. The clinician's effectiveness is due to his or her systematic and reasoned approach to understanding the question at hand, using a sequential and logical approach to data collection, and basing their decision or recommendation on the transparent and clearly communicated synthesis of all relevant information. Thus, use of these strategies is a necessary component of clinical judgment, especially in complex diagnosis, classification, and systems of supports situations in which the complexity of the person's functioning precludes standardized assessment, legal restrictions significantly reduce opportunities to observe and assess the person, historical information is missing and cannot be obtained, or there are serious questions about the validity of the data.

A second purpose of using these four clinical judgment strategies is to avoid thinking errors that can lead to faulty reasoning and, thereby, impact negatively the clinician's decision or recommendation. The following section describes potential thinking errors with which the clinician should be familiar and avoid.

Avoiding Thinking Errors

Table 8.2 summarizes thinking errors that are discussed in more detail in Norman (2005), Papadakis, Teherani, and Banach (2005), and Redermeier (2005). Each of these thinking errors can result in not understanding or aligning the data collected to the question at hand, not completing or accessing a thorough history and broad-based assessment

TABLE 8.2

Common Thinking Errors

Affective error: your feelings, such as incorrect stereotypes, misplaced empathy, or what you wish were true

Anchoring error: the first bit of information anchors your mind on an incorrect decision or recommendation

Availability error: what happened recently or most dramatically

Blind obedience: what the authority said

Commission bias: do something, anything

Confirmation bias: you find what you expect to find

Diagnosis momentum: piling on after an initial diagnosis

Framing effects: mistakenly influenced by the context

Premature closure: deciding too soon

Representativeness error: what is typically true

information, overlooking important personal or environmental factors that impact a person's functioning, and/or reaching a decision prematurely without a thorough analysis and synthesis of all available information. Collectively, these thinking errors reduce the quality, validity, and precision of the clinician's decision or recommendation.

Although one can speculate on the multiple causes of thinking errors, the current literature suggests the following three primary causes:

- Cognitive dissonance, which exists when related cognitions are inconsistent and/or contradictory with one another. This inconsistency produces tension, and one reduces tension by altering one's cognition (Festinger, 1957). For example, having an ID is incorrectly thought to be inconsistent with competency; therefore, because the person has a diagnosis of ID, the assumption is that he or she is incompetent.

- Incompatible mental models, which are defined as deeply ingrained assumptions, generalizations, and images we have to understand the world and form the basis of thought and action (Senge, 2006). In the field of ID, there are two contradictory mental models: a focus on defectology and person-centered traits and characteristics versus an ecological, multidimensional model of human functioning (see Figure 2.1).

- Fundamental attribution error, which refers to the observer's bias in favor of explaining other's behavior on the basis of internal characteristics rather than environmental factors (Hewstone, 1990). An example is the belief that the person's behavior is due to his or her ID rather than environmental factors.

CLINICAL JUDGMENT STRATEGY 1: UNDERSTAND THE QUESTION

The collection and analysis of information begins with a clear understanding of the question at hand, specifically, whether the question relates to diagnosis, classification, or planning individualized supports. Typically, three questions are asked of clinicians: (a) Does the person have ID? (diagnosis); (b) Is the person competent to stand trial, be his or her own guardian, consent to sexual activities, and/or retain child custody? (classification); or (c) What supports are required to assist this individual with ID to be as competent and successful as possible? (planning supports). If the clinician does not clearly understand the question, his or her construction of an assessment strategy will likely be flawed, the answer will not be responsive to the question, the professional's judgment will not be precise or accurate, and the clinician's integrity will be compromised. To prevent this from happening, the assessment framework presented in Table 3.1 summarizes the alignment of each question-related function (diagnosis, classification, systems of supports) to the purposes of that function and to exemplary measures and tools that can be used to answer the questions.

Questions Related to Diagnosis

If the question pertains to eligibility for services, benefits, or legal protection, the focus of the question is generally on diagnosis. Correctly answering this question requires that the person being assessed meets the three diagnostic criteria of ID:

1. *Significant limitations in intellectual functioning* as assessed on an individually administered standardized measure and a resulting score that is approximately two standard deviations below the mean, considering the standard error of measurement for the specific assessment instrument used and the strengths and limitations of the instrument.

2. *Significant limitations in adaptive behavior* as assessed on a standardized measure of adaptive behavior that is normed on the general population, including people with ID and people without ID, and a resulting score that reflects performance that is approximately two standard deviations below the mean of either (a) one of the following three types of adaptive skills: conceptual, social, or practical or (b) an overall score on a standardized measure of conceptual, social, and practical skills.

3. *Age of onset before age 18.* ID is manifested during the developmental period. This period is conceptualized as the period of the life cycle prior to adulthood that is characterized by rapid changes and development in cognitive, social, and practical skills. The cutoff is set at 18 years because this age generally corresponds to the end of high school in the United States and the time when many persons assume adult roles. Eighteen years should not be viewed as the end of one's development because brain plasticity is clearly demonstrated in typical individuals and persons with ID learning new conceptual, social, and practical skills. Furthermore, the cutoff of 18 for a diagnosis of ID need not cause confusion with the cutoff age of 21 years for eligibility for services under the Developmental Disabilities Act (1990); ID is only one of several diagnoses that may result in a developmental disability. The purpose of the age of onset criterion is to distinguish ID from other forms of disability that may occur later in life.

Questions Related to Classification

If the question pertains to grouping for supports or services, communication about selected characteristics (e.g., etiology), or the person's competency, the focus of the question is on classification. Three issues determine what information will be needed to answer classification-related questions. First, what is the purpose for classification? Typical purposes include grouping for service reimbursement or funding, research, services or supports, and communication about selected characteristics. Second, who will use the classification information? Typical users include researchers, clinicians, and/or practitioners. Third, on what basis should classification be made? Depending on its purpose, and as discussed in chapter 7, classification systems can be based on one or more of the elements of a multidimensional model of human functioning: intellectual abilities, adaptive behavior, health, participation, context, and supports (see Figure 2.1).

It is important to realize that classification is used today for more than its historic purpose of grouping on the basis of IQ range bands or adaptive behavior limitations scores. In addition to a diagnosis, clinicians are increasingly being asked classification questions regarding whether the diagnosed person is competent to be a witness, stand trial, consent to sexual activity, parent a child, be his or her own guardian, and/or retain child custody. As clinicians are asked these classification questions, they will need to go beyond the analysis of assessments of intellectual functioning and adaptive behavior that were necessary for diagnosis. They will also need to analyze data from specialized assessments focused on these questions for individuals with ID, such as the Competence Assessment for Standing Trial for Defendants With Mental Retardation (CAST-MR; Everington & Luckasson, 1992) or a guided list of inquiries, such as that developed by Stavis and Walker-Hirsch to provide information and documentation regarding the individual's consent to sexual activity (Luckasson & Walker-Hirsch, 2007).

Questions Related to Developing Supports

If the question pertains to enhancing human functioning and personal outcomes, the focus of the question is on planning and implementing individualized supports. Examples include what supports are necessary to assist this individual with ID to be as competent as possible as a witness, to parent a child, to act as his or her own guardian, to retain child custody, or to experience enhanced personal outcomes. Two guidelines are important to follow in planning and implementing individualized supports: (a) support decisions should be made on the basis of a profile of the pattern and intensity of needed supports obtained from a standardized measure of support needs and (b) the sources of support can include the person him/herself, family and friends, colleagues, neighbors, and recognized services provided by professionals and agencies (see chapter 9).

CLINICAL JUDGMENT STRATEGY 2: CONDUCT OR ACCESS A THOROUGH HISTORY

A thorough history is essential for diagnosis, classification, and supports planning in ID. Such a history should include three components: social, medical, and educational.

Social History

A social history must do more than describe the significant events in a person's life. Specifically, it must contain sufficient detail to allow the clinician to thoroughly investigate, collect, and organize all relevant information about the person's life, including developmental trajectory of the potential ID; functioning at home and in the community; and relationships at home, with neighbors, and with others. In addition, in a thorough social history, there should be exploration of all contacts with agencies with which the individual has been involved, including out-of-home care, juvenile facilities, and social welfare systems.

For a thorough social history, the clinician should take a holistic approach that focuses on the individual's limitations. Although not a part of the diagnosis, exploration of relative strengths may assist the clinician to formulate hypotheses about needed supports. Compiling a thorough social history is especially important when stakes are high, such as in many legal and guardianship cases, when classification and supports planning play a significant role in the person's life or when a retrospective diagnosis is sought.

Medical History

A medical history should include a thorough review of all records related to health of family members; prenatal, perinatal, and postnatal circumstances of the individual's birth; any early concerns or diagnoses; all medical intervention, including the prescription of drugs; genetic or other screenings; injuries; family involvement with alcohol or other drugs; and exposure to toxins. In addition, in the medical history the clinician should review all developmental disorders; physical or mental health disorders; and challenging, difficult, and/or dangerous behaviors.

Educational History

School records are typically available across the elementary, middle, and high school years. An educational history should include (a) mapping out the grades earned across the school years, looking for consistency of low grades in the core academic areas, such as reading, math, English, civics-government, and science (only in the upper grades); (b) indicating any grade level failed or repeated; (c) summarizing teachers' social and behavior ratings; (d) identifying when periodic achievement assessment happened (instruments and results); (e) identifying results of hearing, vision, and any other schoolwide screening; (f) searching for failure/performance patterns that normally would trigger parent/teacher conferences, prereferral meetings, or referrals for special education considerations; (g) identifying the outcome of any eligibility assessment(s) and whether an Individualized Education Program (IEP) was developed; if special education was provided, reporting the diagnosis (typically a developmental delay label is used until age 9), the years given, the type of placement (resource room, self-contained, separate school); (h) noting any services that might be viewed as substitutes to special education, which could indicate difficulties in cognitive adaptive behavior (e.g., remedial reading, chapter 1 services); (i) looking for other evidence of difficulties in cognitive adaptive skills besides grades and test performance (e.g., student often late to class or confused about schedule, difficulty following classroom directions, poor record of handling homework, failing driver education); (j) looking for difficulties in practical adaptive skills (e.g., poor grooming, inability to use money correctly, getting lost in school or on school grounds, unable to tell time); and (k) looking for evidence of difficulties in social adaptive skills (e.g., follows others, lack of self-direction, few friends, gullible, does not understand social humor).

Role of a Thorough History in a Retrospective Diagnosis

It is sometimes necessary to assess the functioning of the individual in his or her past in those situations where a diagnosis of ID becomes relevant, even though the individual did not receive an official diagnosis of ID during the developmental period. A retrospective diagnosis may be required, for example, when clinicians are involved in determining eligibility for adult rehabilitation services, evaluating individuals for Social Security disability, or evaluating individuals involved in legal processes, such as guardianship petitions, competence determinations, or sentencing eligibility questions. In these potential situations, the clinician must use other sources of information, including possible obtainable testing data and the person's history, in order to determine the manifestations of possible ID prior to age 18.

When a thorough history is used to provide information for a retrospective diagnosis, the diagnosis should be based on multiple data points that not only give equal consideration to adaptive behavior and intelligence scores but also reflect an evaluation of the pattern of test scores and factors that affect scores, such as motivation, sensory/motor impairments, and anomalies in the structural features of either the assessment and/or norming sample used at the time of the assessment. In addition, the following five guidelines should be followed in developing a retrospective diagnosis:

- Be aware of legal findings and definitions and clarify any legal question and the form that the recommendation should take.

- Be sensitive to language differences and culturally based behaviors and beliefs. Thus, one needs to investigate and understand the culture, the degree of acculturation, and the language competency of the individual as well as the ways they affect the person. However, do not allow cultural or linguistic diversity to overshadow or minimize disability.

- If adaptive behavior assessments were used and reported in the records reviewed, weigh the extent to which the assessments (a) used multiple informants and multiple contexts; (b) recognized that limitations in present functioning were considered within the context of community environments typical of the individual's peers and culture; (c) measured important social behavioral skills, such as gullibility and naïveté; (d) used an adaptive behavior evaluation that included behaviors that are currently viewed as developmentally and socially relevant; and (e) recognized that adaptive behavior refers to typical and actual functioning and not to capacity or maximum functioning.

- If intellectual functioning assessments were used and reported in the records reviewed, weigh the extent to which the assessments (a) used a standardized and individually administered intelligence test; (b) was the then most recent version of the standardized test used, including the most current norms; (c) took into consideration the standard error of measurement of the instrument when estimating the person's true IQ score; and (d) where a test with aging norms was used, correction was made for the age of the norms (i.e., the Flynn Effect, see chapter 4).

- If indicated, it might be necessary to develop a contemporary assessment in order to show similarities and changes in functioning over the life span.

CLINICAL JUDGMENT STRATEGY 3:
CONDUCT OR ACCESS BROAD-BASED ASSESSMENTS

The purpose of broad-based assessments is to not only answer the question(s) set before the clinician but also permit a full picture of an individual's functioning. This information is critical in those situations in which personal characteristics or environmental factors result in formal assessment that is less than optimal due to its unreliability, invalidity, incompleteness, and/or inappropriateness. These situations require the clinician to develop one or more working hypotheses that are confirmed or not confirmed through information obtained from broad-based assessments that include, in addition to standardized psychometric instruments, alternative assessment strategies and/or direct input from the individual or knowledgeable informants.

Alternate Assessment Strategies

Alternative assessment strategies are not meant to replace formal assessment using appropriate standardized instruments. However, there are times when information obtained from formal assessment instruments does not validly answer the question asked due to lack of opportunity, lack of appropriately normed tests, significant functional limitations of the person, contradictory information, and/or cultural and linguistic factors. In these situations, the clinician's hypothesis can be tested through the proper use of direct observation of the person's behavior or evaluation of the individual's social competency.

Direct observation. As an assessment strategy, direct observation should focus heavily on functional systems assessment (i.e., what the person actually does and how the person interacts with his or her environment, with an emphasis on adaptive behavior). Guidelines for direct observation include (a) the use of multiple informants who know the person well and observe the person in multiple contexts, (b) observations that are based on multiple occurrences of the behavior and not a single event or experience, (c) an explanation of the method used (e.g., averaging across observers) to reconcile different observation scores, (d) the recognition that limitations in present functioning must be considered within the context of community environments typical of the individual's age peers and culture, (e) the understanding that adaptive behavior and challenging behavior are independent constructs and not opposite poles of a continuum, and (f) the recognition that adaptive behavior refers to typical and actual functioning and not to capacity or maximum functioning.

Evaluation of social competency. Many important behaviors, such as gullibility and naïveté, are not measured on most current adaptive behavior scales. The presence or absence of appropriate social behaviors or social competence is critical in each clinical function: diagnosis, classification, and/or planning supports. In the evaluation of social competence, the focus should be on whether or not the person accurately interprets others' emotions and intentions on the basis of available cues; generates appropriate social strategies in response to social problems; and demonstrates knowledge of social scripts and schemes, such as anticipating the consequences of carrying out different strategies for resolving particular social problems in a given social context (National Research Council, 2002; National Research Council, Committee on Disability Determination, 2002).

Direct Input From the Individual or Knowledgeable Informants

The principles of equity, empowerment, and inclusion require that the person with ID and their family have significant input into clinical processes. Information based on this input is essential in developing decisions and recommendations about the person. However, clinicians should recognize that because self-ratings have a high risk of error, self-report information should be interpreted in light of the following guidelines: (a) people with ID are more likely to attempt to look more competent and "normal" than they actually are (Edgerton, 1993; Greenspan & Switzky, 2006), which is sometimes incorrectly interpreted as "faking"; (b) people with ID typically have a strong acquiescence bias or inclination to say yes or agree with an authority figure (Finlay & Lyons, 2002); and (c) ID is a social status that is tied closely to how a person is perceived by peers, family members, and others in the community (Greenspan & Switzky, 2006).

To overcome these potential weaknesses in self-reporting, clinicians should seek out direct input from knowledgeable informants. These informants should know the person well, have observed the person across different community environments and situations, and have formally observed the person longitudinally (i.e., over time).

In summary, and in reference to any assessment activity, when an individual's language or culture is diverse, the clinician must take particular care to ensure that any assessment information addresses the individual's abilities or disabilities, not simply their culture or language differences (American Education Research Association, 1999; Lynch & Hanson, 1992). This means that for broad-based assessments, clinicians need to (a) collect relevant information about the person and his or her home environment or language; (b) select suitable assessment instruments that are sensitive to diversity, have norms that are based on diverse groups, and have acceptable psychometric properties; (c) outline necessary assessment modifications or accommodations; (d) involve an evaluator(s) who is/ are sensitive to, and competent in, the person's language or culture; and (e) ensure that the broad-based assessment process is/was implemented in a manner consistent with all legal and ethical guidelines. Most importantly, the individual's disability must not be overlooked; the clinician should not allow cultural or linguistic diversity to overshadow or minimize an actual disability.

CLINICAL JUDGMENT STRATEGY 4:
SYNTHESIZE THE OBTAINED INFORMATION

Overview

Although the clinician is always using clinical judgment regarding the diagnosis, classification, or supports planning for persons with ID, there are four situations in which the critical thinking skills and the synthesis guidelines discussed in this section of the chapter become more apparent:

1. The complexity of the person's functioning, including medical and behavioral conditions, precludes standardized assessment alone. Examples include persons with severe mental health problems or significant challenging behaviors.
2. Legal restrictions significantly reduce opportunities to observe and assess the person in age-appropriate community environments. Examples include the person being in physical restraints, imprisoned, or highly medicated.
3. Historical information is missing and cannot be obtained. Examples include an adult with suspected fetal alcohol syndrome but whose mother is dead, and there is no one who can provide any information about pre- and postnatal environments or an adult who is requesting disability benefits but has no school records that can be obtained and no reliable family or childhood community reports that can be obtained.
4. Test results are either inconclusive or questionable. Persons with ID are frequently evaluated using a variety of assessment instruments, some of which are appropriate and relevant to the question(s) being asked, some of which are outdated, and some of which produce contradictory results.

The synthesis of information involves applying knowledge and experience to the integration of the information and data obtained from the three previously discussed clinical judgment strategies. The purpose of synthesizing the information is to form the basis for a decision or recommendation that can be characterized as precise and accurate. This synthesis requires the use of critical thinking skills and the application of a number of recommended synthesis guidelines.

Critical Thinking Skills Involved in Synthesizing Information

The synthesis of information as a clinical judgment strategy requires critical thinking skills that are increasingly being recognized as the cognitive engine driving the processes of knowledge development and professional judgment in a wide variety of professional fields (Facione, 1990; Facione & Facione, 1996; Halpern, 1998; Nisbett, 1993; Weiten, 2004). Synthesizing the obtained information as a prelude to making a decision and formulating one or more recommendations involves the four critical thinking skills summarized in Table 8.3: analysis, evaluation, interpretation, and inference.

Table 8.3
Critical Thinking Skills Involved in the Synthesis of Information

Analysis: Examine the case, its elements, and its component parts; reduce the complexity of the case into simpler or more basic components or elements. Important subskills include looking for contradictory explanations for findings and contradictory evidence, recognizing the limits of anecdotal evidence, and recognizing the bias in hindsight analysis (i.e., knowing the outcome of events biases our recall and interpretation of events).

Evaluation: Determine the precision, accuracy, and integrity of available information through careful appraisal and study. Important subskills include using evidence-based decision making; assessing the validity of premises, assumptions, and conclusions; seeking confirmation to reduce uncertainty; understanding the limitations of statistical analysis (e.g., correlation does not mean causation) and the fallibility of human memory; avoiding appeals to ignorance (i.e., lack of information on an issue cannot be used to support an argument); and judging the credibility of an information source.

Interpretation: Integrate the available information in light of the individual's beliefs, judgment, or circumstance. Important subskills include recognizing mental models and the way that definitions shape how we think about issues and constructs such as ID, appreciating the limits of extrapolation, understanding how contrast effects can influence judgments and decisions, and understanding the limits of correlational evidence (i.e., relationship vs. causal).

Inference: Form conclusion or recommendation by integrating all of the facts and tested hypotheses. Important subskills include avoiding reification (i.e., the tendency to treat hypothetical constructs as if they were concrete things); avoiding common fallacies, such as irrelevant reasons, circular reasoning, slippery slope reasoning, weak analysis, and false dichotomies; and discarding previously held theories and/or mental models.

Synthesis Guidelines

The following 12 guidelines augment the critical thinking skills listed in Table 8.3.

1. Show clearly that the obtained data are aligned with the critical question(s) asked. Those questions will relate to diagnosis, classification, or systems of supports.
2. Integrate information from multiple sources. A valid diagnosis of ID is based on multiple sources of information that include a thorough history (social, medical, educational), standardized assessments of intellectual functioning and adaptive behavior, and possibly additional assessments or data relevant to the diagnosis. When considering the relative weight or degree of confidence given to any assessment instrument, the clinician needs to consider (a) the technical adequacy of the instrument, including content and construct validity, reliability, stability of the obtained measures; the generalization of scores; predictive validity; and appropriateness to the individual being assessed; (b) the purpose of the test(s); (c) the

conditions under which the test(s) was/were given; and (d) the standard error of measurement of the assessment instruments used. The standard error of measurement is test-specific and is used to establish a statistical confidence interval within which the person's true score falls. The standard error of measurement is estimated from the standard deviation of the test and a measure of the test's reliability. Therefore, anything that reduces the test's reliability (i.e., inconsistency of measurement) or increases the variability of the person's score (e.g., the test's susceptibility to motivation level, sensory/motor impairments, improper test administration, or lack of normative data for socioeconomic status, ethnicity, or language used) affects the instrument's standard error of measurement. The selection of the confidence interval (i.e., 66% or 95%) relates to the question(s) asked, the properties of the assessment instrument used, and the ultimate use of the obtained score(s).

3. Be aware that some factors might inflate test scores, thus suggesting higher scores than the individual's true score. These factors include anomalies in the structural features of the norming sample, gaps in the development of spacing of item difficulties or subtests of a comprehensive adaptive behavior measure, and pure error variance (Jacobson & Mulick, 2006).

4. Be aware of the potential *false positive* (where the person is diagnosed as an individual with ID but in actually is not) and *false negative* (where the person's true ID is not diagnosed; Greenspan & Switzky, 2006). To overcome a potentially incorrect diagnosis, clinicians need to (a) equate the relative importance of adaptive behavior and intellectual functioning in making a diagnosis of ID; (b) factor in the standard error of measurement of the assessment instruments; and (c) incorporate information from multiple sources, including a thorough history.

5. Explore the possible reasons for differences in data, including poorly trained examiner(s), improper generalizations of test scores administered for other purposes, improper selection of tests, making mistakes in scoring, administration of the same test too close in time, not using the most recent version of the assessment instrument, and examiner bias.

6. Recognize the effects of personal characteristics and environmental factors that can affect test results. As discussed by Jacobson and Mulick (2006), these include (a) personal characteristics, such as concurrent sensory, motor, or mental disabilities; fatigue or illness; high anxiety levels; and the person's motivational history of interaction in assessment situations and (b) environmental factors or conditions, such as educational deprivation, socioeconomically linked language experience, and subcultural biases within the examiner.

7. In the synthesis of school-related factors, determine whether the assessment(s) focused heavily on functional systems of assessment with an emphasis on adaptive behavior. Analogously, in the evaluation of academic competence, the focus should be on the actual academic content or academic standards assessed.

8. In the synthesis of information related to the evaluation of social competence, the focus should be on social perception, the generation of appropriate social strategies

in response to social problems, and the individual's knowledge and use of social scripts and schemes, such as anticipating the consequences of one's behavior.

9. Recognize the impact of *practice effect*, which refers to gains in IQ scores that result from a person being retested on the same test. Practice effect gains occur even when the examinee has not been given any feedback on his or her performance regarding test items, nor do practice effects reflect growth or other improvement on the skills being assessed (Kaufman, 1994).

10. Recognize that self-ratings have a high risk of error because people with ID are more likely to attempt to look more competent and "normal" than they actually are, as well as frequently exhibit an acquiescence bias.

11. Do not use past criminal behavior or verbal behavior to infer level of adaptive behavior or about having ID. Greenspan and Switzky (2006) discussed two reasons for this guideline: There is not enough available information, and there is a lack of normative information.

12. Recognize that a number of reasons might explain the lack of an earlier, official diagnosis of ID, including (a) the individual was excluded from a full school experience; (b) the person's age precluded their involvement in specialized services, such as special education programs; (c) the person was given no diagnosis or a different diagnosis for political purposes, such as protection from stigma or teasing, avoidance of assertions of discrimination, or conclusions about the potential impact on benefits of a particular diagnosis; (d) the school personnel's concern about overrepresentation for data reporting purposes of specific diagnostic groups within their student population; (e) parental desire to avoid a label; (f) contextual school-based issues, such as availability or nonavailability of services and potential funding streams at that time; and (g) the lack of entry referral into the diagnostic-referral process due to cultural and linguistic differences or for other reasons.

SUMMARY

Over the last 2 decades, we have seen major changes in public policy, legal decisions, and service delivery practices that confront clinicians with having to make difficult (and often high stakes) decisions and recommendations related to diagnosis, classification, and/or developing individualized supports for persons with ID. The required task is often compounded by thinking errors that bias one's decision or recommendation and having to make decisions based on incomplete information or situational factors that result in uncertainty, imprecision, and ambiguity. To overcome these challenges, in this chapter we discussed the rationale and parameters to four clinical judgment strategies: clarify and state precisely the question set before the clinician, conduct or access a thorough history, conduct or access broad-based assessments, and synthesize the information based on critical thinking skills and a number of synthesis guidelines. The purpose of these strategies is to assist clinicians in making accurate, valid, and precise decisions and recommendations within the framework of best practices in ID, professional ethics, professional standards, and clinical judgment. The amount of emphasis on clinical judgment in any particular case will vary depending on the type and amount of available information, the complexity of the issue, and the presence of one or more challenging conditions or situations.

Making a valid and credible decision or recommendation involves not just employing the four clinical judgment strategies discussed in this chapter but also requires avoiding thinking errors (Table 8.2) and employing critical thinking skills involved in the synthesis of information (Table 8.3). In addition, a valid and useful decision or recommendation is also based on person-centered standards that include community presence, choice, competence, respect, community participation, and satisfaction. These standards should have broad person-referenced outcomes that can be applied across age and situations and be flexible enough to reflect changing personal characteristics and environmental factors.

Each case will dictate how the decision and/or recommendation is communicated. It might involve a written report, the completion of eligibility determination forms, input into the development of an IEP or Individual Support Plan (ISP), or formal testimony. Regardless of the required format, the decision or recommendation should (a) be clear on the intended product and the form it should take; (b) be communicated clearly, including what data were used to answer the question and how the data collected were aligned with the question(s) asked; and (c) reflect one's competence in clinical judgment by explaining how the process used resulted in meeting the three characteristics of good clinical judgment: systematic (i.e., organized, sequential, logical), formal (i.e., explicit and reasoned), and transparent (i.e., apparent and communicated clearly).

Part III

Systems of Supports

Overview

Public policy and organizational practices toward people with intellectual disability (ID) have focused over the last 30 years on their inclusion and participation in society. This movement, which is reflected in programs related to supported employment, supported living, community living, and inclusive education, has been augmented by the supports paradigm that provides the framework for assessing an individual's support needs and developing individualized systems of supports. More specifically, since the mid-1980s, the supports paradigm has led to at least three significant changes in policies and practices regarding persons with ID. First, the supports orientation has brought together the related practices of person-centered planning, personal growth and development opportunities, community inclusion, self-determination, and empowerment. Second, the judicious application of individualized supports has resulted in enhanced human functioning and personal outcomes. Third, the pattern and intensity of a person's support needs is being used as a basis for agency and systems planning and resource allocation. Within this context (and in this *Manual*), supports and support needs are defined as follows:

- *Supports*: resources and strategies that aim to promote the development, education, interests, and personal well-being of a person and that enhance individual functioning
- *Support needs*: a psychological construct referring to the pattern and intensity of supports necessary for a person to participate in activities linked to normative human functioning

As discussed in the four chapters composing this section of the *Manual*, there are four major implications of conceptualizing ID as a state of functioning instead of an inherent trait. First, any person-environment mismatch that results in needed supports can be addressed through the judicious use of individualized supports rather than focusing solely on "fixing the person." Second, the extent to which these individualized supports are based on thoughtful planning and application, it is likely they will lead to improved human functioning and enhanced personal outcomes. Third, as a bridge between "what is" and "what can be," the focus of educational and habilitation service systems shifts to understanding people by their types and intensities of support needs rather than by their deficits. Fourth, although there is a reciprocal relationship between impairments and support needs in that greater personal limitations will almost always be associated with more intense support needs, a focus on reducing the mismatch between an individual's competencies and the requirements of the environments within which they live, rather than focusing on deficits, is more likely to identify the systems of supports needed to enhance human functioning and personal outcomes.

Throughout these four chapters, readers will also find a discussion of best practices about the assessment of individual support needs and developing individualized systems of support. Chief among these guidelines are the following:

- Understanding a person's support needs is directly related to a constitutive definition of ID because of the focus placed on the fit between a person's state of functioning and the demands of the environment within which the person lives. In that respect, disability is neither fixed nor dichotomized; rather, it is fluid, continuous, and changing, depending on the person's functional limitations and the supports available within the person's environment. Furthermore, individual functioning results from the interaction of supports within the domains of intellectual abilities, adaptive behavior, health, participation, and context.

- An assessment of the person's pattern and intensity of support needs is essential to the development of person-centered plans. The primary purpose for providing supports to persons with ID is to enhance human functioning and personal outcomes, such as those listed in Table 13.1.

- The assessment of support needs can have different relevance, depending on whether it is done for purposes of classification or planning of supports.

- A *systems of supports model* addresses multiple human performance elements that are interdependent and cumulative. As presented in this section and throughout the *Manual*, a systems of supports is defined as the planned and integrated use of individualized support strategies and resources that encompass the multiple aspects of human performance in multiple settings. A systems of supports model provides a structure for the organization and enhancement of human performance elements that are interdependent and cumulative.

- Individualized supports should be provided in natural environments and based on the principles of inclusion and equity.

- A supports model needs to depict the relationship between the mismatch between one's competency and environmental demands and the provision of individualized supports that lead to improved personal outcomes.

- The intensity of a person's support needs reflects an enduring characteristic of the person rather than simply a point-in-time description of the need for a particular type of support.
- Service planning that involves identifying services a person needs to access is not a substitute for individual supports planning that involves developing specific supports a person needs in order to function in activities and settings consistent within his or her preferences.
- Prevention is a form of support.
- Prevention supports focus on primary, secondary, and tertiary strategies directed toward biomedical, social, behavioral, and educational risk factors.
- Comprehensive community health supports are responsive to the physical and mental health needs of persons with ID, are aligned with the ecological, multidimensional conception of disability, and are consistent with the definition of *health* as a state of complete physical, mental, and social well-being.
- Comprehensive community health support standards relate to accessing high quality mental and physical health care, receiving affordable health care, based on self-determination and respect, and participating in health promotion and wellness activities.

CHAPTER 9

SUPPORT NEEDS OF PERSONS WITH INTELLECTUAL DISABILITY

> **Support needs refer to the pattern and intensity of supports necessary for a person to participate in activities linked to normative human functioning.**
> **Supports are resources and strategies that aim to promote the development, education, interests, and personal well-being of a person and that enhance individual functioning.**

OVERVIEW

This chapter is focused on the concept of supports and the construct of support needs as they pertain to people with intellectual disability (ID). *Supports* are "resources and strategies that aim to promote the development, education, interests, and personal well-being of a person and that enhance individual functioning" (Luckasson et al., 2002, p. 151). *Support needs* is "a psychological construct referring to the pattern and intensity of supports necessary for a person to participate in activities linked with normative human functioning" (Thompson et al., 2009, p. 135).

The chapter begins with a discussion of the centrality of support needs in terms of understanding people with ID, along with the significance of a supports orientation to social-ecological models of disability. In the remaining five sections of the chapter, we discuss (a) the concept of supports and the construct of support needs; (b) the measurement of support needs; (c) supports and human performance; (d) a five-component process for assessing, planning, and delivering supports; and (e) approaches to individualized planning.

CENTRALITY OF SUPPORT NEEDS TO UNDERSTANDING PEOPLE WITH ID

Individual Differences and Support Needs

Although people have much in common, it is also true that they differ. The field of individual differences focuses on ways that people are different on dimensions such as personality, motivation, self-concept, intelligence, and adaptive behavior (C. Cooper, 2002). An underlying premise of this *Manual* is that people with ID are different from the general population due to the nature and extent of supports they need to participate in community life.

Justifications for identifying people with ID are based on ways in which low intelligence and limitations in adaptive behavior become manifested in daily life. Namely, people with ID experience great challenges in their learning and development, frequently have difficulty participating in activities of daily life in their communities, and are particularly vulnerable to exploitation by others. The centrality of supports to understanding people with ID is evident when considering these manifestations.

Social-Ecological Model and Support Needs

According to the social-ecological model of disability, described in chapter 2, disability is understood as a multidimensional state of human functioning in relation to environmental demands (Institute of Medicine, 1991, 2007; World Health Organization, 2001). Understanding a person's support needs is directly related to a constitutive definition of ID because of the focus placed on the fit between a person's state of functioning and the demands of the environment in which the person lives. In that respect, disability is neither fixed nor dichotomized; rather, it is fluid, continuous, and changing, depending on the person's functional limitations and the supports available within the person's environment. When ID is understood from a social-ecological perspective, less attention is paid to solving problems that can be evidenced within the person (i.e., increasing personal competence to levels commensurate with others) and more attention is paid to solving problems that are evidenced in the poor fit between the person's capabilities and behavioral requirements of his or her environment. Therefore, based on a social-ecological model of disability, people with ID are different from most others in the general population due to the nature and extent of supports they need to participate in community life.

CONCEPT OF SUPPORTS AND THE CONSTRUCT OF SUPPORT NEEDS

Conceptualizing ID as a multidimensional state of human functioning in relation to environmental demands makes understanding the pattern and intensity of people's support needs essential. Supports and support needs are defined as follows:

- Supports are "resources and strategies that aim to promote the development, education, interests, and personal well-being of a person and that enhance individual functioning" (Luckasson et al., 2002, p. 151).
- Support needs are "psychological construct[s] referring to the pattern and intensity of supports necessary for a person to participate in activities linked with normative human functioning" (Thompson et al., 2009, p. 135).

Understanding Supports

Supports can be technologies, such as a personal digital assistant (PDA) that shows the steps to follow in completing a job task or an augmentative communication device that enhances a person's communication skills through icon input and voice output. Supports can be people, such as a bus driver who prompts a person when it is time to get off at a certain stop or a paid job coach who works one-on-one with a person in a community job. Supports can be referenced to the person or the environment. Support provision needs to be based on the assessed support needs of an individual (i.e., not based on what a program or organization historically provides) and provided with the anticipation that individualized supports will lead to improved human functioning and/or desired personal outcomes.

Supports Model

The supports model shown in Figure 9.1 depicts the relationship between the mismatch between one's competencies and environmental demands and the provision of individualized supports that lead to improved personal outcomes. There are four implications of this model that conceptualizes ID as a state of functioning and addresses a potential person-environment mismatch. First, a *mismatch* between personal competency and environmental demands results in support needs that necessitate particular types and intensities of individualized supports. Second, to the extent that these individualized supports are based on thoughtful planning and application, it is more likely that they will lead to improved human functioning and personal outcomes. Third, as a bridge between what is and what can be, the focus of educational and habilitation service systems shift to understanding people by their types and intensity of support needs instead of by their deficits. Fourth, although there is a reciprocal relationship between impairments and support needs in that greater personal limitations will almost always be associated with more intense support needs, a focus on reducing the mismatch between people's competencies and the environmental requirements where they function, rather than a focus on their deficits, is more likely to lead to identifying, developing, and arranging supports that enhance personal outcomes.

Figure 9.1 also illustrates two related global functions of individualized supports. The first function addresses the discrepancy between what a person is not able to do in different settings and activities and what changes/additions make that person's participation possible. The second function of individualized supports focuses on enhancing personal outcomes by improving human functioning. Both of these functions need to be thoughtfully aligned.

For example, sometimes planning teams focus solely on what individuals can and cannot do in a variety of settings and thus arrange supports to empower individuals to do more things. Although this type of planning may lead to an individual's improved functioning, that individual's personal outcomes may not be significantly enhanced. Such planning may expand the activities available to the person and may even increase

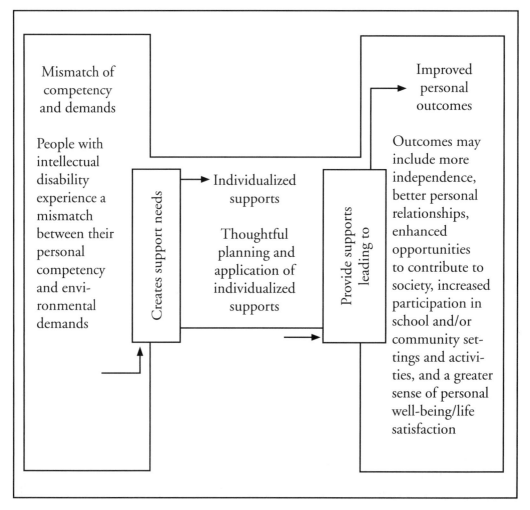

Figure 9.1. Supports model.

participation by the individual. However, if these activities are not based on the person's preferences and priorities, any improvement in personal outcomes may be negligible. Equally misguided would be to focus only on personal priorities and preferences without thoughtfully considering the gaps between a person's competence and his or her environmental demands. This approach to planning increases the risk that supports will be arbitrarily applied. For example, an individual may want to live in his or her own home in the community but may need some support due to safety related concerns. A "throw in everything plus the kitchen sink" approach to supporting the individual might involve supplying staff inside the home who do all the cooking, cleaning, and transporting 24 hours a day, 7 days a week. Such excessive support provision will not enhance the life experiences of the individual and will certainly result in wasting finite resources.

Therefore, it is important to thoughtfully analyze and align both personal priorities and areas of need when planning and delivering supports.

Understanding Support Needs

Whereas supports are resources and strategies that promote personal development and enhance functioning, support needs is a psychological construct referring to the pattern and intensity of supports a person requires to participate in activities associated with normative human functioning. Multiple psychological constructs have been identified regarding both states and traits of humans. For example, anxiety, intelligence, happiness, and morality are all psychological constructs on which there are extreme points (e.g., euphoric and depressed) as well as many points in between—just like the construct of support needs. The support needs construct is based on the premise that human functioning is influenced by the extent of congruence between individual capacity and the environments in which that individual is expected to function. Addressing this congruence (i.e., ensuring person-environment fit) involves understanding the multiple factors that shape human performance, determining the profile and intensity of needed supports for a particular person, and providing the supports necessary to enhance human functioning.

A person's intensity of support needs reflects an enduring characteristic of the person rather than simply a point-in-time description of the need for a particular type of support. People with ID require the provision of ongoing, extraordinary (when compared with their peers with no intellectual disability) pattern and intensity of supports. Providing supports to people with ID enables their functioning in typical life activities in mainstream settings but does not eliminate the possibility that they will continue to need ongoing supports. Put another way, if supports were removed, people with ID would not be able to function as successfully in typical activities and settings.

The *concept of need* generally refers to a condition characterized by the absence of some requisite necessity. Within the professional literature pertaining to health, the concept of need has traditionally referred to a condition characterized as "a disturbance in health and well-being" (M. Donabedian, 1973, p. 62). Within psychology, need can be defined as "what is necessary for an organism's health and well-being" (Harré & Lamb, 1988, p. 409) or a motivated state resulting from "a feeling of unfulfillment or deprivation in the biological system . . . evidenced by a drive to complete such a lack" (Colman, 2001, p. 631). As discussed by Thompson and colleagues (Thompson et al., 2002; Thompson et al., 2004b), support needs are identified based on input from the individual and other respondents. Global (i.e., overall) support needs can be understood in at least four distinct ways (Bradshaw, 1972; Van Bilzen, 2007):

- *Normative need* or *objective need*: what a professional, expert, or social scientist defines as need in a given situation based on an individualized assessment; a professional standard is compared to an individual's actual situation.

- *Felt need*: what the person wants or perceives as needed. This felt need for support can be obtained by asking the person what is needed.
- *Expressed need or demand*: a felt need that has turned into action. An expressed need for support may be a person requesting services.
- *Comparative need*: obtained by studying the characteristics of a population in receipt of a particular service. If there are people with the same characteristics not receiving service, they are in need of that service.

A person's support needs do not necessarily or exclusively reflect a disturbance of human capacity; rather, the person's support needs reflect a limitation in human functioning as a result of either personal capacity or the context in which the person is functioning. Like other psychological constructs, the level of a person's support needs (like the level of a person's motivation or shyness) is inferred and not directly observable.

MEASURING SUPPORT NEEDS

An individual's support needs can be measured with varying degrees of accuracy by self-report and other report indicators of the intensity of support needs, such as is accomplished using the Supports Intensity Scale (SIS; Thompson et al., 2004a, 2004b). The SIS is the only standardized support needs assessment currently available. The standardized portion of the instrument is composed of 49 items relating to life activities in six subscales. There are also eight items included in a supplemental scale focused on self-advocacy and self-determination. In addition, 29 items are related to exceptional supports needed to either maintain or improve medical conditions or prevent negative or damaging consequences from challenging behaviors.

Future progress in accurately measuring support needs will have both theoretical and practical significance. As expressed by W. Thompson (cited by Syndenham, 2003, p. 4), "When you can measure what you are speaking about, and express it in numbers, you know something about it; when you cannot measure it, when you cannot express it in numbers, your knowledge is of a meager and unsatisfactory kind." The social sciences differ in important ways from the hard sciences, and there will never be as precise a measure for constructs like support needs as there is for concepts such as temperature and weight. However, the further development of tools to measure the pattern and intensity of support needs is a worthy endeavor in and of itself.

A reliable tool to measure support needs has practical significance for planning teams. It is a piece of the puzzle needed to develop person-centered plans. Later in this chapter, a five-component planning process is presented, and the ways that information from a comprehensive assessment of support needs contributes to a successful planning process is discussed more fully.

Because support needs assessment and adaptive behavior assessment are both concerned with typical performance in everyday activities, the two can be confused. It is important to understand that assessing a person's support needs is not the same as assessing aspects of personal competence. Whereas adaptive behavior scales assess the adaptive skills that a person has learned (and thus measures achievement or performance associated with personal competence), support needs assessment scales measure an individual's extraordinary supports that are needed to participate in the activities of daily life. Table 9.1 shows critical conceptual differences between the two types of assessment.

TABLE 9.1

Comparison of Scales Measuring Adaptive Behavior and Support Needs

Feature	Adaptive behavior scale	Support needs scale
Uses	To diagnose intellectual disability and to identify relevant educational and training goals that can be listed on individualized education/training plans	To determine a person's support needs in different areas of life (i.e., support needs profile) and relative to others with ID; to develop individualized support plans
Item stems	An array of adaptive behaviors or skills needed to successfully function in society	An array of life activities in which a person engages when participating in society
Item responses	A person's level of mastery or proficiency in relation to adaptive skills	The intensity and pattern of extraordinary supports a person needs in order to participate in life activities
Additional items	Some scales include indicators of problem behavior	The intensity of supports required to maintain/improve medical conditions and prevent negative/damaging outcomes of challenging behaviors

SUPPORTS AND HUMAN PERFORMANCE

Human functioning is enhanced when the person-environment mismatch is reduced and personal outcomes are improved. Because such functioning is multidimensional, considering supports as a means to improve human functioning provides a structure for thinking about more specific functions of support provision. Human performance technology (HPT) theorists have posited that human functioning results from interactions between a person's behavior and his or her environment (Gilbert, 1978). For example, Wile (1996), who created an HPT model by synthesizing five other leading HPT models, suggested that human performance was influenced by the following seven elements: organizational systems, incentives, cognitive supports, tools, physical environment, skills/knowledge, and inherent ability. Examples of the types of support that could correspond to each of Wile's human performance

TABLE 9.2

Examples of Supports That Correspond to Elements in Wile's (1996) Model of Human Performance Technology (HPT)

HPT element	Example
1. Organizational systems	Passing laws and public policies offering incentives to hire persons with disabilities Establishing industry standards for constructing and remodeling home and community settings based on principles of universal design
2. Incentives	Developing a behavioral contract involving positive reinforcement of behaviors to keep one's house clean and sanitary Increasing opportunities to engage in preferred activities as the result of earning more money because of good performance on a job
3. Cognitive supports	Reminders from a coworker to transition to different work activities
4. Tools	Using an augmentative and alternative communication system device to increase expressive communication Using a calculator to enable accurate money exchanges when shopping
5. Physical environment	Providing a less-distracting section of the classroom for test taking Lowering file cabinets for filing by a person who uses a wheelchair
6. Skills/ knowledge	Teaching a person how to use a local health club Using social stories to prepare a person for a visit to doctor's office
7. Inherent ability	Exercising to enhance physical vitality and endurance Using intrinsic motivation to do well in an activity or setting Matching jobs and other activities to an individual's relative strengths

elements are listed in Table 9.2. Wile noted that some of these elements are external to the person (elements 1–5), whereas others (elements 6 and 7) are internal.

Wile's (1996) seven elements are interdependent in terms of human performance and more accurately should be thought of as being cumulative. Therefore, from a supports perspective, solving a problem for any single element may be of limited value if problems with the other elements are ignored. As Edyburn (2000) pointed out when relating Wile's model to decision making in the area of assistive technology, getting a tool (element 4) to improve performance would have a negligible impact if a person lacked motivation (element 2) to be productive on the task for which the tool was to be used. Based on Wile's HTP model, supports should not be delivered to address discrete life activities or separate events or be based on specific support individuals (e.g., job coaches, teachers). Rather, systems of supports should be conceptualized where multiple aspects of human performance are considered in regard to multiple settings.

It is not difficult to envision what a systems of supports would entail when considering the human performance elements in Table 9.2. Consider the case of a man with ID working on a community job. The man could be hired through an on-the-job training program offered by a state vocational rehabilitation agency (element 1, organizational systems). This person may be motivated to do well on the job because of opportunities for recognition and advancement (element 2, incentives) but may require assistance from coworkers on specific job tasks that are difficult (element 3, cognitive supports). Also, this employee could use assistive technologies to work more efficiently (element 4, tools) and may need to have the physical environment modified slightly in order to complete certain job assignments (element 5, physical environment). Also, task analyses of aspects of the job might need to be developed and then taught (element 6, skills/knowledge). Efforts, we hope, were made to assess the person's vocational preferences prior to job placement so that the individual was matched to a job that was reasonably consistent with his unique talents (relative strengths) and personal interests (intrinsic motivation; element 7, inherent ability). This example illustrates how each element of human performance was addressed through a systems of supports, and, therefore, would provide the worker with a good opportunity to be successful on this job.

An interesting implication of Wile's (1996) model is the role supports play at the organizational level. Although public policy is not considered an individualized support, it is evident that laws and regulations can have tremendous influence on people's lives (see chapter 13). For example, consider the passing and subsequent reauthorization of the Individual With Disabilities Education Improvement Act (2004) and its effect on opportunities provided to children with disabilities in the nation's schools. Prior to 1975, it was legal in many states to deny a child with special needs access to a public education. Although federal and state legislation, as well as local policies, would never be listed as distinct supports on individualized plans, it is important to acknowledge the influence that policymakers and advocacy organizations have on the quality and quantity of supports that are available.

FIVE-COMPONENT PROCESS FOR ASSESSING, PLANNING, AND DELIVERING SUPPORTS

Supports are a universe of resources and strategies that enhance human functioning. No individual will need all of the types of supports that are available. A person's support needs differ both quantitatively (in number) and qualitatively (in nature). Planning teams are in the best position to identify the types of supports that people need. In Figure 9.2, a five-component sequential process is provided for (a) identifying what the person

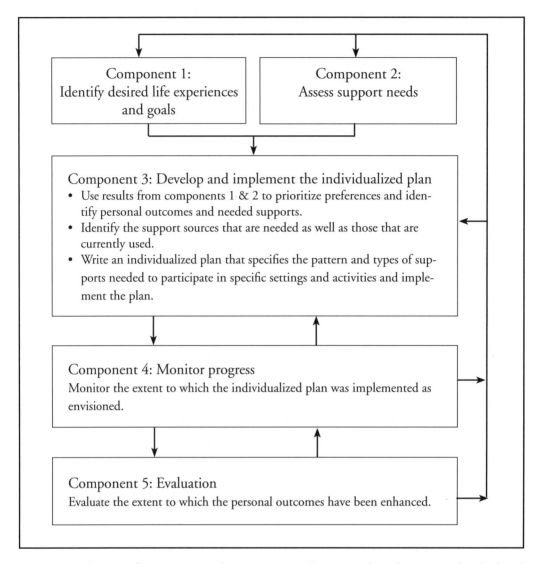

Figure 9.2. Process for assessing, planning, monitoring, and evaluating individualized supports.

most wants and needs to do, (b) assessing the nature of support a person will require to accomplish what he or she most wants and needs to do, (c) developing an action plan to garner and deliver supports, (d) initiating and monitoring the plan, and (e) evaluating personal outcomes. This support planning and implementation process has evolved from a planning process originally developed by Thompson et al. (2002, 2004b).

Component 1: Identify Desired Life Experiences and Goals

The first component of this support process requires the use of person-centered planning processes. A hallmark of person-centered planning is its focus on the individual's dreams, personal preferences, and interests. The primary purpose of a person-centered planning process is to find out what is important to a person, and it is essential that discussions are not constrained by available services or by perceived barriers such as fiscal restrictions or limitations in a person's skills (O'Brien & O'Brien, 2002). As a team planning method, person-centered planning has been shown to yield better outcomes for adults with ID than traditional methods of service planning (Holburn, Jacobson, Schwartz, Flori, & Vietze, 2004; Robertson et al., 2006). Person centered planning processes involve the person with the disability and people important to that person. The desired outcome of such planning is a unified vision of a person's life going forward. This vision takes into account those aspects of the individual's current life that are favorable (i.e., aspects to maintain) and adds elements that will enhance his or her life in the future (i.e., aspects to change).

Component 2: Determine the Pattern and Intensity of Support Needs

The second component of the support process involves assessing the person's support needs. As one example, the Supports Intensity Scale (Thompson et al., 2004a) is a standardized measure used to evaluate an individual's support needs across seven life activity domains as well as to identify exceptional medical and behavioral support needs. However, any method that a planning team finds useful for assessing support needs could be used, including direct observation of the person in a variety of life activities and structured interviews with the person and his or her family members. The critical information to gather is the nature of the extraordinary supports that a person would require to engage successfully in an array of activities, especially those associated with the life priorities identified through person-centered planning.

Component 3: Develop the Individualized Plan

The third component of the process builds on the first two components to develop an individualized support plan. Here, the discussion shifts from "someday" to "now," and it is important that an optimistic and realistic plan of action be designed and implemented. Because a plan cannot address all priorities effectively at one time, some personal priorities identified in Component 1 may need to be tempered, and some difficult choices may need to be made. However, the result of Component 3 should be "an unambiguous, individualized plan that specifies (a) the settings for and activities in which a person is likely to engage during a typical week, and (b) the types and intensity of support that will be provided (and by whom)" (Thompson et al., 2004b, p. 81).

Component 4: Monitor Progress

The fourth component of the process, monitoring, requires that planning teams monitor the extent to which the person's individual plan was implemented. Monitoring should be ongoing and systematic in terms of periodically scheduled meetings to consider the congruence between what was planned and what has actually come to pass.

Component 5: Evaluation

The final component, evaluation, focuses on the extent to which desired life experiences and goals and personal outcomes are being realized. This involves examining the individual's life experiences through the lens of personal outcomes. It is important to acknowledge that personal preferences and priorities can change over time, and completing this component of the process will assure that the plans get revised when they no longer continue to meet the person's needs. Also, aggregate data on personal outcomes can provide organizations and state systems with information regarding the extent to which systems are meeting the needs of individuals. Outcome evaluation frameworks for person-referenced, family-related, and societal outcome domains are found, respectively, in Tables 13.1–13.3.

In summary, this five-component process for assessing, planning, monitoring, and evaluating supports requires a significant investment of time and energy. A comprehensive planning process is essential for arranging supports that are aligned with individual needs and desired outcomes of people with ID. Planning teams can always return to previous components in the process when needed. For example, if Component 4 (monitoring) revealed the plan was not implemented due to unforeseen complications, the planning team would want to return to Component 3 and revise the plan. Also, the cycle of components should be repeated as individuals grow and change and require revised support plans. The process always begins with assessing personal interests and the profile and intensity of needed supports; proceeds to team planning, implementation, and monitoring; and ends with an evaluation of personal outcomes.

APPROACHES TO INDIVIDUALIZED PLANNING

Individualized planning terms and documents differ widely as reflected in Individualized Support Plan, Individualized Service Program, Individualized Program Plan, Individualized Education Program, Individualized Transition Plan, Individualized Written Rehabilitation Plan, Individualized Habilitation Plan, Person Directed Plan, and Individualized Family Service Plan. The word or words sandwiched between "Individualized/Person" and "Plan/Program" may indicate something significant (e.g., age group or approach to planning), or for all practical purposes may mean very little. Some planning documents include legally mandated sections, others are structured by core philosophical values, while still others are artifacts of past practices and traditions that have evolved over time. Although specifying what a planning document should include is beyond our scope in this chapter, it is instructive to distinguish among the different approaches to planning and consider the need to include support planning as a part of any individualized plan.

Service Plans and Support Plans

Services can be defined as organized means for delivering supports, instruction, therapies, or other forms of assistance (Thompson et al., 2009, p. 143). For example, advocacy services provide a means for people to access a variety of advocacy supports, and such supports could range from legal assistance to assuring that planning team members consider an individual's preferences; educational services provide instruction that enhances intellectual development and provide opportunities to learn new skills; health services offer preventive medical care, treatment of health problems, as well as therapies, such as occupational or physical. Not all services will provide the same scope or quality of supports. Differences between service providers might be due to having different missions and purposes or could be the result of different levels of proficiency.

Based on the definition of services, service planning should focus on the types of services that need to be accessed as well as the general scope of involvement (hours) that a person should have with the provider. Because services are portals to supports and other forms of assistance, it is important for communities to have coordinated systems of services. A service planning component in an individualized plan is necessary to identify service providers who can deliver needed supports or other types of assistance.

However, service planning is not a substitute for support planning. Simply identifying hours of service or specifying programs in which an individual is going to participate is unlikely to result in individualized supports or enhanced human functioning and optimal personal outcomes. Thus, distinguishing between support planning and service planning is not just an issue of semantics. Planning teams need to identify services an individual needs to access, but this is not the same as developing the patterns and intensities of specific supports a person needs to function in activities and settings consistent with his or her preferences.

Achievement Plans and Support Plans

Support plans also differ from achievement plans. Achievement plans are a prominent part of Individual Education Programs (IEPs) and Individualized Written Rehabilitation Plans documents where the focus is on learning and/or achieving observable and measurable skills. The purpose of public education and vocational rehabilitation services is to change people in a positive way. Therefore, achievement plans target skill acquisition and levels of mastery. However, although support plans might involve accessing educational settings for purposes of learning new skills, the focus of support planning in such a case would be on assuring participation and/or accessing learning opportunities. Unlike achievement plans, support plans are not characterized by long-term goals and short-term behavioral objectives that specify achievement milestones for an individual. Rather, the function of support plans is to identify the resources and strategies that will bridge the gap between the challenges that a person with ID experiences in life activities (i.e., person-environment mismatch) and the life experiences and opportunities (i.e., outcomes) that the individual values.

In the case of children who are attending school, IEP teams are legally bound to include achievement plans in IEP documents (e.g., measurable learning goals as well as benchmarks for progress monitoring). However, IEP planning forms and processes should also include individualized support plans (see chapter 14). For example, planning for the types of accommodations that will be made to support a child to access the general education curriculum and receive an education in the least restrictive environment are applicable to students with ID. Although support planning should not necessarily dominate the focus of all IEPs and Individualized Written Rehabilitation Plans, the need for support planning should not be dismissed.

SUMMARY

This chapter was focused on the concept of supports and the construct of support needs as they pertain to individuals with ID. The chapter began with a discussion of the centrality of support needs in terms of understanding people with ID, along with the significance of a supports orientation to a social-ecological model of disability. In subsequent sections of the chapter, we discussed the concept of supports and the construct of support needs; the measurement of support needs; supports and human performance; a five-component process for assessing, planning, and delivering supports; and the currently used approaches to individual planning.

As discussed in parts I and II of this *Manual*, the diagnostic criteria and procedures described provide an operational means to identify a set of individual differences that are consistent with the operational definition of ID. Adaptive behavior scales and intelligence tests remain the cornerstones of diagnosis because of their relatively long history of use as well as their psychometric properties that provide evidence of measurement reliability and validity. However, these measurement tools have not been particularly useful for purposes of planning supports to meet individual needs because they do not provide information on the most salient difference between people with ID and others in the general population, namely, the nature and extent of supports needed to participate in community life.

Only through continued conceptual and practical advances in understanding the support needs of people with ID will future operational definitions of ID become better aligned with the constitutive definition of ID that has emerged from a social-ecological model of disability, where the focus is on the person-environment fit. As discussed in this chapter, planning and providing supports is the key to addressing the gap between a person's capabilities and the repertoire of behaviors and skills he or she needs to successfully participate in all facets of daily life.

CHAPTER 10

PREVENTION AS A FORM OF SUPPORT

> Prevention can be considered from three perspectives: primary prevention increases the person's state of health, secondary prevention links identification with intervention, and tertiary prevention improves overall functioning. The multifactorial risk factor approach for determining the etiology of intellectual disability presented in chapter 6 provides opportunities for primary, secondary, and tertiary prevention. These opportunities are delineated as specific individualized supports that are targeted toward each etiologic risk factor and the interaction among risk factors that are present in a particular individual.

OVERVIEW

Prevention is a concept that has several different meanings when it is applied to the field of intellectual disability (ID). As such, the word "prevention" can mean different things to different people. Distinguishing among these different meanings is critically important to avoid misunderstanding. In this chapter we outline a way of thinking about prevention that is consistent with the systems of supports described in this section of the *Manual*. To that end, the four purposes of this chapter are to present (a) a tripartite classification approach to prevention (primary, secondary, and tertiary), (b) three additional perspectives on prevention, (c) a discussion on the concept of prevention supports, and (d) how prevention supports can be developed for persons with ID. The concept of prevention as a form of support presented in this chapter links the multifactorial etiologic factors influencing the manifestation of ID to an individualized program of supports designed to prevent or reduce the impact of the risk factors and their interactions present in a particular case.

PRIMARY, SECONDARY, AND TERTIARY PREVENTION

One important meaning of the prevention concept derives from the classification of prevention into *primary*, *secondary*, and *tertiary* categories. This classification was originally applied to disease prevention and thus reflects a medical approach to some extent (Gordan, 1987). However, it also has important implications for the supports orientation described later in this chapter, and, therefore, it is important to understand it within that context as well.

Primary Prevention

Primary prevention refers to strategies that prevent the development of the disease, condition, or disability itself. Individuals should experience a greater degree of health (in the broad sense) as a result of these strategies. One example of primary prevention is helping alcoholic mothers to stay sober during pregnancy, thereby preventing the child from developing fetal alcohol syndrome. Another example involves childhood immunization against diseases such as measles or Hemophilus influenza, thereby preventing the child from developing meningoencephalitism, which leads to ID. Another example involves strategies to encourage children to wear bicycle helmets, thereby preventing traumatic brain injuries. In each of these examples, the child is healthier as a result of the primary prevention activity.

Secondary Prevention

Secondary prevention refers to strategies that prevent the emergence of symptoms or disability in individuals who have an existing condition or disease. In this category, individuals have an underlying condition that cannot be prevented directly. For example, a person who is born with phenylketonuria (PKU) has a mutation in the PKU gene that is present in every cell of the body. This DNA abnormality will be present throughout the person's lifetime. Secondary prevention in this case is the special dietary management that is provided to an individual who is born with the PKU mutation, starting at birth, which prevents the accumulation of toxic metabolites that would otherwise cause ID. People with PKU who adhere to the diet will still have PKU, but they should not experience symptoms or disability from it. Another example of secondary prevention involves the broad range of screening programs developed to identify individuals with a variety of conditions before those conditions have already resulted in symptoms or disability. These screening programs are justified when identification is linked to effective intervention. (It is generally considered unethical to screen asymptomatic children for the presence of conditions that are not treatable.) Thus, the secondary prevention strategy necessarily encompasses both the screening process as well as the intervention. Universal newborn screening for PKU, and prompt dietary treatment of any child who tests positive, is the classic model for this approach, which has been widened greatly over the years to encompass developmental and behavioral screening as well. Universal screening of young infants for early indications of developmental delay and prompt provision of effective early intervention services represent another form of secondary prevention when it helps the child to achieve more typical developmental milestones subsequently. Another example involves close monitoring of infants who have an older sibling with autism (because the recurrence risk for a subsequent sibling is around 10%). Intensive intervention is then provided if the infant begins to show signs of atypical development as early as 6 to 12 months of age, in the hope that this early identification and intervention will prevent the emergence of symptoms of autism in the younger sibling. In each of these examples, the critical aspect of strategies for secondary prevention is the linkage of identification of persons at risk with intervention to prevent the emergence of disability.

Tertiary Prevention

Tertiary prevention refers to strategies that reduce (but cannot completely eliminate) the consequences of a disability on overall functioning. These strategies do not prevent the disease or disability itself but rather seek to minimize the effects of the condition or to prevent other conditions or complications that may emerge as a result of the disease or disability. Tertiary prevention seeks to improve overall functioning, which can be understood according to the model of the *International Classification of Functioning, Disability, and Health* (World Health Organization, 2001). According to this system, impaired functioning (disability) results from the interaction of physical impairments, activity limitations, and participation restrictions. Tertiary prevention strategies can address each of these categories. For example, a person with Down syndrome is at risk for developing thyroid disease, which can cause a variety of symptoms as the child grows up. Periodic thyroid function testing of people with Down syndrome can thus prevent the physical impairments that can arise as a result of thyroid disease. In another example, behavioral supports that help an individual with ID to overcome problem behaviors and develop appropriate vocational skills and attitudes can prevent the activity limitations that the person might otherwise experience. Similarly, strategies that promote social inclusion (such as community and recreational supports) can prevent functional impairment due to participation restrictions. In each of these examples, tertiary prevention strategies are used to reduce the impact of the disability. The key aspect of this type of prevention is the emphasis on improved overall functioning.

ADDITIONAL PERSPECTIVES ON PREVENTION

In addition to the tripartite (primary, secondary, tertiary) approach to prevention just discussed, there are three additional perspectives found in the literature. These perspectives are the prevention of secondary health conditions, the selective termination of pregnancy, and an ecological/interaction perspective.

Prevention of Secondary Health Conditions

Secondary health conditions are defined as additional physical or mental health conditions that can result from a primary health condition but are not a diagnostic feature of that condition (Institute of Medicine, 2007). Confusion may arise, however, because the words *primary* and *secondary* have different meanings in this context compared to the way the same words are used in the tripartite classification of prevention described earlier. Understanding this distinction is very important because both contexts are encountered frequently in public health policy and practice. Properly understood, prevention of secondary health conditions is actually one aspect of tertiary prevention. Tertiary prevention encompasses a variety of strategies to improve overall functioning, including prevention of secondary health conditions (physical impairments), prevention of secondary behavioral conditions (activity limitations), and prevention of secondary social conditions (participation restrictions). Prevention of secondary health conditions is very important throughout the life span, but it represents only one type of opportunity for using prevention concepts to support individuals with ID and their families. Prevention of secondary conditions, in general, should be considered a subcategory of the broader concept of prevention as a form of support that is discussed in a later section of this chapter.

Selective Termination of Pregnancy

The concept of prevention has taken on a somewhat different meaning in popular usage, and it is this meaning that has driven much of the debate in recent years. Prevention in this sense refers to strategies to prevent the birth of individuals with disabilities, usually through selective termination of pregnancies that are expected to result in the birth of a child with a disability. This meaning of prevention is linked to advances in genetics and reproductive technology (Swenson & Brock, 2007). Thus, widespread screening early in pregnancy is recommended to determine whether the fetus has Down syndrome (American College of Obstetrics and Gynecology, 2007). The vast majority (up to 90%) of fetuses with Down syndrome detected in this way are aborted. As genetic advances allow more conditions to be diagnosed prenatally, more fetuses with these various genetic conditions will likely be aborted. However, new reproductive technologies can prevent the need for selective termination of affected pregnancies. For example, families known to be at risk for having a child with a genetic disorder could choose to undergo preimplantation genetic diagnosis, which involves in vitro fertilization and growth of multiple embryos prior to implantation in the uterus. When the embryos have reached an early stage of development, it is reasonably safe to remove a few of the embryonic cells and test them to see whether they have the genetic disorder for which the family is at risk. Any embryo that is found to be affected is then donated or discarded, and only those embryos that are not affected are implanted into the mother's uterus. This procedure can effectively prevent the birth of individuals with certain genetic conditions without requiring the selective termination of the pregnancy.

This prevention perspective has been at the root of an increasingly polarized debate in public, scientific, political, and religious circles. Much of that debate is beyond our scope in this chapter, and it is sufficient here to acknowledge that it exists. Social and religious groups that oppose abortion oppose this kind of prevention, while those that favor abortion support the availability of these genetic and reproductive techniques. Advocates for people with disabilities, and people with genetic disorders themselves, are concerned that a society that seeks to prevent their birth may also be devaluing their existence as human beings (Swenson & Brock, 2007).

The critical point to be emphasized is the distinction between primary prevention and prevention of the birth of individuals with disabilities. Primary prevention always involves the continued existence and survival of the individual in a healthier state than the person would have been otherwise. Any strategy that involves discarding embryos or aborting fetuses with genetic conditions cannot be considered a form of primary prevention. This chapter is focused on prevention as a form of support for individuals and families affected by ID. The meaning of prevention as used here is limited to primary, secondary, and tertiary prevention as defined earlier and does *not* include preventing the birth of individuals with disabilities.

Ecological/Interaction Perspective

An *ecological/interaction approach* involves an awareness of how individuals interact with their environments and an understanding of how risk factors interact during an individual's life span (Coulter, 1992). Intellectual disability is the functional consequence of the interaction between individual limitations in intellectual skills and adaptive behavior with the demands and expectations of the personal and social environment. Prevention supports for persons with ID can improve functioning when they enhance intellectual skills and/or adaptive behavior (e.g., using biomedical, educational, or behavioral supports) or adjust environmental demands to facilitate performance of desired activities and social inclusion (e.g., using social and educational supports).

Understanding how risk factors interact across the life span is essential for the design of effective prevention supports. Support strategies that focus on only one risk factor may fail because they do not address other interacting risk factors. For example, a pregnant woman who is very poor may not be able to afford prenatal care and may become homeless after the child is born. If the child is born with a disability, she may not be able to access appropriate medical and developmental services. A biomedical prevention support that only provided prenatal care would not address these other social and educational risks, and the child's functioning may be affected adversely as a result. Effective multifactorial prevention supports in this case would also include social supports to help the mother obtain stable housing, behavioral supports to help her take care of her child with a disability, and educational supports to improve the child's developmental skills as much as possible.

The effect of poverty might be different at a later time in the person's life span, however. When the child (who now is recognized as having ID) grows up and leaves school, he or she may be unable to find employment or stable housing and be forced to live at the margins of society, might not eat well or get good medical care, and could be exposed to dangerous situations. This individual may experience social isolation or rejection, with resulting mental health issues as well. Thus, the interaction of biomedical, social, behavioral, and educational risk factors will be different for this person as an adult from what it was when he or she was a child. Clearly, effective multifactorial prevention supports would also need to be different for this person as an adult compared with this person as a child.

Another important aspect of an ecological/interaction perspective involves the distinction between genetics and genomics, and how this distinction influences individual health and well-being. *Genetics* focuses on individual genes and their biomedical effects, one at a time. Normal genes produce normal proteins that then perform normal activities within the cell. Abnormalities within single genes (such as mutations, deletions, expansions, or duplications) result in abnormal proteins (reduced in quantity or quality), which then are unable to perform the required cellular activity. For example, a mutation in a sodium channel gene may cause the abnormal sodium channel protein to be less effective at regulating sodium concentrations across the cell membrane. Genetics is the science that studies the nature, mechanism, and consequences of these individual gene disorders. Clinical genetics applies this knowledge to human disorders. If a person has the appropriate genetic abnormality for a particular disorder (e.g., a sufficiently large expansion of the gene for fragile X syndrome), then that person will develop clinical symptoms of the disorder. Not much can be done to prevent the abnormal gene from having this adverse effect.

Genomics, in contrast, considers all of the 20,000 or more genes as parts of a single dynamic system that is constantly changing and adapting to internal and external forces. Various genes are activated or inactivated from time to time during the life span, depending on a variety of poorly understood factors. One aspect of genomics seeks to understand how to activate advantageous genes and inactivate deleterious genes. In another aspect of genomics, researchers study how individuals can reduce the impact of deleterious genes by intentional activities, such as medical treatment or changes in behavior. For example, genomic studies may demonstrate that an individual has a number of genetic abnormalities that, taken together, increase the person's risk of developing heart disease. If that person smokes, drinks, and/or eats excessively; avoids medical care; and ignores the early signs of chest pain, then the person may die from a heart attack or become severely disabled and unable to function. On the other hand, if that same person with the same genomic abnormalities does not smoke or drink and adheres to a heart-healthy diet, obtains medical treatment to lower cholesterol level, and is alert to any warning signs of heart disease, then the person may live a long and healthy life. In this example, multiple internal (genomic) and external (social and behavioral) risk factors interact to determine whether the individual will experience symptoms of impaired functioning. Prevention supports can potentially address many of these interacting risk factors and, thereby, help the individual avoid death and disability.

PREVENTION SUPPORTS

The idea of prevention as a form of support was originally introduced to integrate prevention concepts with the AAIDD (then AAMR) diagnostic, classification, and systems of supports (Coulter, 1996). When AAIDD (formerly AAMR) defined ID as a problem in functioning and not as a disease (Luckasson et al., 1992), the question for prevention became how to prevent this problem in functioning instead of how to prevent a disease. Traditional medical model approaches to disease prevention were no longer adequate. A new way of thinking was required to identify what caused the problem in functioning in the first place. The multiple risk factor approach to etiology was first developed in 1992 to outline the various factors that might put an individual at risk for having this particular problem in functioning. The current version of this risk factor approach to etiology was described in chapter 6. Within this approach, the issue of how to prevent the problem in functioning can be reformulated as how to prevent these various risk factors from operating in the lives of individuals and families in such as a way as to cause ID. The key insight was the realization that the way to prevent these risk factors from causing ID was to support the individual and family.

Table 10.1 presents an overview of how the tripartite classification of prevention described earlier integrates with prevention supports. Within each category of risk factors, opportunities are identified for supporting individuals across the life span. These support opportunities are further classified as representing primary, secondary, or tertiary prevention according to the concepts and strategies outlined in this chapter. Prevention supports in Table 10.1 are consistent with the criteria listed earlier: primary prevention supports result in improved personal health, secondary prevention supports link identification with intervention, and tertiary prevention supports focus on improving overall functioning.

One very important implication of this supports approach to prevention is that it is focused on the individual and family. In the past, prevention strategies have often been focused on public policy development, public health agencies, health care professionals, and community providers. For example, a government agency might decide that all children should be screened for lead poisoning. The success of this effort to prevent lead poisoning might then be measured by how many children were tested and how many had high lead levels. Unfortunately, once a child is poisoned with lead, subsequent treatment to remove the lead does not change the outcome all that much. This "successful" prevention program might not actually prevent disability in the children who tested positive for lead. Focusing on the individual and family would involve identifying families at high risk, testing their homes and other environmental sources for lead, removing families from places where lead is found, and helping them find safer places to live so that their children will not be exposed to lead in the first place. The success of such a program would be measured by how many high-risk families (such as those living in older homes likely to contain lead) were helped to find safer homes for their children, and how many children did *not* test positive for lead.

According to the World Health Organization (1993, 2001), *health* is defined as a state of complete physical, mental, and social well-being. *Wellness* refers to the state of being healthy or having an optimal state of well-being. In reference to Table 10.1, wellness can now be seen as the individual's experience of prevention. Each of the supports outlined in each risk factor category are designed to assist a particular individual or family. Furthermore, the ultimate measure of the success of these individually designed prevention supports is the extent to which they enhance the individual's experience of personal wellness (Coulter, 1996).

TABLE 10.1

Etiology and Prevention of Intellectual Disability: A Multifactorial and Intergenerational Model

Type of prevention/ recipient of service	Risk factor category			
	Biomedical	Social	Behavioral	Educational
Primary prevention	Examples of prevention supports			
Parent of child with ID	Lead screening Nutrition	Prevention of domestic violence	Acceptance	Social skills
Parent of teenager with ID	Nutrition	Family support	Mature self-care	Sexuality
Parent to be	Prenatal care and screening Prenatal nutrition	Emotional and social support	Avoidance of substance use (or treatment)	Parenting
Primary and secondary prevention	Examples of prevention supports			
Newborn with (or at risk for) ID	Metabolic screening	Promotion of parent–child interaction	Parental acceptance of child	Referral of at-risk newborn for services
Child with (or at risk for) ID	Nutrition Lead screening	Family support Avoidance of abuse and neglect	Avoidance of accidents and injuries Special education Vocational training	Early intervention
Tertiary prevention	Examples of prevention supports			
Adult with ID	Physical and mental health care Prevention of obesity	Community inclusion	Exercise and fitness Leisure activities	Employment

DEVELOPING PREVENTION SUPPORTS

Step 1: Develop a Comprehensive Program

The first step in the development of a comprehensive program of individualized prevention supports is to describe all of the etiologic risk factors present in a particular case as well as the interactions among them. This process was discussed in chapter 6 and an example of such a list was provided for a child with fetal alcohol syndrome. Table 10.2 shows the etiologic risk factors that were identified in this case.

Step 2: Describe Prevention Strategies

The second step is to describe prevention strategies that address each identified risk factor and the interactions among them. These strategies should be designed to reverse or reduce the impact of each risk factor and intervention, if possible. Table 10.2 also shows how prevention strategies might be identified that would provide individual and family

TABLE 10.2

**Relating Etiology to Prevention and Support
for a Child With Fetal Alcohol Syndrome**

Category	Risk factors present	Prevention supports
Biomedical	1. Fetal alcohol syndrome 2. Congenital heart disease	1. Nutritional support 2. Medical and surgical treatment of heart disease
Social	1. Family poverty 2. Homelessness 3. Inadequate parenting skills	1. Family support 2. Parental job training 3. Parenting skills development
Behavioral	1. Parental substance abuse 2. Child abuse or neglect	1. Treatment for alcoholism 2. Domestic violence prevention
Educational	1. Lack of adequate early intervention services	1. Enrollment in early intervention
Interactions among risk factors	1. Maternal poverty and substance abuse causing lack of prenatal care and fetal alcohol syndrome 2. Homelessness causing lack of adequate early intervention services	1. Treatment for alcoholism and job training promotes good prenatal care and avoidance of alcohol use during pregnancy 2. Family support and job training results in stable home and enrollment in local early intervention program

supports for this child with fetal alcohol syndrome. Many of these prevention strategies can be accomplished at the local or personal level and thus become part of the systems of supports for that individual.

Step 3: Evaluate Progress

The third step in the development of prevention supports is to evaluate the progress or success of the prevention support program. Changes can then be made as needed to ensure that the individual and family are experiencing greater wellness as a result of this program.

The following examples demonstrate how the process works in real life. A 3-year-old boy is brought to the doctor by a couple who want to help him. They belong to a religious society that operates an orphanage in South America, where the boy was abandoned by his mother when he was 1 year old. They obtained a medical visa to bring him to the United States for treatment and are now looking for help. The boy is severely malnourished, nonverbal, and nonambulatory. He was diagnosed with cerebral palsy by a neurologist and is believed to have ID by the educational intake team. Etiologic risk factors for his ID include biomedical (cerebral palsy, malnutrition), social (lack of infant care, family poverty, institutionalization), behavioral (parental abandonment, social deprivation), and educational (lack of any early intervention or therapy). Interactions include his birth mother's poverty, inability to care for him, and the orphanage's inability to provide nourishment, emotional stimulation, educational intervention, or therapy for his cerebral palsy. A comprehensive program of prevention supports targeted at these risk factors include routine medical care (including immunizations and health screening); orthopedic management of his cerebral palsy; good nutritional support; extension of his visa to ensure he continues to receive care; social supports for the caretaking couple; potential adoption when he is legally free; enrollment in a specialized preschool program; and provision of extensive physical, occupational, and speech therapy. After receiving these supports for 1 year, he is thriving, gaining weight, socially interactive, happy, and making significant developmental progress. His social situation remains unsettled, however, and needs continued work.

Another example involves a 45-year-old woman with Down syndrome who has functioned well all of her adult life. She lives with her husband (who also has ID), and they receive social supports to help them remain as independent as possible. She has enjoyed good health (other than taking medication for hypothyroidism) and has been employed at a local grocery store for years. Recently, her husband has noticed that she is more forgetful at home, and the grocery store manager has noticed that she is increasingly confused and disorganized at work. A neurologist administers a variety of tests and concludes that she is in the early stages of Down syndrome–related dementia. Etiologic risk factors in this case address her current level of functioning. Although she has always had ID, the development of dementia has increased her level of disability. The interaction of biomedical (Down syndrome, hypothyroidism), social (married life, social supports, inclusion), behavioral (stable employment, community involvement), and educational (involvement in her church's bible study group) risk factors has changed as she has grown from a child into adulthood and middle age.

Now the interaction is changing again as this woman faces the inevitable decline in her overall functioning. A comprehensive program of prevention supports targeted at the risk factors that are present at this stage of her life include neurological care (seizure monitoring and medication to treat dementia), rehabilitative care to provide supports for activities of daily living, and psychological supports (to manage the emotional aspects of dementia). Supports are also necessary for her and her husband to provide income and health insurance when employment is no longer possible, legal assistance to consider future plans (wills, proxies, treatment preferences), and family support to help her relatives cope with the change in her situation. One year later, she is doing as well as one might hope for given the situation, but her husband remains depressed and is not responding well to his therapy. Her psychiatrist plans to start treating him as well.

The comprehensive supports described in these examples could be seen as simply elements of good care. The unique aspect of this approach, however, is the way that formulation of the multifactorial etiologic diagnosis provides a structure for implementing primary, secondary, and tertiary prevention strategies that translate into individualized supports. Furthermore, this approach helps to ensure that important risk factors and interactions are not overlooked. What seems like good care may address only the most obvious issues and fail to address all of these other issues. The approach to prevention and support presented in this chapter is designed to help individuals with ID experience the greatest possible degree of personal well-being.

SUMMARY

In this chapter we described the various meanings of prevention, emphasizing the classification of prevention into primary, secondary, and tertiary. The concept of prevention supports was described as a way to link the multifactorial etiologic diagnosis with primary, secondary, and tertiary prevention to an individualized program of supports designed to prevent or reduce the impact of the risk factors and interactions present in a particular case. Several examples were described to illustrate how the process can result in better care and a greater degree of personal well-being for an individual with ID.

The material and examples presented in the chapter are relevant to understanding the true meaning and purpose of prevention as it relates to ID. Prevention will not directly reduce or eliminate the population-based prevalence of ID. However, prevention efforts can reduce the prevalence of specific disorders causing ID. For example, universal interventions to prevent mothers from drinking alcohol during pregnancy would reduce the prevalence of ID due to fetal alcohol syndrome (a form of primary prevention). Similarly, newborn screening for PKU and early dietary treatment would reduce the prevalence of ID caused by PKU, although it would not reduce the prevalence of PKU itself (a form of secondary prevention). These types of prevention strategies may not reduce the population-based prevalence of ID, but they do benefit the individuals involved and thus can be considered a form of support. These examples also demonstrate the true purpose of prevention, which is to provide individual and family supports that are sufficient to improve the individual's overall functioning.

CHAPTER 11

MENTAL AND PHYSICAL HEALTH-RELATED SUPPORTS

> Health is a state of complete physical, mental, and social well-being. Comprehensive community health supports optimize health and the well-being of persons with intellectual disability.

OVERVIEW

There have been significant changes in our understanding of—and approaches to—health and mental health factors associated with *intellectual disability* (ID). Different conceptualizations of disability have included medical (with the major focus of pathophysiology), functional (disruption of functional activities), social (disability created by social environment and as a natural part of human diversity), public health (a disparity in access to health care or impact of environment), and integrated health (disability as intersection of person and environment; Krahn, Putnam, Drum, & Powers, 2006).

Our purpose in this chapter is to outline the components of a comprehensive community health supports model that are responsive to the physical and mental health needs of persons with ID; aligned with the current conceptualization of disability; and consistent with the World Health Organization's definition of *health* as a state of complete physical, mental, and social well-being and not merely the absence of disease or disability (World Health Organization, 2001). As discussed in this chapter, community health supports incorporate the following types or categories of well-being that, taken together, comprise what is recognized as health: physical well-being; mental, emotional, and behavioral well-being; social and environmental well-being; and spiritual well-being. Thus, an active and effective health supports system incorporates the principles of holism, normalization, and self-determination and reflects both the functional basis of disability and the supports paradigm. Reflective of those principles and components, the seven sections of the chapter are (a) the premises and standards of community health supports, (b) types of health concerns, (c) health-related support needs, (d) community resources, (e) health-related support activities, (f) health outcomes, and (g) a listing of potential resources.

COMMUNITY HEALTH SUPPORTS: PREMISES AND STANDARDS

Premises

Figure 11.1 provides a conceptual framework for understanding the multiple components of health in a general sense and community health supports specifically. In later sections of the chapter, we discuss in more detail three of the components shown in Figure 11.1: support needs, support activities, and health outcomes. This section of the chapter covers four premises of community health supports (CHS) as reflected in the remaining components shown in Figure 11.1: health is a dynamic process, health promotion is multifaceted, health supports are community based, and evaluation of CHS is a continual process.

Health is a dynamic process. Health is the dynamic composite of physical, mental, emotional, behavioral, social, environmental, and spiritual well-being. It is dynamic because every human is in constant physiologic movement, from intracellular actions to interpersonal and intrasocietal actions. The health status of an individual reflects the integration

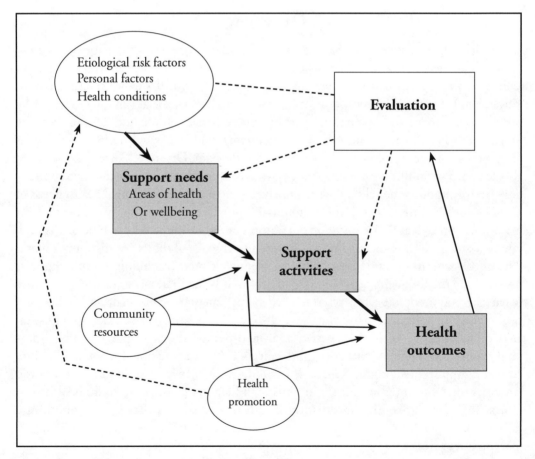

Figure 11.1. Community health supports model.

of all aspects of their functioning: physical, mental, emotional, behavioral, social, environmental, and spiritual. Health is not an absence of disability; rather, disability is part of the human condition. In this sense, everyone is more or less healthy and aspires to optimal health in all of these areas of well-being. The CHS model reflects this dynamic nature of health, while at the same time realizing that individuals with ID often need extraordinary supports to achieve optimal health. The model presented in Figure 11.1 provides a framework to develop, deliver, and evaluate those extraordinary supports.

Health promotion is multifaceted. Within a comprehensive CHS model, health promotion needs to be approached from the broader perspective of health as defined previously: health is a state of complete physical, mental, and social well-being. This multifaceted approach to health promotion focuses on (a) promoting exercise and physical activity, proper nutrition, and healthy lifestyles; (b) reducing stress through effective stress management strategies that include increased predictability, control, and empowerment; and (c) accessing social capital that maximizes connections among people to form mutual support systems, community ties, and social networks.

Thinking about health promotion, and in reference to Figure 11.1, one's health status is improved by employing health-promoting activities within community settings. Activities are determined by the needs and interests of the individual, and this occurrence is dependent on resources. The resources may be naturally occurring, such as having space to take walks or attend local concerts or may be provided as a service, such as physical therapy (PT) sessions or day habilitation. Critical components to achieving and sustaining good health outcomes are evaluating the appropriateness and effectiveness of all health promotion activities and making changes when necessary in the pattern and intensity of the individualized supports provided.

Health supports are community based. Community health supports apply the principle of *normalization* to all aspects of health, stressing that all needed health supports are obtained from the same sources as those provided to everyone else in the community (Nirje, 1969; Wolfensberger, 1972). It is also consistent with the community imperative and adds that all people—even those with the most complex physical and mental health needs—can live well in the community if they receive needed comprehensive community-based health supports; such health supports also reflect the supports paradigm and incorporate the functional model of human functioning discussed in chapter 2. According to Coulter (2005), a support activity fosters physical, mental, emotional, behavioral, social, and/or spiritual well-being when it helps the individual to manage physical or mental impairments in order to perform self-chosen activities that promote participation in desired social roles within the community of choice.

Providers of CHS recognize that disability is a problem in functioning and not an innate trait, disease, or brain disorder. Individuals with ID exert control over their destiny; power is shared between health providers, individuals with ID, and their families or guardians as appropriate. Health supports and services should be provided in typical community settings. Institutions, segregated housing, or substandard living environments are not considered typical community settings. Health supports should be designed to assist individuals to function within those community settings; CHS supports require that individuals with ID receive the same type of high quality health services and supports as everyone else. Different types and intensity of supports are provided for different types of disablement; acute disability may be a temporary state or may become a long-term disability. At different stages of life, people may require different types and different intensities of support. One obvious situation is when children grow through adolescence, when they deal with puberty and changing body size, increased complexities of social interactions, and often increased independence. As people transition from pediatric to adult systems of health care, there is an assumption that every adult can make their own best choices and anticipate the outcomes. The supports for ongoing services that allow individuals with ID to function well in community settings often receive funding from different agencies than those in place for children, require different reporting mechanisms, and must be geared to provide support across many more decades.

Evaluation is a continual process. Community health supports are both dynamic and multifaceted. Therefore, from an evaluation perspective, one needs to focus on more than just the individual's health. From this perspective, evaluation is an ongoing process that provides information to all stakeholders about the impacts of personal factors (including etiological risk factors and health conditions), the individual's support needs, individualized support activities, and health outcomes. This information is then used to determine where additional (or potentially fewer) supports are required to maximize the person's well-being.

Standards

The purpose of CHS is to identify and provide needed supports in order to optimize the person's health and well-being. Seven standards that provide the framework for these needed supports are presented in Table 11.1. These standards reflect national and international goals of community health care for persons with ID (Coulter, 2005; Meijer, Carpenter, & Scholte, 2004; Office of Surgeon General, 2002).

TYPES OF HEALTH CONCERNS

Physical Well-Being

Good health requires clean water, good nutrition, rest, clear air, and exercise. Many negative environmental factors (e.g., air pollution) and personal habits (e.g., not brushing teeth) add to biological predispositions that impede good health. Physical health concerns include general health/illnesses and additional conditions with known risk patterns, such as chromosomal disorders, inborn errors of metabolism, cerebral dysgenesis, intrapartum and neonatal disorders, head injury, brain infection, demyelinating disorders, degenerative disorders, seizure disorders, toxic-metabolic disorders, and malnutrition (see chapter 6). The results of accumulated disorders create added factors of health disparities

TABLE 11.1
Comprehensive Community Health Support Standards

1. **High quality**: People with ID will have access to high quality health care that is universally available, appropriate, timely, coordinated, comprehensive, and provided within the communities in which they live. This includes primary care as well as all types of specialty care and related health supports.

2. **Health care financing**: People with ID will receive affordable health care that promotes their inclusion within the life of their communities.

3. **Self-determination**: People with ID and their families will partner with health care providers and will access and use health information in order to make well-informed, freely chosen decisions about their own health goals, services, and health promotion activities.

4. **Training**: People with ID will be treated with respect by health care providers who are well trained in the provision of health services and supports for adults and children with ID.

5. **Wellness**: People with ID will participate in the full range of health promotion and wellness activities available to other children and adults in the community, including, but not limited to, activities that promote physical fitness, emotional well-being, social and environmental health, and spiritual growth.

6. **Knowledge**: Knowledge about the health status of individuals with ID will be identified, evaluated, and expanded across the life span. Research needs to be of high quality, reliable, and relevant to the lives of persons with ID.

7. **Mental health**: People with ID will have access to comprehensive mental and behavioral health services/supports and other allied services/supports to meet their needs within the community.

and can place the person with ID at a greater risk for illnesses, a greater need for more frequent health care evaluation and treatment, and/or an increased risk of morbidity and mortality.

Mental and Behavioral Well-Being

Traditionally, allopathic/Western medicine has assumed that the absence of disorders of thinking, feeling, and perception in the general population is a sign of normalcy. This is reflected in the attention to pathological conditions, such as anxiety disorders, posttraumatic stress, psychoses, personality disorders, specific sexual disorders, substance abuse and dependence, and alterations in responsive behavior due to medical conditions. In other medical frameworks, such as traditional Chinese medicine or specific Native

American tribal healers, the focus is on supporting and preserving healthy energy in the entire body, or even the universe, through individual action.

Behavioral concerns include behavioral manifestations of abnormal mental states as well as behaviors needed to achieve good overall health and well-being. Effective health promotion requires both an interest and motivation to pursue habits and activities that lead to good physical and mental health and knowledge about specific health promotion activities. As with the general population, people with ID are at risk to self-medicate against life's negative experiences. These experiences are effectively treated only by a combination of treatment strategies, specialist services, education, and social engagement (Taggart, McLaughlin, Quinn, & McFarlane, 2007).

Social and Environmental Well-Being

Meaningful social relationships that are appropriate to an individual's psychological and chronological age are part of the social network comprised of family, friends, neighbors, and coworkers. Interpersonal safety, trust, and reciprocity are essential for people to develop and function in healthy ways. Children require safe, nurturing environments. Adults need to learn how to express their interests, participate meaningfully in society, and protect and nurture younger generations. This is particularly evident in the manner in which societies support the sexual development of their young, which ranges from keeping all matters of sexual activity very private to overtly public displays of sexual maturity (e.g., specific ceremonies and rites of passage) and socially sanctioned sexual unions (implicit by marriage ceremonies). One of the clearest arguments in support of greater community inclusion for individuals with ID is that these social habits and values can be understood through participation in rituals and having questions answered in appropriate ways. Learning how to effectively interact and to appropriately protect oneself is a critical component of increasing freedom from victimization.

The environment has biologic and aesthetic effects on an individual's health. Examples include environments with clear air and safe water, adequate shelter, good nutrition, and space for pursuing individual and communal interests. Such factors are necessary to ensure active participation and reciprocal engagement in a communal social fabric that increases the value of each individual member. When people with or without disabilities are valued, they are less likely to devalue others. A mutual commitment to maintaining and supporting the culture and society over the long term is enhanced by the knowledge and awareness of such interconnections. The less traditional forms of medical care attest to these relationships as part of the connectivity between one's corporal and spiritual selves interacting with the universe.

Spiritual Well-Being

No discussion of health is complete without acknowledging the importance of spiritual and religious beliefs. Organized religions and religious habits and traditions provide solace, moral frameworks, and communities of like-minded individuals. A sense of spiritual connection with humanity or the universe does not require formal recognition of a personal spiritual practice. Spiritual beliefs often assist people in maintaining their physical or mental health; recognizing that individuals have spiritual needs and abilities distinct from their intellectual abilities is important for understanding their overall functioning.

HEALTH-RELATED SUPPORT NEEDS

Health-related problems in functioning for persons with ID arise from a number of potential causes. Some of these causes are medical, some behavioral, and some are related to psychiatric disorders. As discussed in this section of the chapter, health-related problems in functioning require the assessment of the pattern and intensity of exceptional medical and behavioral support needs and the analysis of the potential causative sources of difficult behaviors. This information is then aligned with available community resources and leads to the development of health-related support activities.

Support Needs Assessment

A comprehensive and well-validated system for describing an individual's support needs is provided by the Supports Intensity Scale—SIS (Thompson et al., 2004b). In addition to assessing the pattern and intensity of support needs in seven major life activity areas, the scale also determines exceptional medical and behavioral support needs such as those listed in Table 11.2. In reference to the support needs listed in this table, the SIS assesses how much support is needed to maintain or enhance the exceptional medical needs listed and how much support is needed to prevent or minimize the exceptional behavioral needs listed. As discussed by Thompson et al. (2009), assessment of the person's pattern and intensity of support needs should be repeated as individuals grow and change and require revised support plans.

Causative Sources of Difficult Behaviors

Difficult behaviors expressed by individuals with ID are often the actions that grab unwanted public attention or create feelings of danger and apprehension for family members and direct care staff. For people who are nonverbal, behavioral disruption may indicate a very mild annoyance to a serious medical or mental condition (Lowe et al., 2007). The task for an attending family member, staff, or professional is to assess the likely reasons for the disruptive behavior and to address the individual and environmental contributions to the situation in which it arose.

Table 11.3 lists some of the causative sources for difficult behavior. Each of these categories requires assessment, and they are not mutually exclusive of another category. Internal triggers are clearly state changes within the individual and changes that typically lead to irritable, explosive, or unpredictable behavior. These triggers frequently require detailed assessment for potential causes. Examples include searching for Lyme disease as a cause of fever or considering pain from stones in a shoe in a person with autism.

Table 11.2

Exceptional Medical and Behavioral Support Needs

Exceptional Medical Needs
Respiratory care: inhalation or oxygen therapy, postural drainage, chest physical therapy, suctioning
Feeding assistance: oral stimulation of jaw positioning, tube feeding, parental feeding
Skin care: turning or positioning, dressing of open wounds
Other: protection from infectious diseases due to immune system impairment, seizure management, dialysis, ostomy care, lifting and/or transferring, therapy services
Exceptional Behavioral Needs
Externally directed destructiveness: assaults or injuries to others, property destruction (e.g., fire setting, breaking furniture), stealing
Self-directed destructiveness: self-injury, pica, suicide attempts
Sexual: sexual aggression; nonaggressive but inappropriate behaviors, such as exposing self in public, exhibitionism, inappropriate touching or gesturing
Other: tantrums or emotional outbursts, wandering, substance abuse, maintenance of mental health treatment

Persistently threatening environments that should be safe are particularly anxiety provoking, such as when one is abused or neglected, subsequently demonstrating aversion to going to sleep, excessive startle responses, and persistent disinhibition of irritability and anger throughout the day due to fatigue.

A number of mental illnesses manifest through change in behavior (S. Cooper, Smiley, Morrison, Williamson, & Allan, 2007; Costello & Bouras, 2006; Fletcher, Loschen, Stavrakaki, & First, 2007; Myrbakk & von Tetzchner, 2008; Unwin & Deb, 2008). Careful consideration of possible depressive, anxious, manic, or psychotic disorders must be made using historical information, comprehensive contextual assessment, and family history. Historically, psychiatric illnesses were often overlooked because all difficult behavior in this population was attributed to having ID. Because it has become the standard of practice to acknowledge that mental illness may occur more frequently in people with ID than the general population, there is a tendency to assume that all new behavioral disruption is due to a recurrence or exacerbation of the existing mental disorder. This assumption contributes to incomplete evaluation of these frequent and newly evolving causes of difficult behavior. It is incumbent on *all* members who support or know a person with ID to assure that a thoughtful and comprehensive evaluation of potential sources leading to difficult behavior is accomplished.

TABLE 11.3

Causative Sources of Difficult Behavior

Internal triggers: pain, seizure, sensory, fear, psychosis

External triggers: threats, environmental cues, lack of safety

Trauma: physical, sexual, posttraumatic stress

Limited range of expression: through illness, disability, or habit, different emotions are expressed in few visible expressive behaviors

Differentiation from mental illness diagnoses[a]: overlap of conditions and behaviors;

Behavioral phenotypes (syndromes)

Learned behaviors

Mannerisms: involuntary movement disorder versus unconscious habit

Manifestations of other disease processes: change in arousal due to toxic effects of medications, metabolic problem, dehydration

[a] The *Diagnostic Manual-Intellectual Disability—DM-ID* (Fletcher et al., 2007) is an evidence-based, consensus-based adaptation of *DSM-IV-TR* that reflects the necessary adaptation of psychopathological measures for individuals with ID. Mental illness tends to be underdiagnosed by clinicians, direct care staff, and diagnostic frameworks (S. Cooper et al., 2007; Costello & Bouras, 2006; Merrick, Merrick, Lunsky, & Kandel., 2006; Myrbakk & von Tetzchner, 2008)

COMMUNITY RESOURCES

One of the major barriers to achieving the comprehensive community health support standards summarized in Table 11.1 is the level and availability of public transportation to persons with ID and their families. Access to high quality health care depends on being able to physically encounter well-trained medical staff. In addition, the respective services need to have minimal physical barriers, be respectful of the person with ID and their family/advocate, and provide reliable service. All citizens avail themselves of the social supports of emergency services. Both emergency crews in field operations (e.g., ambulances) and at emergency departments (hospital-based) require training and ongoing feedback about effective communication with individuals who have ID, patterns of medical conditions, and understanding about assessment and treatment of pain in people who are nonverbal. Above all, emergency personnel need to have the mindset that people with ID warrant medical attention at the same standard as the general population. This includes the knowledge that ID places people at increased risk for some conditions, including victimization.

A measure of meaningful participation in community activities is the degree to which individuals with ID are able and permitted to participate in their ongoing health assessment and health care (Hall, Wood, Hou, & Zhang, 2007). Their active and effective participation is one of the means to assure that health care providers continue to learn, adapt practice guidelines, and anticipate health care problems. Regularly scheduled appointments and use of health screening questionnaires can help practitioners look for health conditions, engage their patients with ID in preventative health habits, and initiate effective therapies in a more timely manner (S. Cooper et al., 2006). The unmeasured value of an approach geared toward prevention and anticipation of health care needs is that the staff and family who support people with ID may become more aware of their own health promotion habits.

Standards of health care include varying therapeutic modalities based on scientific evidence. People with ID should receive all the benefits of research and medical therapeutic advances (Lakin & Stancliffe, 2005). As an example, medications should not be withheld because a person has low cognitive ability. However, dosage of medication should be adjusted based on bioavailability, clinical side effects, and age. The importance of training in maintaining community standards of health care includes awareness of treating specific diagnoses, establishing a diagnostic hypothesis and testing the therapeutic response, and preventing undue harm or death.

Explicit in the standards summarized in Table 11.1 is a competent and comprehensive evaluation of the person at initial assessment and continued assessment over the course of treatment. When people in a community find themselves recipients of prejudicial treatment practices, they need to individually and collectively address the deficiencies at the institutional and professional levels. Specific concerns about substandard medical practice are most effectively addressed through discussions with a board of examiners for specific disciplines (e.g., nursing, dentistry, surgery) or for all practitioners within a jurisdiction (e.g., a state, district, or county). These kinds of discussions can occur *before* a fatal event has taken place or a clear case of malpractice is witnessed.

HEALTH-RELATED SUPPORT ACTIVITIES

Once support needs and community resources have been identified, health-related support activities are developed to meet those needs. As discussed in chapter 10, these support activities should address the risk factors that contribute to diminished physical, mental, and social well-being. Health-related support activities should be designed to achieve outcomes that are desired and personally chosen by the recipient of support, following the principle of self-determination. As summarized in Table 11.4, support activities include assessment, individualized supports, and health promotion.

- *Comprehensive assessment* is necessary to accurately determine health conditions and risks for an individual. This framework assumes a holistic view of individual functioning.

Table 11.4
Support Activities for Health

Assessment:

- Comprehensive

- Periodic, appropriate to age, exposure risks, lifestyle

- Concept of life span and prevention

- How patient sees the situation

- Whether clinician uses sedation and if client is prepared for the clinical encounter/exam

- Dental care and prevention

- Treatments that cause behavioral changes (e.g., antiepileptic drugs, steroids)

- Comorbidity evaluations (for potential mental health disorders)

- Mental status examination (for potential mental health disorders)

Standard: Assessment and revision is an ongoing process that also takes into account the individual's changing preferences, personal growth, life situation, and health status.

Individualized supports:

- Medically based supports that maintain or improve exceptional medical needs, such as those listed in Table 11.2

- Positive behavioral supports that produce productive and long-lasting changes to people's behavior by (a) completing a functional assessment to collect and synthesize information to define the problem behavior, determine what maintains it, and describe the environmental context associated with high and low rates of the behavior (Repp & Horner, 1999) and (b) implementing an array of intervention procedures that redesign the environment so that environmental events evoke desirable rather than problem behaviors, teach new skills, deliver rewards following desired behavior, and ensure the safety of all individuals involved (Horner & Carr, 1997; Horner et al., 2005)

- Psychopharmacological treatments that minimize or eliminate the psychiatric/mental illness condition

- Environmentally based strategies that reduce personal stress by increasing both the predictability of environmental events and the person's control over those events

Standard: Support activities must be of high quality, based on current research-based information and best practices, and assessed and revised continually to improve their ability to produce the desired outcomes.

TABLE 11.4 (*continued*)

Health promotion:
- Provide dental care

- Engage in exercise to increase muscle mass, mobility, and endurance and reduce obesity

- Encourage mental stimulation, such as that involved in pursuing interests and learning new facts/material

- Understand and engage in proper nutrition

- Understand and deal with chronic conditions

- Engage in meaningful activities that include making useful contributions to society

Standard: Health promotion activities should recognize longevity and the prevention of secondary conditions, reflect best practices, and be based on the expectation of a full life span, including active participation by the individual in society.

- *Individualized supports* are provided to enhance the person's physical, mental, and social well-being, and, in the process, enhance human functioning.

- *Health promotion* is an important support activity that can enhance personal well-being in a number of ways. Although many health promotion programs have historically excluded persons with ID, the CHS model presented in this chapter recognizes that health promotion is vital for persons with ID. Wellness (the goal of health promotion) is the individual's experience of prevention, and the success of health promotion efforts is measured by the extent to which they enhance personal well-being.

HEALTH OUTCOMES

Health outcomes are determined by the choice of what is being measured. Often the narrowest focus of attention is on a specific medical condition, such as blood sugar level and the risk of developing diabetes. Outcome measures can be reports of an individual's blood glucose on a daily or weekly basis, other measures of glucose in the blood (HgbA1c), or measures of related risk factors, such as weight, body mass index (BMI), fitness, dietary habits, and amount of daily exercise. For populations, these individual measures can be averaged. Outcomes can also be measured by an individual's sense of well-being or overall activity level. In the United States, cities are rated based on opportunities for public recreation. Similarly, individual levels of exercise frequency and variety, exercise tolerance, and general vitality can be a health outcome. For a person who has never liked exercise, this may seem unnecessarily dismissive. Rather, other forms of activity and engagement need to be measured, such as gardening, playing games, or performing arts. For health outcomes to be relevant, they should reflect the values of the individual with ID within their community context and their health supporters' knowledge and skills (Krahn & Drum, 2007). A holistic approach to health outcomes is presented in chapter 13 and summarized in Table 13.1.

People with ID have increased risk for medical problems, including mental health disorders (Hall et al., 2007; Goddard, Davidson, Daly, & Mackey, 2008; Starr & Marsden, 2008). On the one hand, simple prolongation of life span may not be a meaningful objective for any individual. On the other hand, improved quality of daily living may be a tangible result of treating chronic conditions, such as taking medications for psychiatric illness, preventing bone density loss and fractures, or smoking cessation. Some medical conditions are potentially fatal and can be reduced but not abolished. Risk of death from aspiration affects people with motor control disorders, including degenerative neurologic disorders. Accidents and trauma occur in the course of daily living. The risk taken by living more freely in the community means that individuals with ID are also exposed to the risks in the general community, such as motor vehicle accidents, victimization, infectious diseases, sexually transmitted diseases, and chronic conditions due to lifestyle choices (e.g., dietary changes induced by eating fast food).

Consumer outcome measures should demonstrate acceptability, legitimacy, and equity. They should reflect the wishes, desires, and expectations of the person, responsible member of their family, and/or guardian. Legitimate measures meet the ethics, values, norms, laws and regulations of the individual's society or social identity. These outcome measures should reflect just and fair distribution of health care and its benefits among the members of the population. Ongoing evaluation of patient satisfaction with all aspects of care should inform the continuing delivery of care (Parish, Moss, & Richman, 2008).

Functional assessment outcomes measure more objective aspects of health, which include clinical symptoms, physiological-biochemical functioning, physical impairments, performance of physical activities and tasks, pain management, activities of daily living, instrumental activities of daily living, coping behaviors (including adherence to health care regimes and changes in health-related habits), and role performance (marital, familial, occupational, interpersonal).

The integration of health-related supports is difficult to measure for at least four reasons. First, all sources of health supports need to be identified. Second, assessment must be made as to whether access to health care has occurred in a timely fashion and is appropriate to the person's health need. Third, evaluation must be completed regarding insurance-related barriers and supports. Fourth, all health services need to be provided in a consistent manner with clear and measurable goals that are consistent with the individual's goals and values (Andresen, Lollar, & Meyers, 2000; A. Donabedian, 1992; Pulcini & Howard, 1997; Schalock, 2001; Walsh & Kastner, 1999).

LISTING OF POTENTIAL RESOURCES

There are many and varied sources of excellent information to assist the health care professional; service provider organizations; and staff, friends, and family members. Medical textbooks may be the simplest resource for known conditions (Batshaw, 2008; Parker,

Zuckerman, & Augustyn, 2005; Rutter, 2008). Since knowledge is rapidly evolving and the outcomes of health conditions are changing due to improved care practices and longevity of people with ID, readers may want to consult online resources. Professional organizations are also sources of reliable information. Readers are reminded that the source of information for any publication should be documented. Those that appear in medical specialty journals are refereed by peer scientists and clinicians. Articles appearing in these journals meet standards of scientific rigor, including reproducibility and lack of bias.

The issue of what works to treat primary and secondary illnesses related to ID is complex. Evidence-based medicine relies on results from repeated clinical experience and critical evaluation of the literature by experienced clinicians and scientists. Evidence-based practice is the conscientious, explicit, and judicious use of current best evidence in making decisions about individualized health-related supports and integrating individual clinical expertise with the best available evidence from systematic research (Sackett, 1996). Up to date reviews of pharmacological treatments of mental illnesses often rely on these principles to capture the breadth of clinical expertise (Unwin & Deb, 2008). One of the potential limitations of evidence-based medicine includes overvaluing clinical results (which may not be based on objective results from the therapeutic intervention but on a random and unrelated response). Thus, there is considerable weight given to a breadth of clinical experience or expertise.

Information from Web sites and personal communications among families are anecdotes and single-case experiences of effective treatments. The downside to these reported cases is that these are nonrefereed reports and resources. The experience of single cases may not apply to other individuals.

The challenge of finding effective supports for people with ID often involves balancing the results from individual cases and guidance from larger group studies. For any given person, results from each therapeutic intervention and/or individualized support must be assessed. Keeping track of people's responses over years builds an important individualized reference source.

SUMMARY

Health is multifaceted and involves physical, mental, behavioral, emotional, social, environmental, and spiritual well-being. Enhancing the health of individuals with ID requires an array of medical, behavioral, social, environmental, and spiritual health supports to ensure that the individual enjoys a personally satisfying quality of life.

Understanding the services, research, and policy changes needed to assure that these health supports are available for all persons with ID and their families requires a new way of thinking about health and disability. The CHS model discussed in this chapter incorporates the principles of normalization and self-determination, the supports paradigm, and the functional understanding of disability. It is based on a number of key premises and defined by the understanding that a support activity fosters physical, mental, emotional, social, environmental, and/or spiritual well-being (i.e., health) when it helps the individual to manage physical impairments in order to perform self-chosen activities that promote participation in desired social roles within the community of choice.

Applying this new way of thinking leads directly to standards and goals that will realize the vision expressed by community health supports. Achieving these goals will require new research and training as well as major changes in health services delivery systems, health care financing, and health policy. In a rapidly changing and increasingly global world of knowledge, continued vigilance and dedication will be needed to assure that all people with ID achieve optimally healthy and personally satisfying lives.

CHAPTER 12

SUPPORT NEEDS OF PERSONS WITH INTELLECTUAL DISABILITY WHO HAVE HIGHER IQ SCORES

> **Individuals with intellectual disability who have higher IQ scores face significant challenges in society across all areas of adult life, and many individuals who may not receive formal diagnoses of ID or who fall slightly above the upper ceiling for a diagnosis of ID share this vulnerability. Only through an increased understanding of the ongoing strengths and limitations of each individual with ID can we achieve better clinical judgment and identify appropriate supports and, with the provision of individualized supports, accomplish fairness in society.**

OVERVIEW

Our purpose in this chapter is to (a) describe the support needs of individuals with *intellectual disability* (ID) who have higher IQ scores, (b) discuss how intellectual limitation exists along a continuum that reveals many similarities in human functioning limitations between individuals on either side of the definitional dividing line, and (c) reiterate the critical importance of creating accessible, individualized supports for these individuals. Those with ID who have higher IQ scores struggle in society (for more detailed analysis and references, see Snell & Luckasson, 2009). This is true despite the fact that all individuals with ID typically demonstrate strengths in functioning alongside relative limitations. Those with ID who have higher IQ scores comprise about 80 to 90% of all individuals diagnosed with ID. Frequently, they have no identifiable cause for the disability, they are physically indistinguishable from the general population, they have no definite behavioral features, and their personalities vary widely, as is true of all people. Although many of these individuals will need supports, some may be able to live independently, at least for part of the time. Documented successful outcomes of individuals with appropriate supports contrast sharply with incorrect stereotypes that these individuals never have friends, jobs, spouses, or children or are good citizens.

People in this group primarily are identified when they are in school, because school demands place their intellectual and adaptive behavior limitations in clear relief and because schools have a legal obligation to identify disabilities in all children. Beyond school age, however, when activities may be less "intellectual," bureaucracies do not routinely identify people because of intellectual limitations, and needed services and supports are unavailable or rejected. As a result, these people continue to experience significant difficulties achieving success or even a healthy existence in adulthood.

Frequently, the gap between their capabilities and the demands from their environments grows as they leave school, as society becomes more complex, and as the standards for successful adulthood climb. Well-designed individualized supports can help bridge the gap between capabilities and demands, but the reality is that many of these individuals do not have access to needed supports. Thus, life's demands frequently impose overwhelming challenges to those who live with significantly limited intellectual ability and adaptive behavior.

CLASSIFICATION SYSTEMS AND INTELLECTUAL DISABILITY

All people with ID, including those with higher IQ scores, belong to a single disability group (people with ID). However, the application of various classification systems to subdivide the group leads to somewhat different ways of understanding these individuals and their needs. As discussed in chapter 7, classification systems based on relevant criteria should be selected by clinicians and others for explicit professional purposes that benefit the individuals who are classified. For example, service providers may choose classification systems that subdivide the group of people with ID into smaller groups based on support needs, such as using the Supports Intensity Scale assessment to classify individuals by the intensity of their support needs (Thompson et al., 2004a).

The variety of classification systems based on different criteria may partially account for why this group historically has had so many different names. Earlier names, most of which now are highly stigmatizing (e.g., feebleminded, moron, moral idiots [Trent, 1994, p. 20]) were followed by new names taken from then current definitions or classification systems: educable mental retardation and mild mental retardation or names reflecting time periods challenging particular characterizations of this group or an expansion of this group: the "six-hour retarded child" (President's Committee on Mental Retardation, 1969), students with general learning disability (MacMillan, Siperstein, & Gresham, 1996), and the forgotten generation (the combined group of people with ID with higher IQ scores and people without ID but with lower IQ scores, whose IQ scores are just beyond the ID range; Tymchuk, Lakin, & Luckasson, 2001). Generally, the names have followed from the classification system or purpose for classifying.

Similarities to the Borderline Classification

Whatever classification system is used, however, it is critical to point out that the challenges faced by individuals with ID who have higher IQ scores are significant. Thus, references to "mild" are misleading. Moreover, individuals with ID with higher IQ scores (slightly below the ceiling of approximately 70–75) share much in common with individuals without a diagnosis of ID whose functioning is sometimes referred to as *borderline* (individuals who do not technically have ID but who have low IQ scores, above the ceiling of approximately 70–75). Edgerton wrote that "perhaps the most sobering realization is that the majority of these individuals [former 'six-hour retarded children'] are not cited in the research literature nor are they known to the mental retardation/developmental disabilities service delivery system" (Edgerton, 2001, p. 3).

Mild Intellectual Disability Is Misleading

In some ways, it may seem counterintuitive to consider the challenges of individuals with ID with higher IQ scores as being equal to or sometimes greater than those with ID at lower IQ scores. Several factors, however, aggravate their challenges: expectations for performance are higher for people with ID with higher IQ scores than for those with lower IQ scores; the tasks given to them are more demanding because of the higher expectations; and a failure to meet those expectations is frequently met by others blaming the individual or the individual blaming him or herself. Moreover, many individuals with ID who have higher IQ scores attempt to hide their disability or attempt to pass as "normal" or try to appear intellectually capable and thus miss out on or even reject accommodations that might have been available to them if their disability had been declared or identified. In addition, the impact of their ID may be increased by the lack of access to needed mental health care, medical care, dental care, nutrition, and relationship and parenting assistance. Society's increasing lack of neighborly care for one another may hit people with ID in poorer neighborhoods especially hard.

To further describe the challenges faced by many individuals with ID who have higher IQ scores, in this chapter we address areas in which societal threats are especially marked (e.g., education, socioeconomic status, employment, and housing), and the often inadequate response systems regarding individuals with intellectual limitations that increase their vulnerability in everyday life. The chapter concludes with a discussion of the need for a supports framework that spans IQ limitations.

EVERYDAY LIVES OF PEOPLE WITH INTELLECTUAL DISABILITY WHO HAVE HIGHER IQ SCORES

The lifelong experience of having reduced intellectual and adaptive abilities creates a vulnerability that is shared among members of this group. As adults, these people have limited academic skills, are often poor, are underemployed or unemployed, and tend not to live independently. These societal issues impacting their everyday lives are summarized in Table 12.1 and discussed more fully on subsequent pages.

TABLE 12.1

Everyday Lives of People With Intellectual Disability Who Have Higher IQ Scores

Education
- Variability among states in identifying students with ID
- High rates of classroom segregation
- Disproportionality
- Slightly lower rates of leaving school
- Rare declassification

Socioeconomic status
- Significantly reduced income in families with a member with ID
- High rate of single parenting (mother) of child with ID
- Reduced success for individual in obtaining markers of independent economics (e.g., employment, credit cards, checking accounts, driver's license)

Employment
- Low rate of employment
- Low hours, benefits, skill demands
- Low career success
- High need for assistance

Housing
- High poverty and low access to good housing
- Long waits for housing and supports
- Often continue to live with family or other people

Health
- Poorer nutrition
- Higher obesity
- Poor access to health care
- Poor ability to communicate with health providers

Friendships and social behavior
- Reduced ability to form and sustain mutually beneficial friendships without assistance
- High risk of loneliness
- Higher risk of behavior problems if behavioral supports not provided

Table 12.1 (*continued*)

Family well-being
- Most continue to live with parents or others
- Challenges in forming own families due to poverty, learning limitations, poor employment, and fears by others
- Difficulties successfully raising their children without assistance

Rights
- Lack of access to civic education in school and later
- Limited knowledge and disability accommodations in the civil and criminal systems
- Few specialized legal resources
- Low number of affordable advocates with knowledge of disability issues
- Long delay in societal recognition of rights

Social judgment
- Inadequate response systems, interpersonal competence, social judgment, and/or decision-making skills
- Reduced intellectual and adaptive abilities
- Difficulties in problem solving and flexible thinking
- Susceptibility to dangers
- Reduced abilities and adaptation to one's life circumstances
- Vulnerabilities to others who may mislead or harm them

Inadequate social responding and judgment
- Tendency to deny or minimize the ID
- Desire to please authority figures
- Gullibility when others mislead or harm them
- Naïveté or suggestibility

Difficulty in thinking and learning
- Difficulties making sense of the world through consistent, reliable, socially mature levels of planning, problem solving, thinking abstractly, comprehending complex ideas, learning quickly, and learning from experience
- Societal stigma
- History of being feared, devalued, incorrectly stereotyped, and segregated by society

Note. This table is adapted from the appendix in "Characteristics and Needs of People With Intellectual Disability Who Have Higher IQs," by M. E. Snell & R. A. Luckasson, et al., 2009, *Intellectual and Developmental Disabilities, 47,* p. 233. Copyright 2009 by the American Association on Intellectual and Developmental Disabilities, Washington, DC. Adapted by permission.

Education

Polloway, Lubin, Smith, and Patton (in press) traced education for students with ID over the past 25 years. They found little overall variability in the percentage of the school-aged population identified as receiving special education services under the category of mental retardation (0.9%) but great variability from state to state. They described several important national trends. First, in comparison to all other disability groups, children and adolescents with "mental retardation" spend the most time in separate classrooms away from their peers in general education: 51.8% of students receiving special education services under the category of mental retardation versus 18.5% of students in any categorical area. During the 1990s, national rates for including students with ID in general education increased from 27.3% to 44.7%, while rates for separate setting placement decreased from 72.7% to 55.3% but with great variability from state to state. As of the late 1990s, national placement trends reached a stable plateau, but these trends continue to be highly variable across states (Williamson, McLeaskey, Hoppey, & Rentz, 2006).

Second, the U.S. Department of Education (2007) indicated a three to one ratio of being identified with "mental retardation" for African American students in contrast to Caucasian students. Disproportionality is greater for African American students than for any other ethnic group. Also these students have a higher probability of being categorized by schools with the label of "mental retardation" than being categorized with any other high incidence disability. Findings by Skiba, Poloni-Staudinger, Gallini, Simmons, and Feggins-Azziz (2006) and others (Fierros & Conroy, 2002; U.S. Department of Education, 2007) point clearly to this disproportionality: 11% of the school population is African American, while more than 29% of students served under the category of mental retardation are African American. Many factors have been proposed as contributors to the disproportionate number of African American students in special education, including poverty, racism, special education decision-making processes, test bias, unequal opportunity in general education (e.g., educational resources, number of African American teachers), school discipline, and disconnect between school culture and African American culture (Mercer, 1973; Skiba et al., 2008).

Third, dropout rates are generally high for all students with disabilities (approximately 30% across disability groups). Polloway et al. (in press) reported that during the 2002–2003 school year, approximately 28.6% of students with mental retardation left school early. Only 2% of such students were "declassified" from special education, a figure that is lower than for students with learning disabilities (9%) or emotional disturbance (10%). Thus, summarizing these national trends, students served in the category of mental retardation in comparison to other high incidence disability categories spend the majority of their school day in separate classrooms, tend to receive special education services, and remain categorized longer; further, they are 25% more likely to be African American and 33% more likely to drop out before finishing school. Even with these educational system problems, many students and their families thrive while in school, only to suffer insurmountable odds when they leave school and face service discontinuity at best or, more likely, a total lack of needed supports.

Socioeconomic Status

Families of all types with a member who has ID or closely related developmental disabilities (IDD) have significantly reduced income compared to families in the general population; within single-parent households this contrast is even greater (Fujiura, 2003; Lewis & Johnson, 2005). The proportion of single-parent-headed households among those with IDD is twice that of other family households in the United States, with the great majority being headed by women; the economic disadvantage in these household is large (Fujiura, 2003).

Youth with ID several years out of high school had almost no successful experience with credit cards or charge accounts, and only 1 in 10 had a checking account (Wagner, Newman, Cameto, Garza, & Levine, 2005). In contrast with the majority (two thirds) of youth with other disabilities who showed an increase in having drivers' licenses at this same age, only a minority of youth with ID who had higher IQ scores had either driving licenses or permits. These limitations, related both to a disadvantaged socioeconomic status and intellectual and adaptive limitations, can be significant barriers to successful adult independence.

Employment

Youth with ID are less likely than those with learning disabilities to get a job (Wagner et al., 2005). Youth with ID improve in employment 2 years out of high school, though African American youths with any disability are significantly less likely to be employed at this time than Caucasian youths with any disability. Two years out of high school, hours and pay rate increase and the type of jobs held by all youths with disabilities tends to improve, with a significant decline in personal care jobs and an increase in trade jobs, such as plumbing and carpentry. Other commonly held jobs include maintenance, food service, and retail positions.

Although it is true that people with ID who have higher IQ scores are more likely to be employed than people with ID and lower IQ scores, their employment rate (27.6%) is far below the national average in the general community (75.1%) and more often consists of part-time work in entry-level service jobs, with low wages and minimal benefits (Yamaki & Fujiura, 2002). Transportation continues to be a primary difficulty. The median level income for this group "was 20% below the poverty threshold and about one-third of the median total income of the general population" (Stancliffe & Lakin, 2007, p. 437). Despite these bleak statistics, there is optimistic evidence that many of these people with ID who have higher IQ scores can be gainfully employed in the community when given adequate training and on-the-job supports (Mank, 2007) and, when they are supported, to become more self-determined (i.e., when they learn to assume more autonomy and make more personal choices in their lives; Wehmeyer & Palmer, 2003).

Housing

The majority of youth with disabilities (including ID) still live at home 2 years post high school (Wagner et al., 2005). In comparison to the general U.S. population, the income level of people with ID living on their own or with roommates is below the poverty level. "These individuals are simply too poor to afford even the most modest rental housing" (O'Hara & Cooper, 2005, as cited by Stancliffe & Lakin, 2007, p. 436). Although some flexible housing supports exist for people with ID (e.g., rental assistance under Section 8 voucher programs from the Department of Housing and Urban Development), waiting lists are excessive and the application process is particularly challenging to these individuals. In comparison with adults who have disabilities other than ID, people with ID have lower rates of living independently. Although more women with ID who have higher IQ scores live independently than do men in the same category, this finding appears related to a higher marriage rate for these women than for the men (Blackorby & Wagner, 1996; Richardson & Koller, 1996). In other independent living areas, women with ID have less positive outcomes than men in the same category (Rousso & Wehmeyer, 2001).

Health

People with ID and higher IQ scores tend to have higher rates of obesity, poorer nutrition, and be hospitalized more often for longer periods than are adults with no ID (Stancliffe & Lakin, 2007). Health-related challenges for these individuals include accessing health services, affordability, transportation to services, communicating health problems to medical personnel, identifying their disability and their need for support to follow health treatments, and inadequate or nonexistent medical histories (Spitalnik & White-Scott, 2000). Despite these problems appropriate health supports can make a positive difference in healthy lifestyles (Stancliffe & Lakin, 2007).

Friendships and Social Behavior

Greater loneliness in adults with ID and higher IQ scores was reported when individuals lived in larger residences and expressed fear about their living condition, whereas less loneliness was reported when people liked where they lived and reported more social contact (Stancliffe et al., 2007). Boys with ID and higher IQ scores have been reported to exhibit antisocial and delinquent behaviors more frequently than do their male peers without ID (Douma, Dekker, Ruiter, Tick, & Koot, 2007). Despite these findings, behavioral interventions for challenging behavior have been demonstrated as being effective with this same group (Didden, Korzilius, van Oorsouw, & Sturmey, 2006).

Family Well-Being

Similar to their peers without disabilities, a large majority of youth with ID (89%) were reported to be single 2 years after leaving high school (Wagner et al., 2005). Annual incomes of those who were married or living with a partner were $5,000 or less. Few of these people receive the social-sexual teaching that might assist them in their personal lives. Attempts to establish an intimate relationship with another person are often met with restrictions and fear (Walker-Hirsch, 2007).

The vast majority of children and almost half of adults with ID live with their family rather than on their own or with others (Braddock, Emerson, Felce, & Stancliffe, 2001; I. Brown, Renwick, & Raphael, 1999). When they do establish families of their own, it is well-documented that families in which one or both parents have ID/IDD face greater challenges than do other families in raising their children; however, positive outcomes can be enhanced if they receive appropriate supports to navigate adult living; maintain their family; and protect, support, and guide their children (Tymchuk, 2006).

Rights

The ability to know one's rights and make those rights a reality depends on civic education and access to a stable pool of knowledgeable advocates. Limitations in overall education access described earlier result in many people who never have the opportunity to learn about democracy or personal rights with their classmates. A tendency by these individuals to deny their disability and reject services associated with ID may mean that their rights to supports or to fair treatment are not exercised. Assuring justice in the civil and criminal justice system and educating the police, lawyers, and judges who work with these individuals so that needed accommodations can be made (e.g., fair questioning) has not yet been accomplished (Perske, 2008). Moreover, very few legal resources exist for people with disabilities who do not have the finances or ability to hire a private lawyer.

Poverty and unemployment are realities in the lives of most people with ID who are living independently, with the following goals only rarely met: having a reasonable income and ongoing employment, circumventing the restrictive and potentially stigmatizing regulations for acquiring social services, accessing inexpensive transportation, and obtaining affordable housing.

Social Judgment

Individuals with ID who have higher IQ scores are vulnerable to risks due to their sometimes inadequate response systems, interpersonal competence, social judgment, or decision-making skills (Greenspan, 2006a, 2006b; Khemka & Hickson, 2006; Nettelbeck & Wilson, 2001; Patton & Keyes, 2006; Spitalnik & White-Scott, 2000). These challenges are linked to reduced intellectual and adaptive abilities that make it difficult to problem solve and to be flexible in thinking; both limitations create a susceptibility to dangers that is shared among members of this group (Greenspan, 2006a). Some have argued that certain aspects of these characteristics may represent a socialization process and may sometimes be viewed as adaptive responses to stigmatizing and deficient environments (Bogdan & Taylor, 1994; Goffman, 1961). It is likely that both reduced abilities and adaptation to one's life circumstances are involved in these susceptibilities and vulnerabilities.

For some people in this group, these social judgment challenges may mask their disability temporarily, but ultimately these characteristics can contribute to their vulnerability. Research supports possible systematic interventions to counter these characteristics, especially for children and youth, such as teaching appropriate interactions and self-managing conversations with typical peers (Carter & Hughes, 2007). Special educators and parents typically work with these individuals during the school years to teach suitable interpersonal relations, caution with strangers, and social skills, while also encouraging them to dress, talk, and act like their peers. Still, there is a scarcity of effective interventions regarding social judgment by adolescents with ID that effectively prevent abuse by acquaintances or strangers (Nettelbeck & Wilson, 2001) or that teach motivation-based decision making at a developmentally appropriate level (Khemka & Hickson, 2006).

Inadequate Social Responding and Judgment

Four of the contributors to inadequate social responding and judgment in individuals with ID who have some verbal and social skills are denial, a desire to please, gullibility, and naïveté or suggestibility.

Denial or a necessity for passing. Beginning in 1960, Edgerton (1967) followed 110 adults who had been deinstitutionalized from Pacific State Hospital in Los Angeles between 1949 and 1958. He used the phrase *cloak of competence* to describe their strong motivation to explain their hospitalization as due to nerves, surgery, alcoholism, and so forth, and to deny the stigma of the label of ID. Although "passing for normal" was motivated by an attempt to avoid the stigma of being identified as "retarded," after leaving the hospital and returning to the "real world," many of these individuals struggled with the effects of their inadequacy.

Today's motivation for denial by individuals with ID can come from similar motives, such as attempting to avoid the possibility of being placed in self-contained segregated special education classrooms or being associated with services that are openly linked to individuals with ID. Thus, although denial of disability can cause a sometimes dangerous lack of benefits from needed supports, this denial, which may appear to many people with ID and their families as a way to reduce the stigma they experience, may be accompanied by the tendency to exaggerate one's abilities. Individuals with ID may go to great lengths to hide their limitations, making major efforts to attempt to appear as their often mistaken image of "competent" (Perske, 2005).

Desire to please. People with ID may tend to do what others want in an effort to be accepted or liked by them. This can lead to agreeing to do something risky or inappropriate in order to please another person (e.g., exaggerating one's own accomplishments or making false confessions). In stressful situations or under pressure, an individual may acquiesce, due at times to a desire to please or because of inexperience, communication limitations, or fear. Although this trait of overfriendliness can be an asset (it creates a helpful attitude and a pleasant personality with trustworthy individuals), when coupled with gullibility or limited decision making and untrustworthy people, it can result in agreeing without understanding and, thereby, may increase an individual's vulnerability (Greenspan, Loughlin, & Black, 2001; Khemka & Hickson, 2006).

Gullibility. This characteristic, often identified as a cardinal feature of ID, includes occurrences of being successfully fooled, tricked, or lied to by others (Greenspan, 2006a).

When individuals with ID are gullible, it may result in their being taken advantage of, being made fun of without realizing it, or being talked into doing things without understanding the potential consequences (e.g., participating in a practical joke but being left with the blame, confessing to a crime they did not commit; Patton & Keyes, 2006).

Naïveté/suggestibility. This trait appears to others as being overly trusting, immature, innocent, or inexperienced. For example, an individual might believe or agree to what someone says with little or no question, particularly if that person is in a position of power. The person with ID tends not to see or understand the fine points, nuance, or subtlety of novel or complex social situations and behavior. When in settings with predictable routines and trusted people, this characteristic is less visible. Individuals exhibiting this trait have a tendency to quickly look to others for guidance due to their difficulty in understanding a situation and their frequent history of failure in novel situations. This trait may result in making poor choices. The combination of suggestibility and gullibility may increase one's risk of making poor decisions.

Difficulty in Thinking and Learning

The underlying cognitive challenges of having limited intelligence play havoc with ordinary mental processes and may result in having difficulties making sense of the world through consistent, reliable, and socially mature levels of planning; problem solving; thinking abstractly; comprehending complex ideas; learning quickly; and learning from experience. Yet, research has demonstrated that systematic formal instruction can sometimes improve these abilities in some environments, if provided early and consistently and with appropriate supports that are available as needed (e.g., Browder, Trela, Gibbs, Wakeman, & Hallis, 2007; Carter & Hughes, 2007; Snell, 2007). As S. Greenspan (personal communication, December 2007) discussed, however, "even in situations where the warning signs are evident and the consequences of a bad decision are potentially serious" (p. 5), an individual with significant cognitive limitations (ID with a higher IQ) may be unmindful of risk. The motivation to deny their disability or to please others can further distract an individual from being objective or alert to reality, thus contributing to poor decision making.

These potential features of inadequate social responding are not limited to people with ID who have higher IQ scores but are also evident in most individuals with ID and lower IQ scores who have some verbal abilities as well as in many individuals who do not technically fit the diagnosis of ID but who have significantly lower IQ scores than average (borderline). However, these traits appear to be expressed more consistently and overtly in people with ID (Khemka & Hickson, 2006) because of their limited intellectual abilities. It is crucial not to stereotype this heterogeneous group; certainly, not all people in this group are victimized, particularly not those with sustained positive family support. However, many in this group of people with ID and higher IQ scores are not in the service system and thus do not have access to professionals who could assist them in learning to avoid victimization and provide help if victimization occurs.

Many people with significantly limited intellectual functioning and adaptive behavior may be competent learners in some supported settings in which learning is strategically and formally designed and appropriate supports are provided, especially in settings with regular routines (e.g., schools in which good special education supports are provided). Actual or relative strengths often coexist in an individual with ID. With the right supports, functional academic skills can be learned (e.g., purchasing items with the correct amount of money, using a telephone or cell phone, reading a paper to identify what is playing when at a theater) and everyday survival skills can be mastered (e.g., taking the right bus to get to a destination, knowing when to be friendly and with whom). Not all people with ID demonstrate inadequate social responding all the time; appropriate sustained supports are a force that reduces the likelihood that problems will result from these tendencies. Coupled with this, they often have some awareness of their own limitations in comparison to others and are motivated to be socially accepted. Life's expectations frequently impose overwhelming challenges for many people with ID when they confront unpredictable and demanding settings that may be socially confusing or coercive. These same individuals appear more comfortable and successful in predictable and familiar surroundings. For these reasons, individuals with ID are exceedingly vulnerable (socially, academically, practically) unless they are given formal or informal supports and systematic backup protections. As stated by Greenspan (2006b),

> The essence of MR [ID], from the standpoint of definition and diagnosis, is thus found not in the relative absence of especially routine skills but in the relative inability, especially under conditions of ambiguity or stress, to figure out when and how to apply those skills. (p. 176)

INADEQUATE RESPONSE SYSTEMS: STRUGGLING TO SURVIVE OUTSIDE A SUPPORTS FRAMEWORK

The need for supports in individuals with ID is an enduring rather than a temporary characteristic. Identifying a person's specific support needs, however, poses a challenge as these needs are variable, often not directly observable (and must be inferred from indirect assessment and self report), and identification may be resisted by the individual because of fear of stigma or segregation. When those supports are made available to individuals with ID, their functioning in typical life activities in mainstream settings is enabled, but their improvement does not remove the possibility that they will persist in needing ongoing supports. Individualized supports make it possible for people with ID to function with some success in everyday life. Most service systems, however, suffer from high staff turnover due to low pay, limiting needs-based individual funding to only new recipients with ID and providing paid supports through a traditional facility-based service system that determines from averaged service costs for groups of people in specific locations. According to Stancliffe and Lakin, "Such funding is rarely flexible, individually tailored, or portable, because it is not associated with specific individuals or their needs" (2007, p. 440).

A Call for a Supports Framework That Spans IQ Limitations

Rationale for a Continuum of Intellectual Disability

The AAIDD includes all individuals with ID who meet the diagnostic criteria under one term—intellectual disability. Dividing this group into classification subgroups, according to needs for supports, is accomplished with a classification system such as that provided by the Supports Intensity Scale (Thompson et al., 2004a). It is not warranted to develop separate diagnoses or labels for individuals with ID who have higher IQ scores or for those with ID and lower IQ scores (as stated earlier, however, subdividing according to a specific classification system may be warranted). Intellectual ability is a core metric for assessing and describing individuals with ID. By definition, all individuals with ID have significantly impaired intellectual abilities and adaptive behavior; whether at higher IQ or lower IQ, all individuals with ID fall within the definition. The characteristics emerging from significantly impaired intellectual abilities are shared by the entire group of individuals. This universal characteristic of individuals with ID, however, does not mean that they all have similar needs; nor does it deny the existence of actual or relative strengths in individuals with the disability.

Once an individual's IQ is known (which was essential for the diagnosis), nothing further is gained by classification of that IQ score into an IQ band or range. To attempt to create different diagnostic criteria for the already small group of individuals with ID and to separate and identify them into diagnostic groups (e.g., mild ID and moderate ID) is not supported and may introduce additional error to that associated with the assessment of intellectual functioning and adaptive behavior (see chapters 4 and 5). This notion of separate diagnoses would take us backward to the incorrect stereotype that individuals with ID with higher IQ scores have "mild" needs, and those with lower IQ scores have "profound" needs—neither of which provides any specificity for designing individualized supports. Work to improve diagnosis, classification, and systems of supports must continue, however, and it may be useful, as discussed in chapter 7, to have a variety of functional classification systems from which clinicians may choose given that the clinician has (a) specified a particular purpose for classifying and (b) matched the purpose to the attributes of the classification system. Classification systems should be responsive to explicit purposes for categorizing individuals into subgroups.

Nature of the Intellectual Disability "Cutoff"

Individuals who fall outside the category of ID whose functioning is sometimes referred to as *borderline* or *persons with mild cognitive limitations* (people with IQ scores slightly above the ceiling of approximately 70–75) share much in common with individuals diagnosed with ID who have higher IQ scores (slightly below the ceiling of approximately 70–75). They share many of the challenges and vulnerabilities that make life difficult for people with ID. The President's Committee on Mental Retardation (PCMR; now President's Committee for People With Intellectual Disabilities—PCPID) in its 1999

Report to the President referred to this combined vulnerable group of people who have mild mental retardation and borderline disability as the *forgotten generation* or people with *mild cognitive limitations*. Despite their functional limitations, this group may not access services because they do not qualify for a disability label or because they may not seek services for the same reason as individuals with ID with higher IQ scores (stigma, difficulty in navigating the social service system, etc.). The PCMR identified many challenges facing this group, which, despite the lack of an ID diagnosis, are similar to those faced by individuals with ID with higher IQ scores. These challenges are listed in Table 12.2.

TABLE 12.2

Contemporary Challenges Facing People With Mild Cognitive Limitations

1. An increasingly complex, information-based, and technologically demanding society

2. Less "neighborliness" to help people with social, commercial, and governmental settings

3. Barriers related to cognitive limitations are less likely to be "accommodated" than barriers related to physical limitations

4. Changes in public policies that affect low-income, unemployed, and homeless people have a disproportionately negative effect on individuals with cognitive limitations

5. Any changes to existing support programs cause gaps or exclusion because it takes longer to gain information, understand new options, and attempt to reenter a program

6. Desire to avoid additional stigma of a "disability" service system, but lack of skills necessary to enter a generic service (if one exists)

7. Lack of access to a stable pool of knowledgeable advocates

8. Vulnerability to secondary disabilities as a result of poor or no access to health or mental health services

9. Increased stress, loneliness, anxiety, depression, victimization, violence, and maltreatment because of inadequate preparation for independent living, lack of supports, tendencies toward errors of judgment, acquiescence to perceived authority, gullibility, naïveté, and exploitation by others

10. Restricted employment opportunities related to limited academic skills, segregation and lack of social connections, and higher rates of school dropout

Note. This table was adapted from *The Forgotten Generation: The Status and Challenges of Adults With Mild Cognitive Limitations*, A. J. Tymchuk, K. C. Lakin, and R. Luckasson (Eds.), 2001, pp. xxvi–xxvii. Copyright 2001 by Paul H. Brookes, Baltimore, MD. Adapted by permission.

Respect for All People Along the Continuum of IQ Limitations

Many of the problems of individuals with limited intellectual ability are exacerbated by societal contexts in which there is generalized lack of understanding by other people. Along with this lack of understanding, there is often concomitant lack of respect or even presence of fear. Thus, people with intellectual limitations go through life both misunderstood and disrespected. Formation of attitudes begins during the school years, but with less than 11% of students with ID fully included in general education classes across the United States (Smith, 2007), the opportunity for interpersonal interactions to occur between these students and their nondisabled peers are minimal.

Fit Between Human Capacity and Environmental Demands

A wide discrepancy emerges when people with ID who have needed supports are contrasted with similar individuals in the same circumstances who do not have needed supports. Consider a young woman with ID and with a higher IQ who has earned money and is provided supports on how to spend, save, or budget the money. Supports might consist of several years of instruction and supervised practice with shopping and interacting with store employees, along with ongoing assistance at school and home in budgeting. With these specific supports she can learn useful skills that allow choice and control in her life, and she is less likely to be exploited. By contrast, a peer without specific supports continues to be dependent on others for shopping and faces a higher probability of being taken advantage of by others. Individualized supports depend on accurate and ongoing assessment coordinated with family members, along with schools and adult agencies who have the capacity to deliver those supports and monitor their outcomes. A history of inadequate supports contributes to an individual's failure to address the everyday demands in their life and to a thwarted potential.

SUMMARY

In this chapter we described the group of individuals with ID who have higher IQ scores and the societal and social judgment challenges they face in everyday life. Ordinary life demands frequently impose overwhelming challenges to these people who live with significantly limited intellectual ability and adaptive behavior. Intellectual limitation exists along a continuum revealing many similarities in human functioning limitations between individuals on either side of the definitional dividing line. Good professional practices require that any diagnosis of ID in a person be followed by the assessment and provision of needed supports to that person. Merely diagnosing ID is unlikely to improve the functioning of the individual. Historic episodic attention to the people whose IQ scores lie just above the diagnostic cutoff must be converted to a deliberate societal commitment to address their needs in a sustained fashion.

Intellectual disability occurs along a continuum, as does intellectual ability, and must be described and understood in that way. Even with general consensus on the cutoff criteria for diagnosing ID, it is critical to remember that people slightly above the cutoff typically perform similarly to those slightly below the cutoff. Regardless of their qualifying diagnostic test scores, all individuals with ID have significant limitations in intellectual ability and adaptive behavior and require supports that are matched to their individual needs and preferences. This need for supports does not stop at the IQ and adaptive behavior cutoff points in the operational definition of ID.

Individuals with ID who have a higher IQ score face significant challenges in society across all areas of adult life, and many individuals who may not receive formal diagnoses of ID or who fall slightly above the upper ceiling for a diagnosis of ID share this vulnerability. Only through an increased understanding of the ongoing strengths and limitations of each individual with ID can we achieve better clinical judgment and identify appropriate supports and, with the provision of individualized supports, accomplish fairness in society. To realize their potential and reduce suffering in this group of people, our society must create nonstigmatizing, accessible, and individualized supports that apply proven interventions and build on the strengths of these individuals, starting in early childhood. Hence, good professional practices require that any diagnosis of ID in a person be followed by the assessment and provision of needed supports to that person; merely diagnosing ID is unlikely to improve the person's functioning.

Finally, the historic episodic attention to the people whose IQ scores are borderline or just above the diagnostic cutoff must be converted to a deliberate societal commitment to address their needs in a sustained fashion. This will require partnerships by government and relevant advocacy and professional groups. The early work of Edgerton (2001), the President's Committee on Mental Retardation (1999), and others should be integrated into this critical thrust.

PART IV

IMPLICATIONS

OVERVIEW

In the concluding chapter to the previous (10th) edition of this *Manual*, Luckasson et al. (2002) discussed nine major implications for the field of ID. These nine were the need to (a) approach ID (then referred to as *mental retardation*) from a multidimensional perspective; (b) employ an ecological approach to understand and investigate the impact on individual functioning of the person, the environment, and the individualized supports provided; (c) recognize the differences in the relevance of assessment to the three functions of diagnosis, classification, and planning supports; (d) integrate further the supports paradigm into current education and habilitation practices; (e) modify research designs to reflect the current emphasis on inclusion, empowerment, and supports; (f) establish a needs-based approach to eligibility; (g) fund services on the basis of individualized support needs; (h) incorporate current thinking about *intellectual disability* (ID) into legal procedures and the justice system; and (i) address the needs of the *forgotten generation*, defined as persons with ID at the higher IQ levels, those who currently reject or avoid the label but would be eligible for services, or those who are not eligible for the label but experience significant problems due to intellectual limitations.

As reflected in the preceding 12 chapters, since the publication of the 2002 *Manual*, significant progress has been made in reference to each of these nine implications areas. Additionally, the field has also experienced (a) an increased attention to the importance of identifying and capitalizing on the strengths and capabilities of people with ID as a means to promote meaningful participation, community inclusion, and valued personal outcomes (Shogren, Wehmeyer, Buchanan, & Lopez, 2006); (b) a continued decrease in the number of persons with ID living in public or private institutional settings of 16 or more residents (Alba, Prouty, Scott, & Lakin, 2008); and (c) an increased use of community-based nonwork supports (Sulewski, Butterworth, & Gilmore, 2008).

The nine confirmed implications and the three contemporary changes just mentioned provide the context for this final section of the 11th edition of the *Definition, Classification, and Systems of Supports Manual*. The material discussed in the following three chapters is focused on the implications of the best practices discussed in this *Manual* and their application to the areas of public policy, including desired public policy outcomes (chapter 13), (special) education (chapter 14), and support provider organizations (chapter 15). Throughout these three chapters, readers will find a number of application guidelines. Chief among these are the following:

- The development and implementation of public policy is a dynamic process that influences practices but is also influenced by changes in practice and assumptions in the field. This reciprocal relationship is evidenced in the connection between public policy and diagnostic and classification schemes.

- The synergy between public policy and changes in assessment and classification systems has led to an increased recognition of the importance of individualized supports, including the growing emphasis on self-directed funding, person-centered planning, and home-based supports.

- As community-based services have become the predominant mode of service delivery, public managers, advocates, and other stakeholders have worked hard to ensure that supports and services reflect the individual's needs and preferences.

- National and international disability policy is currently premised on a number of principles that are person-referenced (e.g., self-determination, inclusion, empowerment) and systems-referenced (e.g., antidiscrimination, coordination and collaboration, and accountability).

- ID-related professional organizations and service/supports providers throughout the world are increasingly focusing on identifying and assessing outcomes including those related to the person, the family, society, and systems change.

- Enhanced public policy outcomes related to persons with ID and their families can be achieved by (a) establishing best practices; (b) achieving a greater universal use of a multidimensional approach to diagnosis, classification, and supports provision; (c) addressing current policy and system disconnects and implementing more widely the policies that are already in existence; (d) focusing on personal outcomes and their measurement; and (e) using information generated by the assessment of desired policy outcomes to transform service delivery policies and practices.

- Special education services have progressed from congregated, segregated educational services and settings to inclusive educational settings.

- Professionals in special education are increasingly applying an ecological, multidimensional model of ID that includes a focus on individualized educational supports.

- One of the primary strategies ensuring that students with ID can be engaged with the general education curriculum involves the design of instructional materials and activities that promotes flexibility in representing content (i.e., how instructional materials present the content), in presenting context (i.e., how educators and materials deliver content), and in demonstrating content mastery (i.e., how students provide evidence of their learning).

- The focus on providing supports to promote a better fit between a student's capacities and the educational context places greater emphasis on the use of instructional and assistive technologies.
- A systems of supports addresses multiple human performance elements that are interdependent and cumulative.
- Quality improvement is a continuous process with a goal of improving an organization's performance and, thereby, enhancing human functioning and personal outcomes.
- Organizations providing supports to individuals with ID need to be guided by the multiple systems (i.e., micro, meso, and macro) that impact human functioning.
- Organization-level management strategies involved in delivering individualized supports need to be based on strategic thinking, support services as open systems, a focus on the community, and support guidelines.
- Organization-level support provision is based on a multicomponent support process, a systems perspective, and a support team.
- Organization-level management considerations regarding supports include costs and outcomes, quality management, and quality improvement.
- Organization-level supports provision is guided by professional standards and practices.

CHAPTER 13

IMPLICATIONS FOR PUBLIC POLICY

OVERVIEW

Public policy exerts a significant influence on society at large and on people with *intellectual disability* (ID) specifically. The development and implementation of public policy is a dynamic process that influences practice but is also influenced by changes in practice and assumptions in the field. This reciprocal relationship is evidenced in the connection between public policy and diagnostic and classification schemes. On one hand, public policy influences the diagnostic and classification process through state guidelines regarding diagnostic criteria and eligibility requirements. Conversely, changes in classifications systems—and the underlying principles that support them—influence perceptions of the needs and capabilities of people with ID and in turn have an impact on how public systems design and deliver supports and services. Both public policy and classification systems are, in turn, shaped by societal perceptions of disability and by data generated in the field on the outcomes experienced by people with ID.

This synergy between public policy and changes in assessment and classification systems has led to an increased recognition of the importance of individualized supports to the enhancement of human functioning. It has also spawned the growing emphasis on self-directed funding, person-centered planning, and home-based supports (Prouty, Alba, Scott, & Lakin, 2008). Such policies, as embodied in the conduct of public intellectual and developmental disability systems, facilitate society's response to individual support needs and promote person-referenced rather than program-referenced outcomes.

In the present chapter we focus on public policy and the application of the definition of ID and its classification and supports-planning components described in this *Manual* to promote changes in public policy that will lead to the achievement of desired policy outcomes. To that end, the discussions are on (a) social factors that influence public policy and its adoption, (b) the core concepts guiding disability policy, (c) desired policy outcomes stemming from these core concepts, and (d) a framework for implementing the 2010 definition of ID and its classification and supports-planning components to influence desired public policy outcomes. Throughout the chapter, the 2010 AAIDD System will refer to the definition of ID and the diagnosis, classification, and supports-planning components described in chapters 1–12 of this *Manual*. While reading this chapter, it is important that public policy is seen as a critical part of context, the fifth dimension of the proposed AAIDD framework of human functioning (see Figure 2.1).

Social Factors Influencing
Public Policy and Its Adoption

Multiple social factors influence public policy and its adoption and implementation. The goals and purposes of public policy and public service systems for people with ID have significantly changed over time due to changes in both ideology and increased knowledge regarding the nature of disability. In the past, public systems for this population offered only custodial care and treatment in state-operated facilities. As community-based services have become the predominant mode of service delivery, public managers, advocates, and other stakeholders have worked hard to ensure that these supports and services reflect the individual's needs and preferences rather than program and facility needs, preferences, or conveniences. In addition to changes in ideology and knowledge regarding the nature of disability, these changes in public systems have been driven by other factors, including the following:

- *Social and political movements*: general (e.g., civil rights) and disability-specific (e.g., normalization, deinstitutionalization, self-advocacy) social and political movements
- *Attitudinal changes*: changes in how disability is perceived in society resulting from social and political movements and the adoption of an ecological perspective
- *Judicial decisions*: Court rulings affirming the right of individuals with ID to treatment (*Pennhurst State School and Hospital v. Halderman*, 1984; *Wyatt v. Stickney*, 1974), to a free appropriate public education (*Pennsylvania Association for Retarded Children v. Pennsylvania*, 1972; *Mills v. District of Columbia Board of Education*, 1972), and to community based treatment (*Olmstead v. L.C.*, 1999)
- *Statutory changes*: legislation codifying the aforementioned social/political movements and legal rulings (e.g., Individuals With Disabilities Education Improvement Act of 2004 and the American With Disabilities Act of 1990)
- *Participatory research and evaluation frameworks*: the movement toward including people with ID and their families in the evaluation of personal outcomes resulting from services and supports
- *Advances in research regarding the nature of disability that has led to more successful intervention*: the adoption of new techniques and technologies that improve outcomes and enhance our expectations of what people with ID can achieve

Taken together, these social factors have led to significant changes in public policy and practice in the disability field. As shown in Figure 13.1, these social factors are some of the inputs that exert influence on the interactive relationship between public policy and practice.

Core Concepts and Principles Guiding Disability Policy

National and international disability policy is currently premised on a number of concepts and principles that are (a) *person-referenced*, such as self-determination, inclusion,

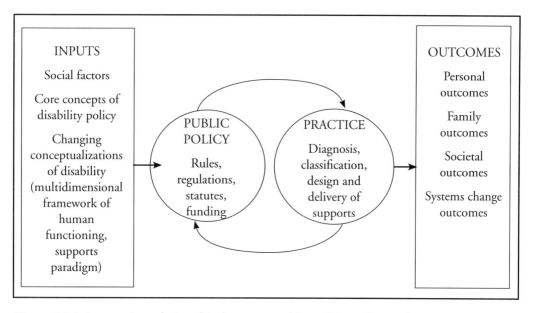

Figure 13.1. Interactive relationship between public policy and practice.

empowerment, individual and appropriate services, productivity and contribution, and family integrity and unity; and (b) *system-referenced* (supports/service delivery), such as antidiscrimination, coordination and collaboration, and accountability (Montreal Declaration, 2004; Salamanca Statement, 1994; Stowe, Turnbull, & Sublet, 2006; H. Turnbull, Beegle, & Stowe, 2001a; H. Turnbull, Wilcox, Stowe, & Umbarger, 2001b). These principles have been operationalized in the United Nations Convention on the Rights of Persons With Disabilities (United Nations, 2006) articles that address the following domains: rights (access and privacy); participation; autonomy, independence, and choice (i.e., self-determination); physical well-being; material well-being (work/employment); societal inclusion, accessibility, and participation; emotional well-being (freedom from exploitation, violence, and abuse); and personal development (education and rehabilitation).

Over time, as our understanding of disability and human functioning has deepened and become more progressive, these evolving core principles have fostered public policy that promotes change based on various types of information (e.g., research, evaluation, quality assurance). They have also increased our interest in generating outcome data that operationalize the core principles guiding public policy. Such data help to assess the efficacy of public policy and practice, which, as depicted in Figure 13.1, creates a feedback loop that impacts public policy and practice over time. For example, the focus on individual choice and control over services and supports has led to the implementation of self-determination, self-directed funding, and the creation of individual budgets based on assessed needs and assets. These rights and entitlements that focus on individual outcomes have in turn lead to ongoing change at the individual, community, and societal level.

Desired Policy Outcomes

Professional organizations and support/service providers throughout the world concerned about people with ID are increasingly focused on identifying and assessing outcomes related to the core concepts and principles of disability policy. There are at least three reasons to focus on desired policy outcomes related to the personal, familial, and societal outcomes described in this section and summarized in Tables 13.1–13.3. First, the outcome domains and exemplary indicators provide a conceptual and empirical link among the core concepts and disability principles, legislative initiatives, and legal trends discussed throughout the chapter. Second, they underscore why the clinical functions of diagnosis and classification are not ends in themselves; rather, as these two clinical functions are integrated into, and aligned with, the provision of individualized supports, the anticipated outcome is the enhancement of human functioning as reflected in one or more outcome domains and indicators described in Tables 13.1–13.3. Third, they recognize the interrelatedness of context with the other dimensions that influence human functioning.

The construct of desired policy outcomes is tied directly to recent legislative and legal trends that have, in turn, shaped the supports and services provided to persons with ID. For example, the intent of recent legislation in most countries has been to ensure rights to education and community living, access to rehabilitation, and employment options and opportunities, technological supports and assistive technology, and person-centered planning. Similarly, legal trends (especially in the United States) have shifted public policy from the preemption of choice to self-determination, from exclusion to inclusion, from segregation to community-based supports, from discrimination to nondiscrimination, and from "paper rights" to rights grounded in established law (Herr, O'Sullivan, & Hogan, 2002). Each of these trends, along with the emphasis on accountability and systems efficiency, has resulted in the conceptualization and measurement of outcomes, such as those suggested later in this chapter.

The core person and system-referenced concepts and principles that guide disability policy have also influenced how we express desired policy outcomes in three important ways. First, as these concepts and principles become embedded in societal attitudes regarding disability, they are the background within which outcome expectations are developed. Second, they form the ideology that motivates policy makers, funders, and other stakeholders to work for the enhancement of valued outcomes for service recipients, families, and the larger society. Third, they constitute a framework for conceptualizing and assessing public policy outcomes, such as the outcome classes we suggest later in the chapter: personal, family, societal, and systems change.

Outcome data can be used for multiple purposes, including analyzing the impact of specific public policies, monitoring the effectiveness and efficiency of supports and services, providing a basis for quality improvement and performance enhancement, meeting the increasing need for accountability, and helping establish the parameters of best practices. The increased use of outcome data as a metric to understand performance is occurring at the same time that we are seeing internationally the emergence of four important trends in the field of ID:

1. A movement from monolithic unitary service delivery organizations to highly complex (and widely varying) support systems composed of multiple levels and types of providers, settings, structures, and dispersed settings
2. A movement from traditional standards and methods associated with compliance and documentation to a quality assessment and improvement methodology that focuses on the systematic collection and analysis of data and information and the implementation of action strategies based on the analysis
3. A movement from management and leadership strategies that are organizational or systems-oriented to strategies that involve managing for results and community integration
4. A movement from traditional discipline-based research strategies to a transdisciplinary approach to research that involves policy makers, researchers, practitioners, and individuals with ID and their families working jointly to produce both scientific understanding and societal applications

Each of these trends suggests the need to measure one or more of the four classes of policy outcomes described next. These outcomes can be used to provide common outcome data across a disparate service delivery system. In addition, such measurement also provides information that can be used for policy evaluation, quality assessment and improvement, quality management and reporting, and transdisciplinary research.

Personal Outcomes

Personal outcomes can be approached from two perspectives. The first is a delineation of valued life domains as reflected in the work of the World Health Organization Quality of Life Work Group (1995) and the United Nations (2006). The second, and complementary, perspective is based on recent work in the field of individual-referenced quality of life that focuses on the identification of domain-referenced quality indicators. The measurement of these respective indicators results in data on personal outcomes (J. Gardner & Carran, 2005; Schalock, Gardner, & Bradley, 2007). The referent for personal outcomes is change in these assessed personal outcomes within the individual over time. The domain-referenced indicators summarized in Table 13.1 are based on the work of Alverson et al. (2006), Colley and Jamison (1998), the Council on Quality and Leadership (2005), J. Gardner and Carran (2005), Gómez, Verdugo, Arias, and Navas (2008), National Core Indicators (2003), Bradley and Moseley (2007), National Council on Disability and Social Security Administration (2000), Schalock et al. (2005), Verdugo, Arias, Gómez, and Schalock (2008), Verdugo, Schalock, Gómez, and Arias (2007), and the U.S. Department of Education (2007).

TABLE 13.1

Person-Referenced Outcome Domains and Exemplary Indicators

Domain	Exemplary indicators
Rights	Human (respect, dignity, equality, privacy) Legal (citizenship, access, due process)
Participation	Participate in the life of their community Participate in integrated community activities Interactions (family, friends, community members) Community/social roles (contributor, volunteer)
Self-determination	Choices (daily routines, activities, personal goals) Decisions (opportunities, options, preferences) Personal control (autonomy, independence)
Physical well-being	Health status (functioning, symptoms, nutrition, fitness) Activities of daily living (self care skills, mobility) Leisure and recreation
Material well-being	Financial status (income, benefits) Employment status (work environment, wages, benefits)
Societal inclusion	Living status (segregated, integrated) Community access and use Connection to natural supports
Emotional well-being	Free from abuse and neglect Experience continuity and security Intimate relationships Friends and caring relationships
Personal development	Education level (achievement, status) Educational environment (time outside the regular class) Postsecondary education Personal competence (cognitive, social, practical skills)

Family Outcomes

Even though the focus of the 2010 AAIDD System is on individuals with ID, the majority of these persons still reside with their family or in a *family home* that is defined as

> a house owned or rented by a family member of a person with an intellectual or developmental disability (ID/DD) in which the individual with ID/DD resides and receives care, instruction, supervision, and other supports from persons other than family members and/or from family members who are paid. (Prouty et al., 2008, p. 82)

Prouty et al. also stated that

> the total number of persons with ID/DD reported to receive services and supports during the 1996–2006 decade increased from 612,928 to 984,662 (a 60.6% increase). Of the estimated 371,374 person increase, 75% was accounted for by growth in the number of persons reported to be receiving services and supports while living with family members. (p. 82)

Families who have a family member with ID and who are providing individualized supports to that person in the home are impacted significantly. This impact is reflected in the evolution of both public policy and the concept of family support plans (A. Turnbull, Brown, & Turnbull, 2004; H. Turnbull et al., 2001a, 2001b). As a result, a companion class of policy outcomes to the person-referenced outcomes just described has emerged within the field of family quality of life. Exemplary domains and indicators are summarized in Table 13.2. These domains and indicators are based on the work of Aznar and Castanon (2005), Isaacs et al. (2007), Park et al. (2003), and Summers et al. (2005). The referent for these outcomes is change over time in the family indicators/outcomes listed.

TABLE 13.2

Family-Related Outcome Domains and Exemplary Indicators

Domain	Exemplary indicator
Family interaction	Spends time together, talks openly with each other, solves problems together, supports each other
Parenting	Helps children, teaches children, takes care of individual needs
Emotional well-being	Has friends who provide support, has time to pursue individual interests, has available outside help to take care of special needs, feels safe
Personal development	Opportunities for continuing education, employment status of parents, educational level of family members

TABLE 13.2 (*continued*)

Domain	Exemplary indicator
Physical well-being	Gets needed medical/dental care, opportunities for recreation and leisure
Financial well-being	Has available transportation, has a way to take care of expenses, family income
Community involvement	Community activities, membership in groups/clubs, community relations
Disability-related supports	Support at school/workplace, support to make progress at home, support to make friends, has good relationship with service provider

Societal Outcomes

Community membership is a useful label for the present service paradigm within the field of ID as it continues to evolve to a supports-based approach. Consistent with the 1992 (Luckasson et al.) and 2002 (Luckasson et al.) AAIDD systems, the 2010 AAIDD System emphasizes attitudes and practices that recognize full citizenship of people with ID, while acknowledging that although ID constitutes a significant limitation to the individual, the goal of a supports-based approach is to facilitate the inclusion of individuals with ID into the full life of the community. With this goal in mind, societal/community indicators are increasingly being used in the field to determine (a) the discrepancy between personal outcomes for persons with ID and community indicators and (b) whether disability related public policies have impacted or reduced that discrepancy. With the increased emphasis in public policy on the rights to education and community living, access to rehabilitation and employment opportunities, and individualized supports to enhance human functioning, it is reasonable that community indicators become the referent at the societal level in the analysis and evaluation of public policy outcomes (Emerson & Hatton, 2008; National Research Council, 2002; Schalock, Gardner, & Bradley, 2007).

Historically, *social indicators*, which refer to external, environmentally based conditions, have been used to facilitate concise, comprehensive, and balanced judgments about the conditions of major aspects of society (Andrews & Whithey, 1976; Kahn & Juster, 2002; Schalock, 2001; Sirgy et al., 2006). Examples include health, social welfare, friendships, standard of living, education, public safety, employment rates, literacy, mortality, life expectancy, housing, neighborhood, and leisure. As discussed by Emerson, Fujiura, and Hatton (2007) and Arthaud-Day, Rode, Mooney, and Near (2005), during the last 3 decades, social indicators associated with subjective well-being, which is considered a key component of the quality of life of persons with ID (Cummins, 2003), have also been used to analyze the impact of economic and social policies. As shown in Table 13.3, there are three significant indicators of subjective well-being as currently conceptualized and measured: a cognitive appraisal of life satisfaction, positive affect, and the absence of negative affect.

TABLE 13.3

Societal Outcome Domains and Exemplary Indicators

Domain	Exemplary indicator
Socioeconomic position	Education, occupation, income
Health	Longevity, wellness, access to health care
Subjective well-being	Life satisfaction, positive affect (happiness, contentment), absence of negative affect (sadness/worry, helpless)

Although the assessment and use of societal outcomes in the field of ID is just emerging, the focus of current efforts is on the three domains listed in Table 13.3: socioeconomic position, health, and subjective well-being. The domains and indicators listed in the table are based on the work of Cummins (2005), Deiner, Lucas, and Oishi (2002), Emerson et al. (2005), Emerson, Graham, and Hatton (2006), Emerson and Hatton (2008), and Mackenbach et al. (2008).

Systems Change Outcomes

The outcome domains and exemplary indicators presented in Tables 13.1–13.3 reflect the intended impact and outcomes of core concepts and disability principles and legislation. The focus on these outcomes also reflects the movement within the field of ID away from a sole focus on diagnosis and classification to an increased focus on the planning and provision of individualized supports that enhance human functioning as reflected in the personal, family, and societal outcomes discussed earlier. Further, they result in information that is responsive to the quality revolution, with its focus on valued outcomes; the reform movement, with its emphasis on outcomes rather than inputs and processes; and the use of outcome-related information as a basis for quality management and quality improvement.

These outcomes can also be viewed as indicators of systems change. As depicted in Figure 13.1, changes in practice or in the public systems that are responsible for the design and delivery of supports and services can impact desired policy outcomes. In addition, data on personal and family outcomes, such as those described in Tables 13.1 and 13.2, can be aggregated at the organization and/or systems level to provide a performance index or a measure of systems change (Bradley & Moseley, 2007; J. Gardner & Carran, 2005; Keith & Bonham, 2005; Schalock et al., 2007). For example, the National Association of State Directors of Developmental Disabilities Services/Human Services Research Institute developed National Core Indicators (2003), which includes a survey of personal rather than programmatic outcomes. Twenty-nine states are currently collecting this information, and data on the outcomes of over 12,000 individuals is currently available. Similarly, accrediting organizations, such as the Council on Quality and Leadership (2005), are using personal outcomes as an essential and integral component of the accreditation process. Provider profiles that include annual summaries of aggregated quality of life-related personal outcomes are also being used in at least two states for meeting accountability and public reporting requirements and providing the basis for quality improvement strategies (Keith & Bonham, 2005).

Outcome data, such as those studied by Braddock and his colleagues (e.g., Braddock, 2002), can also be used to evaluate systems change. For example, in Braddock's longitudinal evaluation of state-level systems change, the major indicators used included (a) distribution of residential services by setting; (b) trends in ID/DD spending (i.e., community services, individual and family support, and public/private institutions); (c) numbers of persons in supported employment; and (d) numbers of persons in supported living and (receiving) personal assistance. Increasingly, there is a need to evaluate two additional systems change indicators: access to services (e.g., transportation and waiting lists) and the availability of specific services across geographical areas.

Collectively, these outcome classes and system change indicators result in information that is responsive to changes in our understanding of ID and our growing recognition of the importance of individualized supports to the enhancement of human functioning. They also reflect one important component of the framework to influence public policy outcomes discussed next.

FRAMEWORK TO INFLUENCE PUBLIC POLICY OUTCOMES

Factors Impacting Outcomes

To understand the potential of the 2010 AAIDD System to influence public policy outcomes, it is critical to understand the multiple factors that influence these outcomes. One set of factors are those depicted as inputs in Figure 13.1: social factors, core concepts of disability policy, and a changing conception of ID. Changes in public policy resulting from these inputs lead to changes in practices, which in turn have an impact on desired public policy outcomes. As also shown in Figure 13.1, a focus on outcomes can reshape the information that is generated by public systems and, therefore, influence the information that guides the development of public policy. Thus, the relationship between public policy and practice is interactive.

A second set of factors are the multiple systems within which people live, are schooled, work, and recreate. As shown in Figure 13.2, which is based in part on Bronfenbrenner's (1979) conceptualization of human development, the inputs (social factors, disability core concepts, and changing conceptions of disability) are operationalized through the multiple contexts within which individuals function: the immediate social setting, including the person, family, and advocates (microsystem); the neighborhood, community, or organizations providing education and supports (mesosystem); and the overarching patterns of culture, society, and sociopolitical influences (macrosystem). The person and these multiple systems interact over time (chronosystem). Thus, each of the outcome classes will be affected by these system filters. For example, at the societal or macrosystem level, the core principle of civil rights can be translated into a commitment on the part of society to concrete outcomes, such as dignity, respect, choice, and equality. At the community or mesosystem level, the principle of rights can be understood (and measured) as the expression of fairness, dignity, and respect by community organizations and support providers to people with ID and their families. At the individual or microsystem level, rights can be understood through the self report of families and people with ID regarding whether their basic human rights have been respected. Finally, over time (chronosystem), changes will occur in how rights for people with ID are understood and expressed across all levels of the system. For example, changes in society (e.g., the civil rights movement)

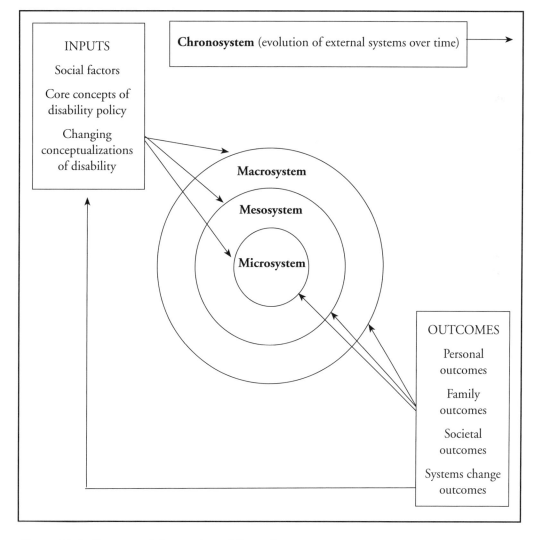

Figure 13.2. Contextual factors in public policy.

can interact with changes in how supports and services are designed and delivered (e.g., more people with ID living in the community), leading to variation in the nature of the rights afforded to them.

Furthermore, the operationalization of each of the inputs at each level of the system influences the operationalization of the inputs over time at the other levels of the system. For example, the core principle of rights may be adopted in public policy at the societal level and filter through to the other levels of the social context (e.g., support providers creating a bill of rights for the individuals they serve; an individual expressing their right to equal access to a public service). However, changes at the micro- or mesosystem level can also filter outward and lead to changes at the societal level (e.g., an individual with disability learning about the rights afforded other groups and beginning to advocate for change in public policy and practice; a support provider organization implementing a consumer-directed model that leads to positive outcomes that it then uses to guide the development of public policy related to consumer-directed supports).

Understanding the multiple factors that influence the adoption and implementation of public policy can exert significant change on practice in the field. For example, the supports model—as a social-political movement/input factor—has changed public policy and led to a shift in the practices used by public systems that provide services and supports to individuals with ID over time. The supports model has also had an impact through each level of the social context by changing public policy, organizational practice, and the outcomes experienced by these individuals and their families (A. Turnbull, Turnbull, Soodak, & Erwin, 2006; A. Turnbull et al., 2004; H. Turnbull et al., 2001a, 2001b).

As discussed in reference to Figures 13.1 and 13.2, policy outcomes are critical to understanding the inputs, throughputs, and outcomes of public policy. As shown in Figure 13.1, outcome data provide essential formative feedback to policy makers regarding the effectiveness of a given policy and important outcome-related information that can be used by organizations and systems for quality management, quality assurance, and quality improvement. As shown in Figure 13.2, there is an interactive relationship between outcomes and the multiple systems (micro, meso, and macro) that impact all individuals. This systems perspective provides the framework for the outcome classes discussed in the previous section of this chapter: personal and family (microsystems level), systems change (mesosystem), and societal (macrosystems level).

Impacting Public Policy Outcomes

The proposed framework for understanding how the 2010 AAIDD System can impact public policy outcomes includes the following six action steps:

1. *Establish best practices in the field of ID*: These best practices involve (a) meeting the three criteria for a diagnosis of ID and understanding the various factors that impact the assessment process and the measurement of intellectual functioning and adaptive behavior (see chapters 3, 4, and 5); (b) using multiple classification

systems to answer respective classification questions (see chapters 6 and 7); (c) assessing the support needs of individuals with ID and providing individualized supports to enhance human functioning and personal outcomes (see chapters 9 and 10); and (d) using clinical judgment and clinical judgment strategies that are based on the clinician's explicit training, direct experience with those with whom the clinician is working, and specific knowledge of the person and the person's environment (see chapter 8).

2. *Achieve greater universal use of a multidimensional approach to diagnosis, classification, and supports provision*: To accomplish this action, it is necessary to understand the approach clearly and align the core functions of diagnosis, classification, and planning/delivery of individualized supports. This will require that the desired outcome of the process of diagnosing and classifying—the delivery of individualized supports that enhance individual functioning and promote desired personal outcomes—be used to guide the application of the multidimensional approach to diagnosis, classification, and supports provision.

3. *Address current policy and system disconnects*: In order to ensure that the individual needs of people with ID are met across the life span, it will be necessary to integrate services, supports, and policies across current service delivery systems. This will require addressing a range of policies and pieces of system infrastructure to create a seamless platform for the delivery of long-term supports from birth through school years into adulthood. In addition, there is a need to address the access to services (as reflected in transportation availability and waiting lists) and the availability of specific services across geographical areas.

4. *Implement more widely the policies that are already in existence*: For many persons with ID, policies that have the potential to promote desired outcomes are "on the books" (e.g., interagency collaboration in the Individuals With Disabilities Education Improvement Act of 2004) but not implemented in practice. Mechanisms such as professional education and training programs, outcome-based management and information systems, and quality improvement strategies (based on the feedback loop depicted in Figure 13.1) should be used to facilitate broader implementation of existing policies.

5. *Focus on personal outcomes and their enhancement*: Personal outcomes should be enhanced through the provision of individualized supports based on (a) understanding the dynamic interaction/interplay among the person, his or her pattern and intensity of needed supports, and his or her environment (as shown in Figure 13.2) and (b) aligning functional characteristics, assessed support needs, and the allocation of resources. These points are discussed in more detail in chapters 2, 9–12, and 14–15.

6. *Utilize formative feedback generated by the assessment of policy outcomes*: Systematic data should be collected on the personal, familial, and societal outcomes described in Tables 13.1–13.3. These data can then be used to evaluate the effectiveness of a given policy, systematically identify necessary changes in public policy and

practice, and develop and implement action strategies for implementing these changes.

SUMMARY

Multiple social factors have influenced the adoption and implementation of public policy toward people with ID. Chief among these factors are social-political movements, attitudinal changes, judicial decisions, statutory changes, participatory action research, and advances in research regarding the nature of disability and successful interventions. Based on an understanding of how these factors impact public policy, we are in a better position to promote policies and practices regarding persons with ID that will enhance their lives and, thereby, better achieve desired public policy outcomes.

In addition to summarizing the social factors influencing public policy and its adoption and the core concepts and principles guiding disability policy, the intent of this chapter has been to delineate clearly desired policy outcomes that we categorize as outcomes related to the person, the person's family, society, and the service delivery system. Once these desired policy outcomes are clearly delineated, policies and practices can be directed at their evaluation and enhancement. One such practice focuses on the use of the 2010 AAIDD System as a framework for impacting public policy outcomes. This framework involves action steps related to best practices, a multidimensional approach to classification and supports provision, augmenting current policies and reducing "policy disconnects," and utilizing formative feedback generated by the assessment of desired policy outcomes at the personal, family, societal, and systems change level.

CHAPTER 14

IMPLICATIONS FOR EDUCATION

OVERVIEW

The definition and classification system introduced in this *Manual* can be of value to educators and applied to students with *intellectual disability* (ID) during their years in school. In this chapter, we discuss (a) the educational characteristics and needs of students with ID and the professionals who teach and support them, (b) historical and current models of special education, (c) definitions and classification systems in education, (d) the AAIDD multidimensional model and supports paradigm as applied to education, and (e) innovative best practices in education.

We begin by describing three people with ID (Nina, Sam, and John) who vary widely in their ages, abilities, and environmental contexts. We will link the concepts addressed in this chapter to these people.

Nina was diagnosed before birth with Down syndrome through an amniocentesis. Before she was born, her parents had met with the early intervention staff and discussed educational services that might be available to their daughter. These services started when Nina was 2 weeks old and an Individualized Family Services Plan was written to guide intervention. Nina is now 3 years old and attends a community preschool program that serves children with disabilities alongside typically developing peers. Nina's special education teacher and her related services support staff (occupational therapist [OT] and speech and language pathologist [SLP]) come to the preschool on a scheduled basis, provide their services that are integrated into the school routine, and meet regularly with the classroom teacher and other team members to plan Nina's educational program and to monitor her progress. Nina's parents and special education teacher have visited the kindergarten class she will attend in 2 years to build successful transition goals into her Individual Education Program (IEP).

Sam is a 10-year-old boy who was born with cerebral palsy and visual limitations; during his preschool years, he was diagnosed with significant developmental delays. Sam received special education services starting at age 2, along with OT and physical therapy (PT) and speech and language services. At age 3, he was placed in an early childhood special education classroom where he received educational and related services but also began exhibiting problem behavior (spitting and refusal to participate). In elementary school he was initially placed in a self-contained classroom for children with multiple disabilities. However, by second grade, when his school district began implementing inclusive practices, Sam received most of the special education and related services supports (OT, PT, SLP) in the context of the second grade scheduled activities and was pulled out for some intensive instruction in the resource room several times weekly. Sam's team worked closely with his parents to plan and oversee his IEP and related progress, and to address his problem behaviors. They involved a Positive Behavior Support (PBS) specialist on the team and designed a support plan that was based on the functions that his problem behavior served. The plan called for teaching him more efficient ways to communicate and improving the classroom conditions that often triggered his problem behavior. Based on his triannual assessment at age 8, Sam's diagnosis was changed from developmental delay to ID; his placement continued to be with his peers in third grade, and his IEP services were delivered to him in that setting. Sam is now in fifth grade, and his team is studying the middle school program in the school district, where inclusive practices were recently initiated with children served under the learning disability category. The teachers in that setting have expressed hesitancy to include someone with ID and other physical disabilities; they are concerned specifically about his means of communicating and responding in class.

John is a young man who lives in a housing project with his mother and grandmother in a large city in northern United States. He was labeled with ID in elementary school after repeatedly failing several grades and most academic subjects. John's speech was not always readily understood by his teachers or peers; however, he received no speech services. At age 9 in fourth grade, he was given special education services on a pull-out basis; by sixth grade, he was placed in a self-contained, cross-categorical special education class. In his first year of high school, John tried out for the football team but was not accepted because of his difficulty attending practice regularly and understanding the rules and the plays. He continued to have difficulty reading and performing in his ninth-grade special education classes. By 10th grade, he started skipping school; he had several contacts with the law, first being caught shoplifting cigarettes for others and later being stopped as a passenger in a stolen car. He quit school midyear in 11th grade. John has never been employed, although he successfully completed two job sampling assignments in 11th grade as part of his transition plan. One summer he worked mowing lawns for several neighbors, but this stopped when he stole tools from the garage of one neighbor. At age 21, he still lives with his mother and grandmother, is unemployed, and spends most of his time with others who have dropped out of school.

CHARACTERISTICS AND NEEDS OF STUDENTS WITH INTELLECTUAL DISABILITY

Although not yet universally implemented, the right to education has become an internationally acknowledged standard for practice for children with ID. For example, participants representing 92 governments at the 1994 United Nations Educational, Scientific, and Cultural Organization (UNESCO) World Conference on Special Needs Education at Salamanca, Spain, passed the *Salamanca Statement and Framework for Action on Special Needs Education* espousing the beliefs that "every child has a fundamental right to education, and must be given the opportunity to achieve and maintain an acceptable level of learning" (UNESCO, 1994, p. viii). The Salamanca Statement

(1994) provides a succinct summary of the ideal to which most countries strive with regard to the education of children with special educational needs, including students with ID.

Who Are Students With Intellectual Disability?

Although criteria for eligibility for special needs education services vary from country to country, there are some factors that span across countries and that assist in designing educational supports for this group of students. First, the majority of students receiving special educational services are students with ID who have higher IQ scores—John clearly falls in this group. Second, the support needs of students with ID range widely as a function not only of the intensity of support needs for any given student but also of the student's age. For example, the support profiles of Nina and Sam are both directed toward their upcoming transitions but otherwise have no similarity. Such potentially diverse needs have led to the recognition that special educational services for students with ID must be individualized, taking into account unique student educational characteristics and providing individualized supports to enable students to achieve those needs.

Who Are Professionals in Education?

There is a wide array of professionals who are involved in the education of students with ID, including special and general educators; related service personnel, such as SLPs, OTs, and PTs; experts in behavioral guidance, counselors, vocational specialists, and transition coordinators; and school psychologists and social workers.

> Nina and Sam have relied on the services of OTs, PTs, and SLPs in addition to special educators, but John's services were limited to special education, even though he needed speech services as well.

Among these professionals, school psychologists or educational diagnosticians are most likely to use the information presented in this *Manual*, because they are responsible for helping to determine eligibility for special educational services.

> Because of school eligibility practices and based on an assessment, Sam's diagnosis was changed when he reached third grade from developmental delay to ID.

Teachers, particularly, but other instructional support personnel as well, are likely to have access to and use information from a diagnostic procedure to plan and implement educational programs. The special educational enterprise is by necessity collaborative in nature if all aspects of a student's educational needs are to be addressed in an educational program. As such, teamwork between school and community professionals and with family members is highly valued. We will return to this issue later in discussing how the supports model can be used in designing educational services for students with ID.

HISTORICAL AND CURRENT MODELS OF SPECIAL EDUCATION

Like many service systems supporting people with ID, special educational services have transformed, or are still transforming, from congregated, segregated services and settings to inclusive educational settings. The earliest attempts at education for people with ID involved efforts to educate youth with ID who lived in institutional settings. Early 19th century efforts in France and across Europe by pioneers such as Itard and Seguin were emulated by progressive reformers in the Americas, Australia, and elsewhere; however, by the late 19th century, the original educative purpose of these institutions was being obviated by the forces of increasing institutional populations and changing populations of people entering institutions. Many felt that the lofty promise of education, the "noble experiment" to eliminate ID, failed when educational methods did not cure mental retardation and when those reintegrated into society still had significant disability and needed support (Trent, 1994). Was it realistic to integrate people with ID into society? Negative myths developed about these individuals as being a danger to the community, and attention turned toward controlling their reproduction. Social pressures pertaining to eugenics and social hygiene led to forced sterilization programs that began in 1880, and these programs continued for much of the 20th century (De Kraai, 2002).

When, in the early decades of the 20th century, the demands for universal access to education opened school doors for more and more children, a nascent movement to provide educational access for students with disabilities emerged, but by and large it did not result in substantial gains with regard to access to education until the post-World War II era. Students with ID, particularly those with more severe impairments, were often the last to gain such access, but by the end of that century, as illustrated by the Salamanca Statement in 1994, there was an international expectation pertaining to the rights of children with disability, including those with ID, to education.

Over the past several decades, however, another almost universal consensus has emerged worldwide pertaining to the education of students with ID; that is, the expectation that every child has a fundamental right to education and that efforts should be made to educate them in inclusive classrooms with their nondisabled peers. The Salamanca Statement calls upon all governments and the international community to (a) adopt as a matter of law or policy the principle of inclusive education, enrolling all children in regular schools, unless there are compelling reasons for doing otherwise and (b) endorse the approach of inclusive schooling and to support the development of special needs education as an integral part of all education programs. In summary, there is an emerging consensus that children and youth with ID be included in general education settings so that they have access to the same educational opportunities available to the majority of children.

USES OF DEFINITIONS AND CLASSIFICATION SYSTEMS IN EDUCATION

For educators and other professionals involved in the education of students with ID, this 11th edition of AAIDD's *Diagnosis, Classification, and Systems of Supports Manual* recommends diagnostic processes that will be familiar to practitioners. The *Manual* also challenges professionals to think differently about ID itself and to apply a multidimensional model and supports paradigm that will fundamentally alter the educational process. In the field of education, the primary application of the definition of ID is in the diagnostic process that is used to help determine eligibility for special education or related services. Diagnostic responsibilities typically reside with school psychologists or educational diagnosticians, who are trained to administer standardized tests and to make diagnoses based on test findings and other factors. These professionals will want to become familiar with information provided in part II of this *Manual* ("Diagnosis and Classification of Intellectual Disability") and are referred to chapters 4–8 for more information on the diagnostic process.

The application of classification systems to the education of students with ID has a more complex and, in most cases, problematic history. As is emphasized in chapter 12 ("Support Needs of Persons With ID Who Have Higher IQ Scores"), students with ID vary with regard to the severity of their impairment, and the educational support needs of students across this range of abilities and limitations likewise varies. Since the earliest attempts to educate students with ID, schools have classified students based upon level or impairment. Classification systems used in more recent times have almost all been linked to IQ ranges and identified by labels pertaining to each IQ range. Students with relatively higher IQ scores, typically between two and three standard deviations below the mean, were classified as *educable* or with *mild mental retardation*; students whose scores fell between three and four standard deviations below the mean were referred to as *trainable* or as having *moderate mental retardation*; those with IQ scores between four and five standard deviations below the mean were classified as having "severe mental retardation" and students with IQ scores lower than that were classified as having "profound mental retardation."

As a result of years of such classification systems, students were frequently grouped according to their level of mental retardation and provided special education services in homogeneous groups, typically in separate classrooms and frequently in special schools. The problems associated with homogeneous grouping by IQ level are myriad and beyond the scope of this chapter or *Manual*. The primary problems, however, have included the routinization of curricular content by level of impairment (and the consequent lack of individualization resulting from such routinization), social isolation and exclusion (and the consequent lack of appropriate role models), low expectations for performance and capacity, and the promulgation of problem behaviors associated with factors inherent to segregated settings. Finally, according to recent federal data, only 2% of students served in the United States under the categorical area of mental retardation are "declassified" from special education; once students in this category start receiving special education services, they almost always continue to need them (Snell et al., 2009).

The 1992 AAMR *Manual* proposed a classification system based not upon IQ ranges, but on the intensity of supports a person needs to function successfully in his or her environment (intermittent, limited, extensive, pervasive [ILEP]). In the 2002 AAMR *Manual*, the AAMR Terminology and Classification Committee retained a "strong commitment to a supports-based classification system" as embodied in a system based on support levels (Luckasson et al., 2002, p. 101), but also acknowledged the variance in classification systems and needs across the life span and disciplines. The present *Manual* continues to recognize that multidimensional classification systems may be necessary in the provision of supports (e.g., to determine funding levels for adult developmental disabilities services), but the use of such systems must result in more benefit than harm to the person with ID. In the cost/benefit analysis of the application of classification systems to education to date, there is evidence that the harm, in the form of social isolation, exclusion, and low expectations, may indeed outweigh the benefits for students with ID.

Classification systems based upon level of disability become less important and, perhaps, irrelevant in school systems that include students with ID alongside their peers without disabilities and that provide needed support to all students in the classroom. It is important, then, that all educators and educational practitioners consider the ways in which the AAIDD multidimensional model, as described in chapter 2, and the supports paradigm, as described in chapter 9, impact educational decision making and practice. This change toward inclusive education has gradually evolved over the past 30 years.

> John's history of special education apart from his peers is quite different from others with ID who are younger. Sam was educated separately until second grade and then included with supports, while Nina was included with peers with no disability at the preschool level.

As we have noted, there is a worldwide acknowledgement that students with ID should be included in schools and classes with their same-aged peers who do not have the disability (Emerson et al., 2007). However, as Emerson et al. noted, "Questions about educational services in the poorest nations tend not to be about appropriateness or quality but rather about availability" (p. 602).

BEST PRACTICES IN THE EDUCATION OF STUDENTS WITH INTELLECTUAL DISABILITY

Three educational practices substantiate the impact of the AAIDD multidimensional model of ID, which includes an emphasis on individualized supports (see Figure 2.1). These three are applications of *Universal Design for Learning* (UDL), the use of educational and assistive technology, and the application of positive behavior supports. These are briefly described here by way of illustrating how the educational process may differ as a function of the new ways of thinking about ID discussed in this *Manual*.

Universal Design for Learning

One of the primary strategies to ensure that students with ID can be engaged with the general education curriculum involves the implementation of principles of UDL as the design of instructional materials delivering content information to students. Historically, content information, particularly in core academic areas, has been presented through print-based formats (textbooks, worksheets) and lectures. Students who cannot read well or who have difficulty with memory or attention, including students with ID, do not have access to the content presented exclusively through these mediums and thus will not have the opportunity to learn that content. Applying principles of UDL to curriculum development can address this barrier by providing multiple means for presenting information and for students to respond to that information. Orkwis and McLane (1998) defined UDL as "the design of instructional materials and activities that allows learning goals to be achievable by individuals with wide differences in their abilities to see, hear, speak, move, read, write, understand English, attend, organize, engage, and remember" (p. 9).

The UDL contributes to progress in the general education curriculum by ensuring that all students can access academic content information and can provide evidence of their learning through more than one means. It promotes flexibility in representing content (how instructional materials present the content), in presenting content (how educators and materials deliver content), and in demonstrating content mastery (how students provide evidence of their learning).

Flexibility in the presentation and representation of content information can be achieved by providing information in a variety of formats, including text, graphics or pictures, digital and other media formats (audio or video, movies), or performance formats (plays, skits). The development of curricular materials in digital (electronic text) formats allows for the use of computers to provide multiple output formats. For example, using specially designed media players, electronic text can be converted to multiple output formats, including electronic Braille, digital talking book format, and sign-language avatars, as well as allowing for output in multiple languages and enabling the user to modify features of the presentation, including font size and color and background color. Similarly, there are multiple ways students can provide evidence of their learning, including written reports, exams, portfolios, drawings, performances, oral reports, videotaped reports, and other alternative means.

There are also pedagogical or instructional modifications that can provide greater access to content information. For example, the use of graphic or advance organizers has been shown to improve the comprehension of students with disabilities. Both graphic and advance organizers are, in essence, flexible ways of presenting content information to students.

> The sixth-grade science teacher found that when he labeled all the areas of the science lab with picture and word directions to facilitate Sam's understanding, the rest of the class understood the procedures better too.

The use of UDL to drive curriculum design is a perfect example of the impact of multidimensional models of disability, such as that presented in this *Manual*, to education. These modifications alter the context, in this case the actual curricular materials, to enable learners with a wide array of abilities and experiences to have access to content information. The UDL improves the "fit" between the student with ID and the curriculum through which content information is presented.

Instructional and Assistive Technology

The focus on providing supports to promote a better fit between a student's capacities and the educational context also places greater emphasis on the use of instructional and assistive technologies. *Instructional technology* involves educational materials that are intended to teach ideas and concepts (e.g., a software program that provides drill and practice in arithmetic operations), whereas *assistive technologies* are tools that help students compensate for their disability; that is, technologies increase, maintain, or improve the functional capabilities (Edyburn, 2000). Sometimes a technology can serve both an instructive and assistive purpose. For example, a student who uses the Writing with Symbols software to write an essay may use it as an assistive technology because they could not write the essay without it, but it also serves as an instructional technology because, by using it, the students learns to write.

Traditionally, the role of technology in special education has been rather narrowly prescribed as of benefit only to students with more severe impairments who need some assistive technology device, such as an augmentative communication device, to accommodate for that student's speech and language deficits. This was consistent with an understanding of ID that focused on fixing the person. Within the AAIDD multidimensional model and supports systems, however, the role of all types of technology, whether they have been developed specifically for a disability population or for the general population, becomes critical to addressing not only the student's capacities but also the educational context. Computer-assisted instruction (CAI), for example, involves the use of computer-based technologies to perform a variety of instructional roles, from initial delivery of content information to drill and practice activities. Research supports the efficacy of CAI with students with and without disabilities, including students with ID (Wehmeyer, Smith, Palmer, Davies, & Stock, 2004). Generic technologies can promote peer interactions by providing a topic of conversation between the student with ID and a peer. Devices like iPods and BlackBerry wireless handheld devices are socially desirable and can facilitate social interactions as well as provide needed supports, such as picture prompts to complete a sequence of job tasks.

> Nina learned to use a visual scene display in preschool to augment her speech; the device was programmed with routine scenes scanned from her day (arrival, centers, circle, recess, snack, bathroom) and spoken messages could be activated by pressing parts of each scene, such as "Let's play housekeeping!" (Fossett & Mirenda, 2007)

Positive Behavior Supports

An ongoing concern for many teachers working with students with ID is managing their classroom to create a nondisruptive learning environment for all students and to deal with challenging behavior problems exhibited by a few students. The field of positive behavior supports reflects another area of intervention and treatment that has advanced from emphasizing the person with a disability as the problem to be fixed to recognizing that treatment and intervention must focus on the social and environmental context and the fit between that context and the individual's limitations. Applying positive behavior supports requires a focus on two primary modes of intervention: altering the environment before a problem behavior occurs and teaching appropriate behaviors as a strategy for eliminating the need for problem behaviors to be exhibited (Carr et al., 1999). Positive behavior supports interventions and support plans are based on a functional behavioral assessment and are directed toward changing the environment in several ways: (a) to prevent the problem behavior by improving antecedent conditions that predict its occurrence, (b) to teach specific skills to replace problem behavior and to expand the individual's general access to reinforcement, and (c) to change the ways others respond to the individual so desired behavior is reinforced and problem behavior is not.

> In second grade when Sam's school implemented inclusive practices with all students, his team worked closely to plan his needed supports. His family was both excited and fearful about the change. Following the five steps for planning supports in Figure 14.1, they started by (a) identifying what they wanted for Sam and what they thought Sam wanted in his life, (b) assessing the kinds of supports Sam would require to accomplish these goals, (c) developing an action plan to gather and deliver the supports, (d) initiating and monitoring the plan, and (e) evaluating personal outcomes. At the time, Sam had no friends; engaged in a lot of problem behavior that seemed to get him attention, albeit negative; had difficulty communicating his wants and feelings; and did not have many academic or other skills or interests beyond his puppy, his family, and watching TV. The team had little trouble identifying goals, but the challenge was to select the goals that could yield the most immediate benefits in Sam's life. Now, 3 years later, this plan has been revised every year and serves to direct his IEP goals, objectives, and support services.

Significantly for educators, the use of positive behavior supports has focused attention on addressing problem behaviors in school settings and in addressing school violence (Horner, Albin, Sprague, & Todd, 2006; A. Turnbull, Brown, & Turnbull, 2006) by providing interventions at an individual, classroom, or whole-school level. Schoolwide positive behavior supports has been demonstrated to reduce office referrals in schools, create classroom environments more conducive to learning, and assist students with chronic behavior problems to improve their behavior. These supports involve the application of behaviorally based approaches to enhance the capacity of schools, families, and communities to design effective environments that improve the fit or link between the students and the environments in which teaching and learning occurs. Attention is focused on creating and sustaining school environments that improve lifestyle results (personal, health, social, family, work, and recreation) for all children and youth by making problem behavior less effective, efficient, and relevant, and desired behavior more functional.

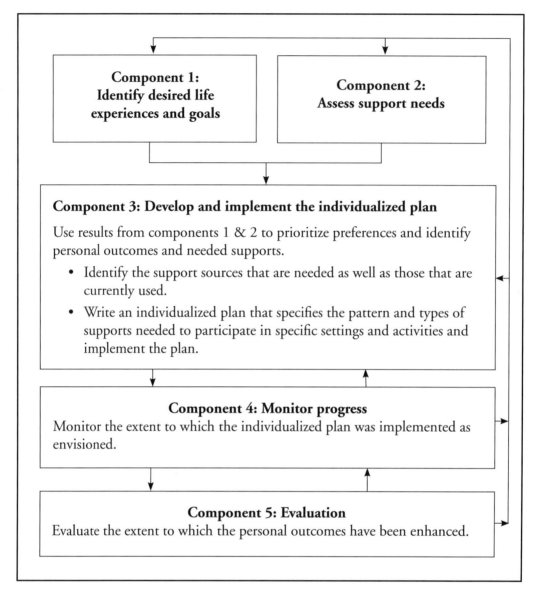

Figure 14.1. Process for assessing, planning, monitoring, and evaluating individualized supports in special education.

SUPPORTS AND THE EDUCATIONAL CONTEXT

Enhancement of Human Functioning

Supports are resources and strategies that aim to enhance individual functioning through the promotion of that person's development, education, interests, and personal well-being. Human functioning is enhanced when the person-environment mismatch is reduced and personal outcomes are improved. Figure 14.1 illustrates the process of individually determining and designing supports with the active involvement of key stakeholders in the process. This approach contrasts with traditional educational service delivery models designed in a top-down manner and delivered in the form of programs, which are often driven as much by the needs of the educational system as by the student's own needs.

> John's educational program followed this path. All students in his special education classroom during middle school received the same special education reading program, and none were taught science or received community-based instruction to learn functional skills and apply academics.

Supports added to a student's school day can take many forms but must be designed to alter the elements of the curriculum, classroom, lesson, or activity to enable that person to be educated with his or her peers without disability. Many supports will be faded once the student participates in an activity with success and shows mastery of new competencies. Supports should always be as unintrusive as possible. Overly intrusive supports can be difficult to eliminate or reduce because they tend to call unnecessary attention to the student and, therefore, run the risk of attaching stigma to a student's participation.

> John did not like going to the special education classroom in high school. It was located near the cafeteria everyone used; other students called it the "retard room."

Sometimes the involvement of peers can help professionals design less intrusive classroom adaptations and accommodations (Janney & Snell, 2004).

> When Nina was in a preschool with peers who did not have disabilities, she required the extensive supports of an OT, PT, and SLP in addition to a special educator to meaningfully participate. Now, as she approaches the transition out of preschool, Nina has learned many of the motor skills and communication skills needed to be an active member of a kindergarten class. Therefore, her support needs have changed and the supports provided to her in the kindergarten class will be different than what was provided when she attended preschool.

Because a supports model requires active and ongoing evaluation of the ecological aspects of the disability, teams who design supports focus heavily on changing aspects of the environment or social context and providing students with skills or strategies to overcome barriers in those environments. Within schools, this contextual focus involves modifications to the classroom, the curriculum, and instructional and social activities.

Addressing Heterogeneity Through Individualized Supports

Educators who seek the best practices for instructing students with ID must keep in mind the extensive heterogeneity of these students. There are many children who, like John, are not identified until after they have been in school for several years and academic achievement problems become a critical concern. These children's outward physical appearance are often no different than typically developing children. There are other children with

ID whose physical appearance is clearly different than others their age due to a recogniz-able syndrome or multiple disabilities, such as Nina's Down syndrome. Such children are usually identified when they are infants or toddlers. For these children, intervention efforts begin early in life and focus on developing basic skills associated with commu-nication and self-care. Adding to the diversity of learners is a range of factors that has a tremendous impact on learning and school success, such as the presence of concomitant disabilities or medical conditions, a child's motivation to learn, the extent of family in-volvement and support, and the quality of the instruction. Because students with ID are such a diverse population, there is a wide array of educational "best practices" that may be appropriate in certain circumstances, depending on a student's abilities, needs, and age. As illustrated in Figure 14.1, educational teams, including family members, must align individualized instructional goals, teaching methods, and educational supports based on the desired life goals and experiences and the assessed learning needs and priorities of each student.

The diversity within the population of students with ID has prompted some to suggest that children with relatively higher IQ scores should be considered under a different dis-ability category than individuals with relatively lower IQ scores (MacMillan, Siperstein, & Gresham, 1996). The variety of teacher certification structures used by different states in the United States reflects the uncertainty of educational systems on how to best pre-pare educators to meet the needs of this diverse population of students. Thirteen states have separate certifications for teachers working with children with "mild/moderate lev-els" and "severe/profound levels" of ID, six states have just one certificate associated with all levels of ID, and the remaining states include certification for teaching students with ID within a multicategorical special education certificate (Education Commission of the States, 2004).

Although children with ID are diverse in many ways, they also have many common-alities in their learning characteristics and educational needs. For example, whether they have relative high or relatively low IQ scores, children with ID, as compared to their typically developing peers, experience difficulty in the areas of cognitive skills (e.g., short term memory, attending to important stimuli, general knowledge, abstract thinking, rate of learning, generalization of learning), academic achievement (e.g., making adequate progress in all content areas, mastering academic skills), social competence (e.g., social interactions, naïveté/gullibility), and communication (e.g., language development, lis-tening and speaking vocabularies; Taylor, Richards, & Brady, 2005). Therefore, all chil-dren with ID need access to educators who understand their learning challenges and are familiar with the extensive professional literature on effective instruction. Each child should have an individualized educational program (IEP) developed by a team of educa-tors who work in collaboration with family members to decide (a) *what* it is that a child needs to learn, (b) *how* (i.e., methods/approaches) to best teach the child, and (c) *where* to teach the child.

Deciding What to Teach

Deciding what to teach a child is contingent on deciding what the child needs to learn. However, even the most thoughtful process requires that educational team members weigh potential benefits that may result from efforts to develop academic competencies against the potential benefits that may accrue from teaching "functional skills" (sometimes referred to as *life skills*). Functional skills include areas such as work habits and behaviors needed to keep a job, social interaction skills needed to participate with others in community settings, and home living skills needed to maintain oneself safely in a community house or apartment. Functional skills are typically not part of the general education curriculum. The choice between teaching functional skills and academic skills can be a false dichotomy. For example, teaching applied money concepts needed to make correct change and balance a checking account are academic skills that are certainly applicable (i.e., functional) to daily life.

Ward, Van De Mark, and Ryndak (2006) coined the term *blended curriculum*, in which academic and functional content are combined to meet students' individualized needs across multiple contexts. Students who receive instruction in a blended curriculum still must have the content individualized, both in terms of academic and the functional skills. Consistent with the first three steps in Figure 14.1, teachers conduct an ecological inventory, or an assessment of activities and skills a particular student needs in current and probable future environments (Ward et al., 2006). This assessment process depends on teachers working closely with other team members—parents, related service providers, and the student him or herself. Individualized academic and functional content that is needed and valued by the student and his or her family receives priority over content that does not meet these criteria. Academic concepts that are not particularly applicable to a person's daily life, or for which the student does not have the prerequisite skills, are not targeted or taught under a blended approach.

One of the biggest challenges in including students with ID in the general education curriculum is that academic skills traditionally are specified by grade level and taught according to a certain schedule. Students with ID usually fall behind in the early elementary grades in mastering the skills at the same rate. If students with ID are to learn skills that are needed to function in life, (a) teams must identify needed academic and functional skills to create a blended curriculum and (b) adaptations must be made on the individualized content through simplification and adapted instructional methods and the application of principals of UDL.

> John would have been more successful learning to read, write, and calculate in ways that were functional to his everyday life had he started elementary school with a blended curriculum and an IEP specifying individually designed supports. Neither John nor his family members were meaningfully involved in planning his educational program, leaving John's mother confused over the school's failure to prepare her son for a job, even after 8 years of special education. John's pattern of skipping school and getting in trouble might have been curtailed if he had experienced success in learning and if his secondary schools had practiced schoolwide positive behavior supports.

In recent years, there has been greater emphasis on students with ID accessing the general education curriculum, which is mostly academically oriented. Despite educational accountability trends that emphasize the teaching and learning of reading, math, and written language, there has never been a mandate for a "one size fits all" approach. Rather, deciding what to teach for an individual child has remained the responsibility of the child's educational team. Educational team members must thoughtfully balance the need for instruction in academic and functional areas and eventually prioritize learning goals so that educational outcomes can be maximized. Among the most important considerations when deciding what to teach (and learn) are a child's age, future plans, current skill level, and learning history (Shelden & Hutchins, 2008; Wehmeyer, Sands, Knowlton, & Kozleski, 2002).

Deciding How to Teach

A comprehensive review of teaching approaches that are useful to educators charged with teaching students with ID is well beyond the scope of this chapter, though some are identified in subsequent sections. However, the importance of teachers being knowledgeable about the array of instructional strategies that have been shown to work with students with ID cannot be overstated. Parents and advocates must insist that teacher-preparation programs produce sufficient numbers of educators who have the professional preparation and expertise necessary to be effective instructors. The shortage of well-prepared special education teachers is severe, chronic, and has persisted for at least 20 years (McLeskey, Tyler, & Flippin, 2004).

Many teaching methods that have been proven effective for learners with ID were developed from principles of applied behavior analysis. Perhaps the most important contribution of applied behavior analysis has been the emphasis placed on collecting data to monitor progress on learning goals. There is no shame in implementing a teaching method that is not successful; teaching students with ID meaningful skills requires perseverance and not every intervention is going to work for all of the children all of the time. However, there is shame in continuing with teaching methods that are not successful. It is critical that educators collect progress-monitoring data on learning goals that an education team has prioritized to determine whether their instruction is effective or if other approaches should be tried. How to teach a child with ID should ultimately be driven by data that show the child's progress or lack of progress.

Once teams prioritize the needed academic and functional skills that a student needs to learn, it may be necessary to adapt the content through a collaborative process of planned simplification. Often, teams will specify needed accommodations (e.g., use of readers and scribes, untimed tests, calculators) to include on a student's IEP. Frequently, team members, including the general education classroom teacher, will determine how instructional approaches might be modified to strengthen the likelihood for success in learning (teaching methods, materials, and the mode of student response; Janney & Snell, 2004).

Deciding Where to Teach

Fifteen years ago, debates regarding where students with ID should be taught were rather heated (see Fuchs & Fuchs, 1994; Wang & Walberg, 1988). L. Brown et al. (1991) calmed the debate by pointing out that very few people were ever in the "100% club" (i.e., never remove a child with a disability from the general educational classroom for any reason) or the "0% club" (never include a child with a disability in the general educational classroom for any reason). The current international legal and moral basis for including students with ID in the general education classroom is strong; currently, most countries have laws that also emphasize that these students must have access to the general education curriculum. Research findings provide evidence that such access is more likely to be gained in the general education classroom, providing a further impetus for inclusive practices (Soukup, Wehmeyer, Bashinski, & Bovaird, 2007; Wehmeyer, Lattin, Lapp-Rincker, & Agran, 2003).

SUMMARY

Considerable effort has been invested in developing approaches to promote the successful inclusion of children with disabilities in general education classrooms. Some of the most popular approaches are often a combination; the success of every approach, however, depends on having collaborative teams of general and special educators and related services staff who receive input from family members and have regular time scheduled for joint planning. These approaches include (a) assessing the general education classroom activities and schedule, (b) modifying classroom instruction and adding needed accommodations that are "only as special as necessary," (c) delivering instruction through coteaching by special educators and general educators, (d) establishing cooperative learning groups and peer mentoring arrangements among students, (e) creating instructional materials based on the principle of UDL, (f) examining student performance data to assess progress and create needed improvements, and (g) carefully employing paraprofessionals to provide direct support in the classroom.

For students with more intense support needs, several authors recommend first conducting an ecological assessment of the focus student's participation in the general education activities and then creating a program planning matrix (Demchek, 1997; Janney & Snell, 2004; Snell & Brown, 2006). The assessment reveals areas where adaptations are needed to increase participation (e.g., use of yes/no switch plate) as well as skills the student needs to be more actively involved (e.g., learning to use the yes/no switch to answer questions and to signal the teacher for opportunity to respond). Team members then list the student's IEP objectives on one axis and the general education schedule on the other. The educational team places an *X* for each part of the day (i.e., activity) where an IEP objective can be taught (each objective will likely be addressed in multiple activities). The ecological classroom assessment and the program planning matrix serve as guides for teaching needed skills in inclusive settings to students whose objectives differ greatly from their classmates.

Whatever approaches are used, success in inclusive classrooms will likely depend on the quality of teamwork, student-referenced and individualized supports, and problem solving among educational team members (Perner & Porter, 2008; Prater, 2007; Snell & Janney, 2005). Meaningful inclusive education relies on a school and classroom culture that values inclusion; a curriculum and instruction that accommodates for a wide range of students; and, as necessary, individualized adaptations that are thoughtfully planned and implemented for individual students who need them (Janney & Snell, 2004). The goal is that students with ID will be members of general education classrooms and participate both socially *and* instructionally alongside classmates.

CHAPTER 15

IMPLICATIONS FOR SUPPORT PROVIDER ORGANIZATIONS

OVERVIEW

The multidimensional framework for understanding *intellectual disability* (ID) discussed in chapter 2 and the systems of supports outlined in chapters 9–12 and 14 of this *Manual* have significant implications for support provider organizations. There is a wide variety of organizations providing services and supports to persons with ID. They range from full residential services to special education schools, supported work agencies, health care agencies that provide supported living, and advisory agencies or broker agencies that primarily engage in service mediation and coordination. Each of these organizations, in turn, is influenced by the social factors impacting public policy, the core concepts and principles guiding disability policy, and the increasing focus on the desired policy outcomes discussed in chapter 13.

In this chapter we discuss the implications of a systems of supports for support provider organizations. These implications are presented as five considerations that are relevant to designing and operating support services: (a) the ecological framework of support organizations, (b) considerations for strategic management, (c) the support process, (d) two service management considerations related to costs and outcomes and quality management, and (e) metaconsiderations for planning and operating support services for persons with ID.

ECOLOGICAL FRAMEWORK OF SUPPORT

Environmental Context

The most dramatic demonstration of the impact of service context on the functioning and well-being of persons with ID was presented by Blatt and Kaplan (1966) in their photographic essay "Christmas in Purgatory." Part I of this historic book shows pictures taken by a hidden camera during their visit to four institutions around Christmas 1965. The alienated and dehumanized situations shown in these pictures were shocking and stood in sharp contrast with the pictures in part II that were taken in a fifth institution (Seaside), showing persons with ID engaged in more normalized and meaningful interactions and activities. From these photographs, it was clearly not the person's disability that explained the dramatic differences in quality of life of the residents; rather, it was the organizational environment and culture.

Modern scientific models of human functioning and ID include the environmental context of the person as a major factor for understanding his or her functioning. Environmental factors make up the physical, social, and attitudinal environment in which people live and conduct their lives. These factors can either act as facilitators that contribute to adapted behavior and typical living conditions or act as barriers that hinder functioning and development (Wehmeyer et al., 2008). For persons with ID who make use of professional support services, these services are an important part of their environment. It is obvious that agencies or programs can make a significant difference to their functioning and quality of life. Understanding the ecology of a support service is a prerequisite for effective management. Service directors and staff are in an excellent position to facilitate the congruence between individuals and their environments of home living, school and education, work, leisure, and community participation. The performance of the support service can be evaluated in terms of this congruence by looking at personal, family, and social outcomes such as those summarized in chapter 13 (Tables 13.1–13.3).

Systems Perspective

Clients with ID who use support services are affected by three ecological systems (Bronfenbrenner, 1979): (a) the immediate microsetting around the client where face to face interactions take place with staff and professionals; (b) the mesosetting of the organization's structure, hierarchy, bureaucracy, and culture; and (c) the sociopolitical or macroenvironment characterized by the broader societal values, rights, and regulations under which the service organization is operating. As shown in Figure 15.1, each ecological level is interactively connected. The support service is a translator and facilitator of macroconditions onto the lives of the clients in the microsettings. Staff competences and attitudes, human resources management, internal allocation of staffing and budget resources, management style, organizational structures, and organizational culture and ethics are factors that can be influenced by the service organization itself in order to optimize positive outcomes for their clients and their families. The embedment of the service organization itself in the macrocontext, however, also shows its dependency on general public policy and culture with regard to supporting persons with ID.

In addition to the micro-, meso-, and macroenvironments, one should be aware of the time dimension (chronosystem; Bronfenbrenner, 1999). The microsystem, therefore, should include an understanding of the person's life history but also of his or her future (dreams, life goals, age development). The mesosystem implies understanding the dynamics of the service organization's history, present environment, and planning horizon. Considering the macrosystem should include an orientation on the past, present, and future direction of human service philosophies and policies. Understanding these philosophies

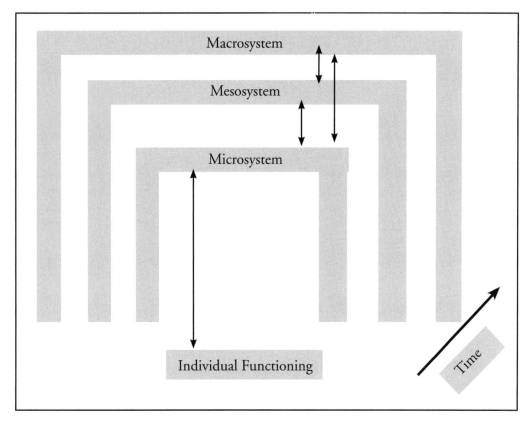

Figure 15.1. Social-ecological model of environments affecting human functioning.

is necessary to understand the forces that are affecting human service agencies generally and support services for persons with ID specifically (Reinders, 2008).

STRATEGIC MANAGEMENT CONSIDERATIONS

Strategic Thinking

Strategic thinking in support service organizations reflects key factors discussed in previous chapters: the social-ecological, multidimensional model of ID, the supports paradigm with its focus on the assessment of support needs and provision of individualized supports, the movement toward equality in basic values and underlying supports for persons with ID, and the inclusion in public policy of core human rights principles and desired person-referenced outcomes. Strategic thinking is concerned with the big picture of the service organization and its position within the broader societal context, not just the daily work process (Ashbaugh, 2008). Such thinking generates ideas about the future of the service and ways to make it more relevant to its stakeholders. Strategic thinking and planning, therefore, implies knowledge of present disability paradigms and models.

Support Services as Open Systems

Traditional services are rather closed systems that provide specialized functions within the boundaries of their organization or system. Even when physically situated in the community, they rarely make use of the resources from the client's natural environment. Support services need to be open systems that facilitate their clients' participation in society, use generic services as much as possible, and provide specialized services only when needed.

As an open system, support services typically are oriented toward the following:

- Enhancing the competencies of the person to participate in mainstream social settings by offering teaching, training, and learning opportunities
- Maintaining the relation between the person and his or her social network of family, friends, and informal relations
- Facilitating the person's use of mainstream home living, school, work, and leisure settings
- Making optimal use of generic services in the areas of health care, education, housing, community living, and employment
- Achieving goals in terms of personal outcomes for their clients

Focus on Community Resources

The management of a support provider organization is not restricted to the use of its inner resources but strives to make use of community resources in achieving desired, person, and family-referenced outcomes. Therefore, critical success factors in the planning and provision of supports should be integrated in the directional strategy or strategic plan of the agency/program at three levels: mission, vision, and values. These three factors need to guide decision making in the organization (Swayne, Duncan, & Ginter, 2006).

- The mission of the support service is a statement of purpose that distinguishes it from other human service organizations and identifies the scope of its operations not only in terms of services delivered (product), target group (market), and geographical area but also in regard to the philosophy and desired public image. Support organizations stress their value as partners of the client and his or her social network to enhance subjective well-being and personal outcomes.
- The vision of the support service expresses the hope for the future, describing what the organization will be like while accomplishing its mission. Visions should be inspiring; be clear; make sense in the community; be stable; and empower employees, persons with ID and their families, and other stakeholders. Support organizations visions should consider the ideas of an open organization, dependable partnership, responsiveness to needs, professional competence, commitment, and creativity.

- Values reflect fundamental service/supports principles. In the context of the AAIDD System described in this *Manual*, these values include social equality, human dignity, respect for the individual, freedom of choice, empowerment of clients and employees, teamwork, valued personal outcomes, evidence-based professional practices, innovation of services, moral integrity, positive contributions to society, and continuous quality improvement.

Support Provision Principles and Guidelines

Because support services operate as part of both the meso- and macrosystem, it is appropriate to be aware of the principles and policy guidelines that are congruent with the basic egalitarian nature of supports. Important support provision principles and guidelines that reflect current best practices in agency-referenced supports provision are summarized in Table 15.1.

TABLE 15.1

Support Provision Principles and Guidelines

- Awareness of clients' fundamental human rights, as formulated in the United Nation Convention on the Rights of Persons With Disabilities (these rights can be used as a general backdrop for developing policies for implementing systems of support that enhance desired personal outcomes for persons with disabilities)

- Awareness of the sociopolitical context of national, state, and/or regional policies and its impact on regulations and service culture

- Individual interdisciplinary assessment with regard to intellectual functioning, adaptive behavior skills, support needs, community participation, physical and mental health status, and environmental context

- Assessment data that offers clear information to clients, family, and other stakeholders

- Assurance that the provision of supports is based on the individual's personal goals and assessed support needs

- Support strategies and resources that operate as a system and are operationalized as a partnership within the context of stable and competent supports teams

- Supports teams that engage in quality improvement strategies and monitor personal outcomes

---

SUPPORT PROCESS CONSIDERATIONS

Two questions dominate all professional activities concerning persons with ID: (a) How can the problems in functioning of this individual be understood? and (b) How can this person be best supported to live a good life? Activities associated with the first question belong to diagnosis, classification, and assessment of functioning. Activities associated with the second question belong to developing and managing supports.

Before engaging in any support activities, service providers should know whether their clients received a valid diagnosis and classification of their disability. They should also make sure that every individual in their service receives regular assessment of strengths and weaknesses in functioning along the five dimensions of the AAIDD functional model of ID (see Figure 2.1). Understanding the disability is a prerequisite for starting a successful support process. Assessment of functioning, however, does not automatically lead to supports. Therefore, the support process should be understood and integrated in the service activities. To that end, in the next three sections we discuss the general structure of the support process, the features of supports as a system, and support as a team process.

Supports Process

The support needs of persons with ID differ both quantitatively and qualitatively. No individual will need all of the supports that are potentially available. Therefore, selecting and implementing appropriate supports is an individual endeavor and implies identifying the person's support needs and then matching appropriate resources and strategies to address these needs. This is the work of a team. As discussed in chapter 9 (and in reference to Figure 9.2), the supports process involves a five-component process. Implementing each of these components (which are summarized below) requires that support provider organizations commit time and resources to the efforts, including the provision of staff training to ensure staff competencies in Individualized Support Plan (ISP) development, implementation, monitoring, and evaluation.

Component 1: Identify desired life experiences and goals. The first component of this support process requires the use of person-centered planning processes. A hallmark of person-centered planning is the focus on the individual's dreams, personal preferences, and interests (Holburn, Gordon, & Vietze, 2007). The primary purpose of a person-centered planning process is to determine what is important to a person, and it is essential that discussions are not constrained by available existing services or by perceived barriers, such as fiscal restrictions or limitations in a person's skills (O'Brien & O'Brien, 2002). Person-centered planning processes involve the person with the disability and people important to him or her. The desired outcome of person-centered planning is a unified vision for a person's future life; this vision includes a listing of the most important aspects of the person's current life to maintain and the most important changes to make.

Component 2: Determine the pattern and intensity of support needs. The second component of the support process involves assessing the person's general support needs. As one example, the Supports Intensity Scale (SIS; Thompson et al., 2004a) is a standardized instrument used to evaluate an individual's support needs across seven life activity domains as well as identify exceptional medical and behavioral support needs. However, any method that a planning team finds useful to assess support needs could be used, including direct observation of the person in variety of life activities and interviews of the person and their family members within the framework of person-referenced outcomes listed in Table 13.1.

Component 3: Develop the individualized plan. The third component of the support process builds on the first two components to developing an ISP. It is important that an optimistic and realistic plan of action be designed and implemented. It is essential that resources are not only identified but are also available and accessible for the individual. Because an ISP cannot address all priorities effectively at one time, some personal priorities identified in Component 1 may need to be tempered and some difficult choices made. However, the result of Component 3 should be "an unambiguous, individualized plan that specifies: (a) the settings for and activities in which a person is likely to engage during a typical week, and (b) the types and intensity of support that will be provided (and by whom)" (Thompson et al., 2004b, p. 81).

Component 4: Monitor progress. The fourth component of the support planning process requires that support teams examine the progress of the plan. Specifically, teams should monitor closely the extent to which the person's individual plan was implemented. Monitoring should be ongoing and systematic in terms of periodically scheduled evaluations to carefully consider the congruence between what was planned and what was actually delivered.

Component 5: Evaluation. Evaluation is focused on the extent to which desired life experiences and goals and personal outcomes are being realized. The current approach to the conceptualization and measurement of personal outcomes involves (a) delineating outcomes that are of value to the person on one or more objectives of public policy and (b) assessing indicators of the desired personal outcomes on the basis of self-report and direct observation (Schalock, Gardner, & Bradley, 2007). Consistent with the AAIDD System evaluation should focus on the eight person-referenced outcome domains summarized in Table 13.1: rights, participation, self-determination, physical well-being, material well-being, societal inclusion, emotional well-being, and personal development.

Although this five-step support process requires a significant investment of time and energy, these ordered steps are essential when planning and implementing supports for a person with ID. This cycle of steps reoccurs as individuals grow and change and require revised support plans. The process always starts with assessing personal interests and needs for support, proceeds to planning and implementation, then is followed by careful monitoring of implementation, and ends with an evaluation of outcomes. Furthermore, the ISP is the central instrument for formulating and coordinating individualized support processes in the service organization.

Supports as a System

The ecological nature of supports implies that activities at the individual level will be affected by organizational conditions and even by general policy and funding regulations. Since these conditions can either facilitate or impede the individual support process, supports should be seen as a system that affects human functioning in very different ways and at different levels. Therefore, the ISP should focus on a systems of supports that addresses multiple human performance elements that are interdependent and cumulative. As discussed in chapter 9 (see Table 9.2), a systems of supports should optimally include the following performance elements (Wile, 1996):

- *Organizational systems.* Examples include laws, public policies, funding system(s), regulations affecting the supports organization, and the organization's mission, vision, organizational structure, policies, and market position
- *Incentives.* Examples include behavioral contracts, opportunities, compensation and income, feedback on performance, recognition, and encouragement
- *Cognitive supports.* Examples include documentation of service functions, knowledge relevant to the assessment of ID, and competencies regarding the development of systems of support
- *Tools.* Examples include technical aids, information and communication technology, and transportation
- *Physical environment.* Examples include quality of home, work and leisure settings, accessibility of services and settings, and safe and secure environments
- *Skills/knowledge.* Examples include competencies and skills, training, teaching and study activities
- *Inherent ability.* Examples include health, physical vitality and endurance, matching tasks to an individual's relative strengths and interests, and maximizing intrinsic motivation

Supports Team

Because of the interactive nature of supports, the architecture and culture of the support service organization is essential to the successful development and implementation of a systems of supports. One cannot provide a traditional program oriented organization with a modern tool like an ISP and expect supports to work. The *microunit* approach suggested by Nelson, Batalden, and Godfrey (2007) can act as a model for the design of support teams. Transposed to the field of ID, microunits refer to functional support teams that provide services to a well-defined group of clients. This group can be clients living in a specific geographically area, or a specific target group (e.g., persons with severe and multiple disabilities, people with dual diagnosis). Microunits include the relevant stakeholders at the microsystem level (clients, direct support staff, professionals) but also include key elements of the human resources and financial control systems of the service organization. There is no formula for the size of the microunit, but it should encompass all relevant functions to facilitate and account for the delivery of supports to the target group in an autonomous way.

The basic idea behind microunits is that the supports provided by the service/support organization can be no better than the quality of the supports generated by the frontline team. This team shares the same coordinating process (the five component supports process discussed previously), information system, and orientation toward valued personal outcomes. Since they operate at the client-service interface of the organization, they should also maintain relations with relevant settings of their clients such as family, school, work, and leisure. The primary orientation of a supports team in the microunit is to maintain productive client relationships that enhance personal growth and valued outcomes. Microunits can also be seen as building blocks of a larger support organization. The idea of support teams is not just applicable to larger "on-site" service delivery organizations but also to the coordination of supports in the community or in rural areas (Mandal, LeVelle, & Wilson, 2006).

Any supports provider organization requires a structure that is clearly articulated, bears an orientation toward the client's subjective well-being and quality of life, and at the same time is able to cope with organizational control requirements (e.g., human resource management and financial control). In this regard, microunits can provide a model for structuring interdisciplinary support teams that (a) combine the expertise of frontline staff and relevant experts; (b) meet on a regular basis to discuss and evaluate client needs, support strategies, and outcomes; (c) share the same information about the client's assessed needs and available resources; (d) participate autonomously in internal resource allocation and efficiency monitoring; and (e) self-manage and monitor their efforts and results regarding continuous quality improvement.

SERVICE MANAGEMENT CONSIDERATIONS

The support process considerations as described in the previous section are concerned with the service organizations' performance at the individual level. At the system level, however, the organization is concerned with performance with respect to all its clients and also in relation to similar services in the region, state, or nation. This raises questions about cost-effectiveness of services and quality management.

Costs and Outcomes

Throughout much of the world there has been a shift from institutional to community provision of services. In the last two decades funding procedures have also moved from service based funding (reflecting the costs of the place) toward individualized funding and needs-based resource allocation. Individualized budgeting requires a process of determining individual support needs and assigning costs to supports (Zaharia & Moseley, 2008; Kirchner & Moseley, 2007; Fortune et al., 2005). The Supports Intensity Scale (Thompson et al., 2004a) is increasingly being used in this process (Schalock, Thompson, & Tassé, 2008).

Funding programs influence service configurations and management. Within the support service organization, the ISPs should ideally drive the spending of individual budgets. This requires a business model and architecture that is capable to plan and account for both support costs and programmatic outcomes. Moreover, individualized budgets strengthen the role of choice and do not automatically lead to the use of one single congregate service but potentially various services. In that case, coordination of support services related to the ISP has become more important, and facilitators or support provision brokers have evolved (Lord & Hutchison, 2003). A broker organization can be seen as focusing on support needs assessment, assisting persons with ID and their families in both the development of the ISP and obtaining individualized supports that are provided, monitored, and evaluated.

As the funding environment is changing, support service organizations will have to adapt their internal architecture as part of their strategic planning. Since the field is in transition, no definite models can yet be suggested as standards or best practices. Since relationships between client characteristics, funding system, service organization characteristics, and service environment are so diverse and complex, no single optimal standard model might ever exist. Research shows that there is no simple relationship between costs and outcomes of services; nor is a clear economy of scale evident (Emerson et al., 2005; Felce & Emerson, 2005). However, the following five factors need to be considered in evaluating costs and outcomes (Lakin & Stancliffe, 2005; Perry & Felce, 2005): (a) provision of transparent information about the support service to facilitate individual and family choices; (b) facilitation of person-centered planning to assess strengths and weaknesses in functioning and support needs; (c) commitment to equitable, understandable, and transparent individualized resource allocation; (d) development of a qualified direct-support workforce with supports team continuity; and (e) quality management viewed as a continuous quality improvement (CQI) process.

Quality Management

In this section we discuss quality management and the importance of CQI. Quality management in human services focuses not only on organization performance (e.g., cost-effectiveness) but also on valued personal outcomes (Sluyter, 2000; Schalock, Gardner. & Bradley, 2007). Support service quality management is a dynamic process that is constantly evolving as a result of client support needs, support outcomes, and staff and management perceptions.

Quality management in human services can benefit from experiences and instruments used in the service industries. One of these tools is the GAP model of service quality (Zeithaml, Bitner, & Gremler, 2006). This model is concerned with the harmonization of client's and provider's expectations and perceptions to avoid service quality gaps. Transposed to support service organizations, this model (in summary) addresses five questions: First, does the management have a clear perception of client's and family's support needs and expectations of the service? Second, do the service design and performance standards reflect the client's needs and expectations? Third, is the support team at the client/service interface qualified and sufficiently enabled (in terms of resources and support from the management) to deliver the requested and intended supports? Fourth, does the support service "promise" to its clientele and the community as expressed in their external communication (brochures, Web sites, personal communications) match the actual client's support experiences and outcomes? Fifth, what is the congruence between client's and family's expectations of needed supports and their actual experiences of supports received (client satisfaction)?

Each of these questions can be evaluated on the basis of data obtained through surveys, interviews, and/or focus groups. The framework for these evaluations is basically the same as the quality of life framework that is influencing and directing the support needs assessment and support outcome evaluations (Schalock, Bonham, & Verdugo, 2008). This means that quality evaluations to a great extent can be integrated into the support process as discussed previously in the section entitled "Support Process Considerations." It should be obvious that quality management is not restricted to service managers or a special department, but that it should be a daily and continuous concern for improvement in the organization. Moreover, CQI should include multiple stakeholders including persons with ID.

A number of key concepts from the management literature underlie the use of the supports paradigm to facilitate CQI. Chief among these are the following: First, *total quality management* involves teamwork, consumer orientation, and data-based decision making. Second, a *learning team* is characterized by its being open to change; organizations learn through their individual members and by constantly monitoring support goals and support outcomes as a function of their team activities. Third, CQI necessitates *right to left thinking*, wherein an organization starts with identifying desired personal outcomes and asks, "What needs to be in place for these outcomes to occur?" Fourth, organizations need to be *aligned both vertically and horizontally* in order to maintain a clear relationship between an organization's mission and staffing patterns (vertical alignment) and among clients' needs, support provision, and anticipated outcomes (horizontal alignment). Fifth, perceptions of client, family, and staff need to be included and integrated into the evaluation of service quality. Sixth, *state of the art organization design* includes two important concepts: microunit and self-managing groups. These six key concepts provide the conceptual basis and framework for the 10 continuous quality improvement strategies summarized in Table 15.2.

Table 15.2

Continuous Quality Improvement Strategies

1. Commit the organization to a systematic assessment of the clients' desired life experiences, personal goals, and the pattern and intensity of needed supports from a multidimensional perspective.

2. Use individual and aggregated data based on this assessment to determine needed staff competencies and staff utilization patterns.

3. Use the individual's profile of needed supports as the basis for the Individualized Supports Plan (ISP) that incorporates the individual's support needs within the context of their interests and preferences.

TABLE 15.2 (*continued*)

4. Evaluate personal outcomes from three perspectives: (a) Did the person-referenced outcomes occur, and if so, to what degree? (b) What were the significant predictors of those outcomes? and (c) What is the client's satisfaction with the outcomes and related service performance?

5. Use the microunit approach as the building block for quality improvement and align quality measures for internal benchmarking.

6. Use the evaluation data from No. 4 to provide important information about the organization's effectiveness and to decide on further changes and human resource/staff development activities that are needed for additional enhanced outcomes to occur.

7. Use the information from No. 6 to communicate with key stakeholder groups and interface with the larger service delivery system.

8. Monitor client as well as staff experiences and expectations about the service using the GAP model or the evaluation of personal and family-referenced outcomes such as those summarized in Tables 13.1 and 13.2.

9. Celebrate success and use the concept of continuous quality improvement and the results that occur from its use as a motivational tool to demonstrate that organizations can change and that an effective change strategy is beginning with the end (i.e., desired personal outcomes) in mind and then working backward to the supports that need to be in place for those outcomes to occur.

10. Assure consistency between the organization's mission, vision, values, team performance goals, processes, and the quality system.

METACONSIDERATIONS FOR PLANNING AND OPERATING SUPPORT SERVICES FOR PERSONS WITH INTELLECTUAL DISABILITY

Support services belong to the ecological realm of the mesosystems. Mesosystems exist, however, within the realm of macrosystems that represent not just rights and regulations but also the sociopolitical climate and values of society. Along with the changes in services for persons with ID (from institutions to community services) and funding systems (from service-based to individualized funding), the sociopolitical and socioeconomic climate has changed throughout much of the world. Understanding this broader context is important to policy making and to realizing effective support delivery systems. Understanding the forces in the overarching climate is also important for support service managers and administrators to direct the culture of their organizations in the context of strategic management. Two emerging themes and issues related to the macrosystem are impacting how organizations are planning and operating support services for persons with ID: neoliberalism and professionalism.

Neoliberalism

Reinders (2008) observes a transformation in the culture of professional services to people with ID. Traditionally, professional expertise (of various disciplines such as medical, psychological, educational, social work, and nursing) represented a central authority in the field of ID. It provided the knowledge, standards, protocols, and practices to direct the caregiving process with a reasonable degree of autonomy and independence for many decades. In the last decade, this situation has changed in that professionals are now perceived more as employees of the service and are expected, therefore, to act in the interest of the organization's goals and targets. They are no longer "pure" professionals but "hybrid" professionals (Noordegraaf, 2007). The relationship with the people they serve has also changed, so that the latter have become "clients" and "consumers."

Reinders (2008) also discussed these changes against the backdrop of neoliberalism and new public management. Neoliberalists regard the market as the prime regulatory instrument in the public domain: public goods, such as the well-being of persons with ID, are seen as products that are open to market mechanisms of demand, supply, and price. Features of new public management are market mechanisms; decentralization; quality control; measures of performance; and an emphasis on results, efficiency, and cost-effectiveness. As a result, professionals (from direct support staff to specific experts) need to spend considerable time and energy in detailed administration, documentation, and completing surveys that diminishes the time spent with clients. Service provision has become an economic issue (DiRita, Parmenter, & Stancliffe, 2008).

In this context, management is seen as a profession in its own, separate and different from the professional support activity. As a result, there is a risk that management will get dissociated from the primary core process. Nevertheless, the success of professional support services for persons with ID will always depend on the knowledge, skills, commitment, and ethics of professionals who are driven by a sincere concern for the people and families they serve.

Another problem with neoliberalism is its insistence on reducing public expenditures. Although increasing expenditure does not solve social problems by itself, they cannot be solved without money. The real point of management, however, would be to optimize, not minimize, expenditure (Swenson, 2008, p. 633). Returning to Blatt and Kaplan's (1966) essay referred to in the first section of this chapter, it is true that per capita daily costs in the Seaside residential facility were higher (almost double) than those of the four institutions of discussed in part I. This shows that decent human conditions and quality of life come with a price; they come with moral obligation as well as economic calculation.

Professionalism

An advantage of a more market orientation of services for persons with ID is that the focus of service delivery moves to the person and the families around the person with ID. Services rightfully are becoming more client driven and offer more space for client's choice and self-determination. In light of neoliberalism, however, the role of the professional could develop into just responding to the person's wants and delivering what is being asked on the basis of technical and billable interventions. This would result in supports being considered as products and not as human services. This is not what clients and families expect from true professionals. As Maister (1997) noted, "Professionalism however is predominantly an attitude, not a set of competencies. A real professional is a technician who cares" (p. 16). Chapter 8 contains a discussion of professional responsibilities in more detail.

Professionalism in ID support service provision is interactive in nature; supports are always the result of a dialogue between support-receivers and support-givers (Widdershoven, 2001). The provision of supports in the context of professional services should not be a function of satisfying mere consumer support wants but of meeting client support needs. The formulation of support needs is the result of a common endeavor that involves both client input and professional assessment. The same is true for the process of supports delivery. Therefore, within support provider organizations, conditions should be created that, to the best of our knowledge, foster a productive and satisfying dialogue (Buntinx, 2008). Productive client-professional relationships in support provider organizations should, therefore, avoid the demand-supply model but try to establish a sustainable partnership model.

One practical example of such conditions is the availability of sufficiently stable support teams. Services in the field of ID are facing significant staff turnover (Baumeister & Zaharia, 1987; Braddock & Mitchell, 1992; Larson, Lakin, & Bruininks, 1998), and there is no sign that staffing continuity is improving (Lakin & Stancliffe, 2005, p. 330). However, we note that a significant part of support staff discontinuity as experienced by clients and families is not related to external (labor market) factors but to the service organization's design and management practices (Buntinx, 2008). Thus, for creating conditions to integrate client as well as professional and managerial interests, the microunit concept as mentioned previously deserves attention. By integrating support processes, cost-effectiveness, and CQI practices into the same microunit, the supports team may be in a better position to maintain quality, continuity, and flexibility. Microunits that operate within a holistic/multidimensional framework can efficiently be integrated into a wider service environment because the different support teams share the same general procedures and client outcome orientation. The application of multipurpose instruments such as the Support Intensity Scale (Thompson et al., 2004a) can play a role in reducing bureaucracy because the same instrument is useful for identifying support needs, developing an ISP, and allocating resources. In addition, the support provider organizations should be sensitive to integrating moral responsibilities in the way they organize and manage themselves. A professional support service needs to be a reliable and dependable partner of persons with ID and their families along with other members of their community.

SUMMARY

In this chapter we addressed the challenges, opportunities, and current best practices regarding the provision of individualized supports from the perspective of support provider organizations. The context for the chapter is those components of the AAIDD System described in earlier sections of this *Manual*: the multidimensional nature of ID; the supports paradigm, with its focus on the assessment of support needs and the provision of individualized supports; and the emphasis in current public policy on the principles of human rights and the desirability of valued personal outcomes for persons with ID.

Imbedded within each section has been four key concepts that provide a basis for current practices and a benchmark for future activities: *mental models, assessment, service/ support delivery practices*, and *quality improvement*. Mental models are deeply ingrained assumptions, generalizations, and images we need in order to understand the world (Senge, 2006). They form the vision and culture of an organization and serve as the basis for leadership, values training, service/supports delivery, outcome evaluation, and quality improvement. Assessment is the foundation for individualized supports, evidence-based practices, and quality improvement. Assessment involves the measurement of support needs and personal outcomes. Service/supports delivery practices include the services and supports that are provided to persons with ID. Their use involves the alignment of resources and strategies to produce enhanced personal outcomes through best practices. Quality improvement represents an organization or system's capacity to improve performance and accountability through systematically collecting, analyzing, and synthesizing data and implementing action strategies based on this process. The continuous quality improvement strategies discussed in this chapter (see Table 15.2) are based heavily on the concept of organizational learning that has been developed to promote change within bureaucratic organizations, which frequently by their very nature have regulation or policy-defined structures that limit the consideration of new ideas (Ashbaugh, 2008).

GLOSSARY

AAIDD System: The systematic approach to the diagnosis, classification, and systems of supports for persons with ID described in this *Manual*. The approach is based on current knowledge regarding the etiology of ID and an ecological, multidimensional framework that is used as a basis for assessment, classification, and developing individualized systems of supports.

Adaptive behavior: The collection of conceptual, social, and practical skills that have been learned and are performed by people in their everyday lives.

Age of onset: The period during which ID first originates. As defined in this *Manual*, age of onset is prior to age 18.

Alternative assessment strategies: Assessment strategies used in conjunction with appropriate standardized instruments when information obtained from formal assessment instruments does not validly answer the question being asked. Two such strategies are direct observation and the evaluation of social competency.

Assessment: The process in the field of ID that involves systematically collecting information and data for decisions, recommendations, and communication related to three assessment functions: diagnosis, classification, and developing individualized supports.

Assistive technology: Use of mechanical or electronic devices that reduce the mismatch between a person's competency and cognitive, social, and practical demands of their environments.

Best practices: Research-based knowledge, professional ethics, professional standards, and clinical judgment applied to persons with ID.

Blended curriculum: Academic and functional content are combined to meet the student's individual needs across multiple contexts.

Classification: The process of dividing into subgroups that which has been included in a term through its definition. The dividing into subgroups is done according to stated principles and uses. All classification systems have as their fundamental purpose the provision of an organized schema for the categorization of various kinds of observations and a way to (re)organize information. A classification system (a) has to serve a purpose, (b) be based on relevant information, and (c) is used to better understand a person.

Clinical judgment: A special type of judgment rooted in a high level of clinical expertise and experience. Clinical judgment emerges directly from extensive data and is based on training, experiences, and specific knowledge of the person and his or her environment.

Clinical judgment strategies: A set of procedures/actions used to enhance the quality, validity, and precision of the clinician's decision or recommendation in a particular case. The four clinical judgment strategies discussed in this *Manual* are understanding the question, conducting or accessing a thorough history, conducting or accessing broad-based assessments, and synthesizing the obtained information.

Clinician in intellectual disability: A person who (a) has relevant training, (b) engages in clinical activities (diagnosis, classification, developing individualized supports), and (c) uses professionally accepted practices, such as those described in this *Manual*.

Comprehensive community health supports: Individualized supports provided within one's community that are responsive to the physical and mental health needs of persons with ID; aligned with the current ecological, multidimensional conception of disability; and consistent with the definition of health as a state of complete physical, mental, and social well-being.

Conceptual skills: Adaptive skills that include language; reading and writing; and money, time, and number concepts.

Confidence interval: The statistical interval, or range, within which the person's true score falls. The results of any standardized psychometric assessment must be evaluated and interpreted in terms of the accuracy of the instrument used. Variability in the obtained score(s) can be due to limitations of the instrument used, test-taking attitude of the person being evaluated, examiner's behavior, or other personal factors (e.g., health status of the person) or environmental factors (e.g., testing environment or testing location). Thus, variation in scores may or may not represent the individual's actual or true level of intellectual or adaptive behavior functioning. The term *standard error of measurement*, which varies by test, subgroup, and age group, is used to quantify this variability and provide the basis for establishing a statistical confidence interval within which the person's true score falls. From the properties of the normal curve, a range of statistical confidence can be established with parameters of at least one standard error of measurement (i.e., 66% probability) or parameters of two standard error of measurement (i.e., 95% probability). The selection of the confidence interval (i.e., 66% or 95%) relates to the question(s) asked, the properties of the assessment instrument used, and the ultimate use of the obtained score(s).

Construct: An abstract or general idea based on observed phenomena and formed by arranging parts or elements.

Context: The interrelated conditions within which people live their everyday lives. Context includes environmental factors that make up the physical, social, and attitudinal environments within which people live and conduct their lives and personal factors that include characteristics of a person such as gender, age, race, and motivation. As used in this *Manual*, context represents an ecological perspective that involves at least three different levels: (a) the immediate social setting, including the person, family, and/or advocates (microsystem); (b) the neighborhood, community, or organizations providing education or habilitation services or supports (mesosystem); and (c) the overarching pattern of culture, society, larger populations, country, or sociopolitical influences (macrosystem or mega system).

Constitutive definition of intellectual disability: Defining a construct (e.g., ID) in relation to other constructs (such as an etiological, multidimensional model of human functioning and individualized supports).

Critical thinking skills: Skills involved in the synthesis of information. Four important critical thinking skills discussed in this *Manual* are analysis, evaluation, interpretation, and inference.

Cutoff score: Score(s) that determines the boundaries of the "significant limitations in intellectual functioning and adaptive behavior" criteria for a diagnosis of ID. For both criteria, the cutoff score is approximately two standard deviations below the mean of the respective assessment instrument, considering the standard error of measurement for the specific instrument used and the strengths and limitations of the instrument.

Defining: Explaining the term precisely and establishing the meaning and boundaries of the term.

Developmental disability: A severe, chronic disability of an individual 5 years of age or older that (a) is attributable to a mental or physical impairment or a combination of mental and physical impairment; (b) is manifested before the individual attains age 22; (c) is likely to continue indefinitely; (d) results in substantial functional limitations in three or more of the following major life activities: self-care, receptive and expressive language, learning, mobility, self-direction, capacity for independent living, and economic self-sufficiency; and (e) reflects the individual's need for a combination and sequence of special, interdisciplinary, or generic service, individualized supports, or other forms of assistance that are lifelong or of extended duration and are individually planned and coordinated (Developmental Disabilities Assistance and Bill of Rights Act of 2000 [Public Law 106–402; 102 (8) (a)]).

Diagnosis: The identification of ID based on three criteria: significant limitations in intellectual functioning and adaptive behavior as expressed in cognitive, social, and practical adaptive skills, and age of onset prior to age 18.

Disability: The expression of limitations in individual functioning within a social context that represents a substantial disadvantage to the individual.

Ecological model: A focus on person-environment interaction and its impact on human functioning. Human functioning is facilitated by the congruence between personal competence and environmental demands and the provision of individualized supports.

Egalitarianism: The belief in human equality, especially with respect to social, political, and economic rights.

Etiologic assessment: The search for the etiology of a condition that involves obtaining information about all of the risk factors that might have resulted in impaired functioning in a particular person. This information search involves obtaining as much medical information as possible, performing psychological and physical examinations, and pursuing sufficient laboratory investigations to consider reasonable possibilities.

Etiology: A branch of knowledge concerned with all of the causes of a particular phenomenon. In this *Manual*, etiology is presented as a multifactorial construct composed of four categories of risk factors (biomedical, social, behavioral, educational) that interact across time and affect the individual's overall functioning.

False negative: Person is actually an individual with ID but is incorrectly/falsely not diagnosed as such.

False positive: Person is incorrectly/falsely diagnosed as an individual with ID but actually is not.

Flynn effect: The increase in IQ scores over time. The Flynn Effect raises potential challenges in the interpretation of IQ scores, with the recommendation that in cases where a test with aging norms is used as part of a diagnosis of ID, a correction for the age of the norms is warranted.

Genetics: That branch of knowledge that focuses on individual genes and their biomedical effects, one at a time.

Genomics: That branch of knowledge that considers all genes as part of a single dynamic system that is constantly changing and adapting to internal and external forces.

Genotype: Consists of all of the information contained within the individual's DNA.

Gullibility: This characteristic of many persons with ID includes occurrences of being successfully fooled, tricked, or lied to by others.

Health: A state of complete physical, mental, and social well-being.

Human functioning: An umbrella term referring to all life activities of an individual and encompasses body structures and functions, personal activities, and participation. This *Manual* is based on a multidimensional model of human functioning that includes five dimensions (intellectual abilities, adaptive behavior, health, participation, and context) and the key impacting role played by individualized supports.

Human performance technology: Enhancing human functioning by reducing the mismatch between persons and their environments through the use of strategies related to organization systems, incentives, cognitive supports, tools, physical environment, skills/knowledge acquisition, and building on inherent ability.

Individuals with ID who have higher IQ scores: Persons with ID whose IQ score(s) is slightly *below* the ceiling of 70–75. This group shares much in common with individuals without a diagnosis of ID whose functioning is sometimes referred to as *borderline* (i.e., individuals who do not technically have ID but who have low IQ scores above the ceiling of approximately 70–75.

Informants: *See* **Respondents.**

Intellectual disability: A disability characterized by significant limitations in both intellectual functioning and in adaptive behavior as expressed in conceptual, social, and practical adaptive skills. This disability originates before age 18. The following five assumptions are essential to the application of this definition: (1) limitations in present functioning must be considered within the context of community environments typical of the individual's age, peers, and culture; (2) valid assessment considers cultural and linguistic diversity as well as differences in communication, sensory, motor, and behavioral factors; (3) within an individual, limitations often coexist with strengths; (4) an important purpose of describing limitations is to develop a profile of needed supports; and (5) with appropriate personalized supports over a sustained period, the life functioning of the person with ID generally will improve.

Intellectual disability continuum: Intellectual disability occurs along a continuum, as does intellectual ability, and needs to be described and understood in that way. The AAIDD includes ALL individuals who meet the criteria of intellectual disability under one term: ID. It is not warranted to develop separate diagnoses or labels for individuals who have higher IQ scores or for those who have lower IQ scores. By definition, all individuals with ID have significantly impaired intellectual functioning and adaptive behavior; whether at higher IQ or lower IQ, all individuals with ID fall within the definition.

Intellectual functioning: A broader term than either *intellectual abilities* or *intelligence*. The term reflects the fact that what is considered intelligent behavior is dependent on the other dimensions of human functioning: the adaptive behavior that one exhibits, the person's mental and physical health, the opportunities to participate in major life activities, and the context within which people live their everyday lives.

Intelligence: A general mental capability. It includes reasoning, planning, solving problems, thinking abstractly, comprehending complex ideas, learning quickly, and learning from experience.

Macrosystem, mesosystem, microsystem: *See* **Systems perspective.**

Maladaptive behavior: Behaviors that are challenging, difficult, or dangerous. Maladaptive behavior is not a characteristic or domain of adaptive behavior. Also referred to as *problem behavior* or *difficult behavior*.

Measurement error: *See* **Standard error of measurement.**

Mental retardation: An earlier term for intellectual disability (ID). The term *ID* covers the same population of individuals who were diagnosed previously with mental retardation in number, kind, level, type, and duration of the disability and the need by people with this disability for individualized services and supports. Furthermore, every individual who is or was eligible for a diagnosis of mental retardation is eligible for a diagnosis of intellectual disability.

Multidimensional classification system: An approach to classification based on the five dimensions associated with human functioning (intellectual abilities, adaptive behavior, health, participation, and context) and the pattern and intensity of the individual's support needs.

Multidimensional framework: A framework for understanding ID that depicts how human functioning and the manifestation of ID involve the dynamic, reciprocal engagement among intellectual abilities, adaptive behavior, health, participation, context, and individualized supports.

Naïveté: Overly trusting of others, immature, innocent, or inexperienced.

Naming: Attaching a specific term (e.g., ID) to something or someone. Naming is a powerful process that carries many messages about perceived value and human relationships.

Operational definition: Defining a construct on the basis of how it is observed and measured. In reference to ID, three criteria are used to define ID: significant limitations in intellectual functioning, significant limitations in adaptive behavior, and age of onset before age 18.

Outcomes: Personal, family, or societal changes or benefits that follow as a result or consequence of some activity, intervention, or service.

Participation: The performance of people in activities in social life domains.

Phenotype: The actual observed properties of the individual, including physical, developmental, mental, behavioral, social, and other attributes.

Positive behavior supports: An intervention strategy that involves (a) a functional assessment that defines the problem behavior, determines what maintains it, and describes the environmental context associated with high and low rates of behavior and (b) a focus on two primary modes of intervention: altering the environment before a problem behavior occurs and teaching appropriate behaviors as a strategy for eliminating the need for problem behaviors to be exhibited.

Practical skills: Adaptive skills that include activities of daily living (personal care), occupational skills, use of money, safety, health care, travel/transportation, schedules/routines, and use of telephone.

Primary prevention: Strategies that prevent the development of a disease, condition, or disability.

Professional ethics: A set of principles that describes a system of professional moral behavior and a set of rules of professional conduct recognized in respect to professional behavior.

Professional standards: Authoritative criteria that provide the basis for professional activities such as evaluating professional practices, personnel preparation, accreditation, and quality control.

Quality improvement: An organization or system's capacity to improve performance and accountability through systematically collecting and analyzing data and information and implementing action strategies based on the analysis. Its goal is to improve human functioning and personal outcomes by enhancing policies, practices, training, technical assistance, and other individual, organization, or systems-level supports.

Quality management: Management strategies that focus on organizational performance and valued personal outcomes.

Reliability: The measurement consistency of a test or assessment instrument.

Respondents: People who know the individual well, who have observed the person across different community environments and situations, who have formally observed the person over time, and who provide information to a professional conducting an adaptive behavior interview.

Retrospective diagnosis: A diagnosis of ID made later (i.e., after age 18) in a person's life and where the individual did not receive an official diagnosis of ID during the developmental period. For such a diagnosis, the clinician must use other sources of information, including possible obtainable data and the person's history to determine manifestations of possible ID prior to age 18. Important guidelines for determining a retrospective diagnosis are discussed in chapter 8 of this *Manual*.

Secondary prevention: Strategies that prevent the emergence of symptoms or disability in individuals who have an existing condition or disease.

Services: An organized means for delivering supports, instructions, therapies, or other forms of assistance.

Significant limitations: *See* **Cutoff score.**

Social history: A vehicle to investigate, collect, and organize all relevant information about the person's life, including developmental trajectory of the potential disability; functioning at home and in the community; and relationships at home, with neighbors, and with others. A social history includes the person's medical and educational history.

Social judgment: Judgment based on interpersonal competence, problem-solving skills, and decision-making skills. Individuals with ID are frequently vulnerable to risks due to their lack of social judgment.

Social skills: Adaptive skills that include interpersonal skills, social responsibility, self-esteem, gullibility, naïveté (i.e., wariness), follows rules/obeys laws, avoids being victimized, and social problem solving.

Standard error of measurement: The variation around a hypothetical "true score" for the person. The standard error of measurement applies only to scores obtained from a standardized test and can be estimated from the standard deviation of the test and a measure of the test's reliability. The standard error of measurement, which varies by test, subgroup, and age group, should be used to establish a statistical confidence interval within which the person's true score falls. For example, in reference to an IQ score of 70 (which corresponds to the "cutoff score" of approximately two standard deviations below the mean of the respective assessment instrument), the score of 70 is most accurately understood not as a precise score but as a range of confidence with parameters of at least one standard error of measurement (i.e., scores of about 66–74, 66% probability) or parameters of two standard error of measurement (i.e., scores of about 62–78, 95% probability). Reporting the range within which the person's true score falls, rather than only a score, underlies both the appropriate use of intellectual and adaptive behavior assessment instruments and best diagnostic practices in the field of ID. Such reporting must be a part of any decision concerning the diagnosis of ID.

Standard deviation: An index of the amount of variability from the average (mean) score in a set of data. The standard deviation reflects the dispersion of scores in a distribution.

Standardized measures: Measures of intellectual functioning, adaptive behavior, and support needs that have been developed on the basis of an underlying construct or theory and have demonstrated reliability, validity, and normative comparison groups. *See also* **Technical adequacy**.

Supports: Resources and strategies that aim to promote the development, education, interests, and personal well-being of a person and enhance individual functioning. Services are one type of support provided by professionals and agencies.

Support needs: A psychological construct referring to the pattern and intensity of supports necessary for a person to participate in activities linked with normative human functioning.

Systems of supports: The planned and integrated use of individualized support strategies and resources that encompass the multiple aspects of human performance in multiple settings. A systems of supports model provides a structure for the organization and enhancement of human performance elements that are interdependent and cumulative.

Systems perspective: Integrating into one's thinking and actions the four systems that impact human functioning: (a) microsystem that includes the immediate social setting including the person, family, friends, colleagues, and close support staff; (b) mesosystem that includes the neighborhood, community, or organizations providing services/supports; (c) macrosystem that is the overarching patterns of culture, society, larger population, country, or sociopolitical influences; and (d) chronosystem that reflects the interactions of the person and multiple systems over time.

Technical adequacy: An essential requirement of assessment instruments. Criteria include content and construct validity, reliability, stability of measures, generalization of scores, predictive validity, and appropriateness to the individual/group being assessed.

Tertiary prevention: Strategies that reduce (but cannot completely eliminate) the consequences of a disability on overall functioning.

Thinking errors: Faulty reasoning that negatively impacts the clinician's decision or recommendation. Examples include affective error, availability error, blind obedience, confirmation bias, and premature closure.

Typical performance: What the person typically does, and not what the individual can do, or could do. Typical performance is assessed on adaptive behavior scales and is distinguished from ability and maximum performance that is assessed on measures of intelligence.

Universal design for learning: The design of instructional materials and activities that allow learning goals to be achievable by individuals with wide differences in their abilities.

Validity: The ability of the test or assessment instrument to measure what it was designed to measure.

References

Adams, G. L. (1999). *Comprehensive test of adaptive behavior* (Rev. ed.). Seattle: Educational Achievement Systems.

Alba, K., Prouty, R., Scott, N., & Lakin, K. C. (2008). Changes in populations of residential settings for persons with intellectual and developmental disabilities over a 30-year period, 1977–2007. *Intellectual and Developmental Disabilities, 46,* 257–260.

Alverson, C. Y., Bails, C., Navajo, J. M., Yamamoto, S. H., & Unruh, D. (2006). *Methods of conducting post-school outcomes follow-up studies: A review of the literature.* Eugene: National Post-School Outcomes Center, University of Oregon.

American College of Obstetrics and Gynecology. (2007). Practice bulletin #77: Screening for fetal chromosomal anomalies. *Obstetrics and Gynecology, 109,* 217–227.

American Educational Research Association, American Psychological Association, & National Council on Measurement in Education. (1999). *Standards for educational and psychological testing.* Washington, DC: American Educational Research Association.

American Psychiatric Association. (1952). *Diagnostic and statistical manual: Mental disorders.* Washington, DC: Author.

American Psychiatric Association. (1968). *Diagnostic and statistical manual of mental disorders* (2nd ed.). Washington, DC: Author.

American Psychiatric Association. (1980). *Diagnostic and statistical manual of mental disorders* (3rd ed.). Washington, DC: Author.

American Psychiatric Association. (1987). *Diagnostic and statistical manual of mental disorders* (3rd ed., Rev.). Washington, DC: Author.

American Psychiatric Association. (1994). *Diagnostic and statistical manual of mental disorders* (4th ed.). Washington, DC: Author.

American Psychiatric Association. (2000). *Diagnostic and statistical manual of mental disorders* (4th ed., Text rev.). Washington, DC: Author.

American Psychiatric Association. (2008). *Diagnostic and statistical manual of mental disorders DSM–V: The future manual.* Manuscript in preparation. Available at http://www.psych.org/dsmv.asp

American Psychological Association. (1992). Ethical principles of psychologists and code of conduct. *American Psychologist, 47,* 1597–1611.

American Psychological Association. (1999). *Standards for educational and psychological testing.* Washington, DC: Author.

American Psychological Association. (2002). Ethical principles of psychologists and code of conduct. *American Psychologist, 57,* 1060–1073.

American With Disabilities Act of 1990, 42 O.K. § 12101 et seq.

Andresen, E. M., Lollar, D. J., & Meyers, A. R. (2000). Disability outcomes research. *Archives of Physical Medicine and Rehabilitation, 81,* S1–S4.

Andrews, F. M., & Whithey, S. B. (1976). *Social indicators of well-being: Americans' perception of quality of life.* New York: Plenum Press.

Aronowitz, R. A. (1998). *Making sense of illness: Science, society, and disease.* Cambridge, MA: Cambridge University Press.

Arthaud-Day, M. E., Rode, J. C., Mooney, C. H., & Near, J. P. (2005). The subjective well-being construct: A test of it convergent, discriminant, and factorial validity. *Social Indicators Research, 74,* 445–476.

Ashbaugh, J. (2008). Managing system change in human service agencies. *Intellectual and Developmental Disabilities, 46,* 480–483.

Aznar, A. S., & Castanon, D. G. (2005). Quality of life from the point of view of Latin American families: A participative research study. *Journal of Intellectual Disability Research, 49,* 784–788.

Bach, M. (2007). Changing perspectives on developmental disabilities. In I. Brown & M. Percy (Eds.), *A comprehensive guide to intellectual and developmental disabilities* (pp. 35–57). Baltimore: Brookes.

Batshaw, M. L. (2008). *Children with disabilities* (6th ed.). Baltimore: Brookes.

Baumeister, A. A. (2006). Mental retardation: Confusing sentiment with science. In H. Switzky & S. Greenspan (Eds.), *What is mental retardation? Ideas for an evolving disability in the 21st century* (pp. 95–126). Washington, DC: American Association on Mental Retardation.

Baumeister, A. A., & Zaharia, E. S. (1987). Withdrawal and commitment of basic-care staff in residential programs. In S. Landesman, P. M. Vietze, & M. J. Begab (Eds.), *Living environments and mental retardation* (pp. 229–267). Washington, DC: American Association on Mental Retardation.

Bayley, N. (1993). *Bayley scales for infant development* (2nd ed.). New York: Psychological Corp.

Blackorby, J., & Wagner, M. (1996). Longitudinal postschool outcomes of youth with disabilities: Findings from the National Longitudinal Transition Study. *Exceptional Children, 62,* 399–413.

Blatt, B., & Kaplan, F. (1966). *Christmas in purgatory: A photographical essay on mental retardation.* Boston: Allyn & Bacon.

Bogdan, R., & Taylor, S. J. (1994). *The social meaning of mental retardation: Two life stories*. New York: Teachers College Press.

Borthwick-Duffy, S. A. (2007). Adaptive behavior. In J. W. Jacobson, J. A. Mulick, & J. Rojahn (Eds.), *Handbook on intellectual and developmental disabilities* (pp. 279–291). Washington, DC: Springer.

Braddock, D. (Ed.). (2002). *Disability at the dawn of the 21st century and the state of the states*. Washington, DC: American Association on Mental Retardation.

Braddock, D., Emerson, E., Felce, D., & Stancliffe, R. J. (2001). Living circumstances of children and adults with mental retardation or developmental disabilities in the United States, Canada, England and Wales, and Australia. *MD Research Reviews, 7*, 115–121.

Braddock, D., & Mitchell, D. (1992). *Residential services and developmental disabilities in the United States: A national survey of staff compensation, turnover and related issues*. Washington, DC: American Association on Mental Retardation.

Bradley, V., & Moseley, C. (2007). National core indicators: Ten years of collaborative performance measurement. *Intellectual and Developmental Disabilities, 45*, 354–358.

Bradshaw, J. (1972). A taxonomy of social need. In G. McLachland (Ed.), *Portfolio for health: Problems and progress in medical care* (pp. 34–65). London: Nuffield Provincial Hospital.

Bronfenbrenner, U. (1979). *The ecology of human development: Experiments by nature and design*. Cambridge, MA: Harvard University Press.

Bronfenbrenner, U. (1999). Environments in developmental perspective: Theoretical and operational models. In S. L. Friedman & T. D. Wachs (Eds.), *Measuring environments across the life span: Emerging methods and concepts* (pp. 3–28). Washington, DC: American Psychological Association.

Browder, D. M., Trela, K., Gibbs, S. L., Wakeman, S., & Hallis, A. A. (2007). Academic skills: Reading and mathematics. In S. L. Odom, R. H. Horner, M. E. Snell, & J. Blacher (Eds.), *Handbook of developmental disabilities* (pp. 292–309). New York: Guilford Press.

Brown, I. (2007). What is meant by intellectual and developmental disabilities? In I. Brown & M. Percy (Eds.), *A comprehensive guide to intellectual and developmental disabilities* (pp. 3–15). Baltimore: Brookes.

Brown, I., Renwick, R., & Raphael, D. (1999). *The quality of life project: Results from the follow-up studies*. Toronto: Center for Health Promotion, University of Toronto.

Brown, L., Schwarz, P., Udvari-Solner, A., Kampschroer, E., Johnson, F., Jorgensen, L., et al. (1991). How much time should students with severe intellectual disabilities spend in regular classrooms and elsewhere? *Journal of the Association for Persons With Severe Handicaps, 16,* 39–47.

Bruininks, R. H., Hill, B. K., Weatherman, R. F., & Woodcock, R. W. (1986). *Inventory for client and agency planning.* Allen, TX: DLM Teaching Resources.

Buntinx, W. H. E. (2006). The relationship between WHO-ICF and the AAMR-2002 system. In H. Switzky & S. Greenspan (Eds.), *What is mental retardation? Ideas for an evolving disability in the 21st century* (pp. 303–323). Washington, DC: American Association Mental Retardation.

Buntinx, W. (2008). The logic of relations and the logic of management. *Journal of Intellectual Disability Research, 52,* 558–597.

Butler, M. G., & Meaney, F. J. (Eds.). (2005). *Genetics of developmental disabilities.* Philadelphia: Taylor & Francis.

Campbell, W. W. (2005). *DeJong's neurological examination* (6th ed.). New York: Lippincott Williams & Wilkins.

Carr, E. G., Horner, R. H., Turnbull, A. P., Marquis, J. G., McLaughlin, D. M., McAtee, M. L., et al. (1999). *Positive behavior support for people with developmental disabilities: A research synthesis.* Washington, DC: American Association on Mental Retardation.

Carroll, J. B. (1993). *Human cognitive abilities: A survey of factor-analytic studies.* New York: Cambridge University Press.

Carroll, J. B. (1997). Psychometrics, intelligence, and public perception. *Intelligence, 24,* 25–52.

Carter, E. W., & Hughes, C. (2007). Social interaction interventions: Promoting socially supportive environments and teaching new skills. In S. L. Odom, R. H. Horner, M. E. Snell, & J. Blacher (Eds.), *Handbook of developmental disabilities* (pp. 310–329). New York: Guilford Press.

Cattell, R. B. (1963). Theory of fluid and crystallized intelligence: A critical experiment. *Journal of Educational Psychology, 54,* 1–22.

Ceci, S. (1990). *One intelligence . . . more or less: A bioecological treatise on intellectual development.* Englewood Cliffs, NJ: Prentice Hall.

Centers for Medicare and Medicaid Services. (2005). *Medicaid program general information.* Available at http://www.cms.hhs.gov/MedicaidGenInfo/

Chapman, D. A., Scott, K. G., & Stanton-Chapman, T. L. (2008). Public health approach to the study of mental retardation. *American Journal on Mental Retardation, 113,* 102–116.

Chen, J., & Gardner, H. (1997). Alternative assessment from a multiple intelligences theoretical perspective. In D. P. Flanagan, J. L. Genshaft, & P. L. Harrison (Eds.), *Contemporary intellectual assessment: Theories, tests, and issues* (pp. 105–121). New York: Guilford Press.

Colley, D. A., & Jamison, D. (1998). Post school results for youth with disabilities: Key indicators and policy implications. *Career Development of Exceptional Individuals, 21,* 145–160.

Colman, A. M. (2001). *Dictionary of psychology.* Oxford: Oxford University Press.

Cooper, C. (2002). *Individual differences.* London: Arnold.

Cooper, S. A., Morrison, J., Melville, C., Finlayson, J., Allan, L., Martin, G., et al. (2006). Improving the health of people with intellectual disabilities: Outcomes of a health screening programme after 1 year. *Journal of Intellectual Disability Research, 50,* 667–677.

Cooper, S. A., Smiley, E., Morrison, J., Williamson, A., & Allan, L. (2007). Mental ill-health in adults with intellectual disabilities: Prevalence and associated factors. *British Journal of Psychiatry, 190,* 27–35.

Costello, H., & Bouras, N. (2006). Assessment of mental health problems in people with intellectual disabilities. *Israel Journal of Psychiatry and Related Science, 43,* 241–251.

Coulter, D. L. (1992). An ecology of prevention for the future. *Mental Retardation, 30,* 363–369.

Coulter, D. L. (1996). Prevention as a form of support. *Mental Retardation, 34,* 108–116.

Coulter, D. L. (2005). Comprehensive health supports and health promotion. In K. C. Lakin & A. Turnbull (Eds.), *National goals and research for people with intellectual and developmental disabilities* (pp. 109–124). Washington, DC: American Association on Mental Retardation.

Council on Quality and Leadership. (2005). *Personal outcome measures.* Towson, MD: Author.

Cummins, R. A. (2003). Normative life satisfaction: Measurement issues and a homeo-static model. *Social Indicators Research, 64,* 225–256.

Cummins, R. A. (2005). Moving from the quality of life concept to a theory. *Journal of Policy and Practice in Intellectual Disabilities, 49,* 699–706.

Curry, C. J., Stevenson, R. E., Aughton, D., & Byrne, J. (1997). Evaluation of mental retardation: Recommendations of a consensus conference. *American Journal of Medical Genetics, 72,* 468–477.

Das, J. P., Naglieri, J. A., & Kirby, J. R. (1994). *Assessment of cognitive processes: The PASS theory of intelligence.* Boston: Allyn & Bacon.

Deiner, E., Lucas, R. E., & Oishi, S. (2002). Subjective well-being: The science of happiness and life satisfaction. In C. R. Snyder & S. J. Lopez (Eds.), *Handbook of positive psychology* (pp. 63–73). Oxford: Oxford University Press.

De Kraai, M. (2002). In the beginning: The first hundred years (1850 to 1950). In R. L. Schalock (Ed.), *Out of darkness and into the light: Nebraska's experience with mental retardation* (pp. 103–122). Washington, DC: American Association on Mental Retardation.

Demchek, M. (1997). *Teaching student with severe disabilities in inclusive settings* (Innovations: Research to Practice Series #12). Washington, DC: American Association on Mental Retardation.

Denkowski, G. C., & Denkowski, K. M. (2008). Adaptive behavior assessment of criminal defendants with a mental retardation claim. *American Journal of Forensic Psychology, 26*(3), 43–61.

DePloy, E., & Gilson, S. F. (2004). *Rethinking disability: Principles for professional and social change.* Belmont, CA: Thompson Brooks/Cole.

Developmental Disabilities Assistance and Bill of Rights Act of 2000 (Pub. L. No. 106–402), 42 U.S.C. @5801 et seq.

Devlieger, J. P. (2003). From "idiot" to "person with mental retardation": Defining differences in an effort to dissolve it. In J. P. Devlieger, F. Rusch, & D. Pfeiffer (Eds.), *Rethinking disability: The emergence of new definitions, concepts, and communities* (pp. 169–188). Antwerp, Belgium: Garant.

Devlieger, J. P., Rusch, F., & Pfeiffer, D. (Eds.). (2003). *Rethinking disability: The emergence of new definition, concepts, and communities.* Antwerp, Belgium: Garant.

Didden, R., Korzilius, H., van Oorsouw, W., & Sturmey, P. (2006). Behavioral treatment of challenging behaviors in individuals with mild mental retardation: Meta-analysis of single-subject research. *American Journal on Mental Retardation, 111,* 290–298.

DiRita, P. A., Parmenter, T. R., & Stancliffe, R. J. (2008). Utility, economic rationalism and the circumscription of agency. *Journal of Intellectual Disability Research, 52,* 618–624.

Doll, E. A. (1936). *The Vineland social maturity scale: Revised condensed manual of directions.* Vineland, NJ: Vineland Training School.

Doll, E. A. (1941). The essentials of an inclusive concept of mental deficiency. *American Journal of Mental Deficiency, 46,* 214–219.

Donabedian, A. (1992). The role of outcomes in quality assessment and assurance. *Quality Review Bulletin, 18*, 356–360.

Donabedian, M. P. H. (1973). *Aspects of medical care administration.* Cambridge, MA: Harvard University Press.

Douma, J., Dekker, M. C., Ruiter, K. P., Tick, N. T., & Koot, H. M. (2007). Antisocial and delinquent behaviors in youths with mild or borderline disabilities. *American Journal on Mental Retardation, 112*, 207–220.

Drew, C., & Turnbull, H. R. (1987). Whose ethics, whose code? An analysis of problems in interdisciplinary intervention. *Mental Retardation, 41*, 113–117.

Dunst, C. J., Bruder, M. B., Trivette, C. M., & Hamby, D. W. (2006). Everyday activity settings, natural learning environments, and early intervention practices. *Journal of Policy and Practice in Intellectual Disabilities, 3*, 3–10.

Durand, V. M., & Crimmins, D. B. (1988). Identifying the variables maintaining self-injurious behavior. *Journal of Autism and Developmental Disorders, 18*, 99–117.

Durand, V. M., & Kishi, G. (1987). Reducing severe behavior problems among persons with dual sensory impairments: An evaluation of a technical assistance model. *Journal of the Association for Persons With Severe Handicaps, 12*, 2–10.

Dykens, E. M., Hodapp, R. M., & Finucane, B. M. (2000). *Genetics and mental retardation syndromes: A new look at behavior and interventions.* Baltimore: Brookes.

Edgerton, R. (1967). *The cloak of competence: Stigma in the lives of the mentally retarded.* Berkeley: University of California Press.

Edgerton, R. B. (1993). *The cloak of competence: Revised and updated.* Berkeley: University of California Press.

Edgerton, R. B. (2001). The hidden majority of individuals with mental retardation and developmental disabilities. In A. Tymchuk, K. C. Lakin, & R. Luckasson (Eds.), *The forgotten generation: The status and challenges of adults with mild cognitive limitations* (pp. 3–19). Baltimore: Brookes.

Education Commission of the States. (2004). *Special education teacher certification/licensure and endorsement categories of the states.* Denver: Author.

Edyburn, D. L. (2000). Assistive technology and students with mild disabilities. *Focus on Exceptional Children, 32*(9), 1–23.

Emerson, E., Fujiura, G. T., & Hatton, C. (2007). International perspectives. In S. L. Odom, R. H. Horner, M. E. Snell, & J. Blacher (Eds.), *Handbook on developmental disabilities* (pp. 593–613). New York: Guilford Press.

Emerson, E., Graham, H., & Hatton, C. (2006). The measurement of poverty and socio-economic position in research involving people with intellectual disability. In

L. M. Glidden (Ed.), *International review of research in mental retardation* (pp. 77–108). New York: Academic Press.

Emerson, E., & Hatton, C. (2008). Self-reported well-being of women and men with intellectual disabilities in England. *American Journal on Mental Retardation, 113,* 143–155.

Emerson, E., Robertson, J., Hatton, C., Knapp, M., Walsh, P., & Hallam, A. (2005). Costs and outcomes of community residential supports in England. In R. Stancliffe & K. Lakin (Eds.), *Costs and outcomes of community services for people with intellectual disabilities* (pp. 151–174). Baltimore: Brookes.

Evans, I. (1991). Testing and diagnosis: A review and evaluation. In L. H. Meyer, C. A. Peck, & L. Brown (Eds.), *Critical issues in the lives of people with severe disabilities* (pp. 25–44). Baltimore: Brookes.

Everington, C., & Luckasson, R. (1992). *Competence assessment for standing trial for defendants with mental retardation (CAST–MR).* Columbus, OH: International Diagnostics Services.

Facione, P. A. (1990). *Critical thinking: A statement of expert consensus for purposes of educational assessment and instruction. Research findings and recommendations.* Newark, DE: American Philosophical Association. (ERIC Document Reproduction Service No. ED 315423)

Facione, N. C., & Facione, P. A. (1996). Externalizing the critical thinking in clinical judgment. *Nursing Outlook, 44,* 129–136.

Felce, D., & Emerson, E. (2005). Community living: Costs, outcomes, and economies of scale: Findings from U.K. research. In R. Stancliffe & K. Lakin (Eds.), *Costs and outcomes of community services for people with intellectual disabilities* (pp. 45–62). Baltimore: Brookes.

Festinger, L. (1957). *A theory of cognitive dissonance.* Stanford: Stanford University Press.

Fierros, E. G., & Conroy, J. W. (2002). Double jeopardy: An exploration of restrictiveness and race in special education. In D. J. Losen & G. Orfield (Eds.), *Racial inequality in special education* (pp. 39–70). Cambridge, MA: Harvard Education Press.

Finlay, W. M., & Lyons, E. (2002). Acquiescence in interviews with people who have mental retardation. *Mental Retardation, 40,* 14–29.

Fletcher, R., Loschen, E., Stavrakaki, C., & First, M. (Eds.). (2007). *Diagnostic manual-intellectual disability* (DM-ID). New York: National Association for the Dually Diagnosed.

Flynn, J. R. (1984). The mean IQ of Americans: Massive gains 1932 to 1978. *Psychological Bulletin, 95,* 29–51.

Flynn, J. R. (1987). Massive IQ gains in 14 nations: What does IQ really measure? *Psychological Bulletin, 101*, 171–191.

Flynn, J. R. (2006). Tethering the elephant: Capital cases, IQ, and the Flynn effect. *Psychology, Public Policy, and Law, 12*, 170–198.

Flynn, J. R. (2007). *What is intelligence: Beyond the Flynn Effect*. New York: Cambridge Press.

Fortune, J. R., Smith, G. A., Campbell, E. M., Clabby, R. T., Heinlein, K. B., Lynch, R. M., et al. (2005). Individual budgets according to individual needs: The Wyoming DOORS System. In R. Stancliffe, & K. Lakin (Eds.), *Costs and outcomes of community services for people with intellectual disabilities* (pp 241–262). Baltimore: Brookes.

Fossett, B., & Mirenda, P. (2007). Augmentative and alternative communication. In S. L. Odom, R. H. Horner, M. E. Snell, & J. Blacher (Eds.), *Handbook on developmental disabilities* (pp. 330–348). New York: Guilford Press.

Fougeyrollas, P., Cloutier, R., Bergeron, H., & St. Michel, G. (1998). *The Quebec classification: Disability creation process*. Lac St-Charles, Quebec: The Quebec Classification Disability Creation Process, Québec, International Network on Disability Creation Process.

Fuchs, D., & Fuchs L. S. (1994). Inclusive schools movement and radicalization of special education reform. *Exceptional Children, 60*, 294–309.

Fujiura, G. T. (2003). Continuum of intellectual disability: Demographic evidence for the "forgotten generation." *Mental Retardation, 41*, 420–429.

Gardner, H. (1983). *Frames of mind*. New York: Basic Books.

Gardner, H. (1993). Assessment in context: The alternative to standardized testing. In H. Gardner (Ed.), *Multiple intelligences: The theory in practice* (pp. 161–183). New York: Basic Books.

Gardner, H. (1998). Are there additional intelligences? The case for naturalist, spiritual, and existential intelligences. In J. Kane (Ed.), *Education, information, and transformation* (pp. 111–132). Englewood Cliffs, NJ: Prentice Hall.

Gardner, J. F., & Carran, D. (2005). Attainment of personal outcomes by people with developmental disabilities. *Mental Retardation, 43*, 157–174.

Gilbert, T. F. (1978). *Human competence*. New York: McGraw Hill.

Goddard, L., Davidson, P. M., Daly, J., & Mackey, S. (2008). People with an intellectual disability in the discourse of chronic and complex conditions: An invisible group? *Australian Health Review, 32*, 405–414.

Goffman, E. (1961). *Asylums*. New York: Anchor Books.

Gómez, L. E., Verdugo, M. A., Arias, B., & Navas, P. (2008). Evaluación de la calidad de vida en personas mayores y con discapacidad: la Escala Fumat [Assessment of quality of life in elder people and persons with disabilities: The Fumat Scale]. *Revista Sobre Igualdad y Calidad de Vida, 17*(2), 189–200.

Goodey, C. F. (2006). Behavioural phenotypes in disability research: Historical perspectives. *Journal of Intellectual Disability Research, 50*(6), 397–403.

Gordan, R. (1987). An operational classification of disease prevention. In J. A. Steinberg & M. M. Silverman (Eds.), *Preventing mental disorders* (pp. 50–78). Rockville, MD: U.S. Department of Health and Human Services.

Gottfredson, L. S. (1997). Mainstream science on intelligence: An editorial with 52 signatories, history, and bibliography. *Intelligence, 24*(1), 13–23.

Gould, S. (1978). Morton's rankings of races by cranial capacity: Unconscious manipulation of data may be a scientific norm. *Science, 200,* 503–509.

Greenspan, S. (1981). Social competence and handicapped individuals: Practical implications of a proposed model. In B. K. Keough (Ed.), *Advances in special education* (Vol. 3, pp. 41–82). Greenwich, CT: JAI Press.

Greenspan, S. (1996). There is more to intelligence than IQ. In D. S. Connery (Ed.), *Convicting the innocent: The story of a murder, a false confession, and the struggle to free a "wrong man"* (pp. 136–151). Cambridge, MA: Brookline Books.

Greenspan, S. (1997). Dead *Manual* walking? Why the 1992 AAMR definition needs redoing. *Education and Training in Mental Retardation and Developmental Disabilities, 32,* 179–190.

Greenspan, S. (1999). A contextualist perspective on adaptive behavior. In R. L. Schalock (Ed.), *Adaptive behavior and its measurement: Implications for the field of mental retardation* (pp. 61–80). Washington, DC: American Association on Mental Retardation.

Greenspan, S. (2006a). Functional concepts in mental retardation: Finding the natural essence of an artificial category. *Exceptionality, 14,* 205–224.

Greenspan, S. (2006b). Mental retardation in the real world: Why the AAMR definition is not there yet. In H. N. Switzky & S. Greenspan (Eds.), *What is MR: Ideas for an evolving disability* (pp. 165–183). Washington, DC: American Association on Mental Retardation.

Greenspan, S., & Granfield, J. M. (1992). Reconsidering the construct of mental retardation: Implications of a model of social competence. *American Journal on Mental Retardation, 96,* 442–453.

Greenspan, S., Loughlin, G., & Black, R. (2001). Credulity and gullibility in people with developmental disorders: A framework for future research. In L. M. Glidden

(Ed.), *International review of research in mental retardation* (Vol. 24, pp. 101–133). New York: Academic Press.

Greenspan, S., & Love, P. E. (1997). Social intelligence and developmental disorder: Mental retardation, learning disabilities, and autism. In W. E. MacLean, Jr. (Ed.), *Ellis' handbook of mental deficiency, psychological theory and research* (pp. 311–342). Mahwah, NJ: Lawrence Erlbaum Associates, Publishers.

Greenspan, S., & Switzky, H. N. (2006). Lessons learned from the Atkins decision in the next AAMR *Manual*. In H. N. Switzky & S. Greenspan (Eds.), *What is mental retardation? Ideas for an evolving disability in the 21st century* (pp. 283–302). Washington, DC: American Association on Mental Retardation.

Greenspan, S., Switzky, H. N., & Granfield, J. M. (1996). Everyday intelligence and adaptive behavior: A theoretical framework. In J. W. Jacobson & J. A Mulick (Eds.), *Manual of diagnosis and professional practice in mental retardation* (pp. 129–145). Washington, DC: American Psychological Association.

Gross, B. H., & Hahn, H. (2004). Developing issues in the classification of mental and physical disabilities. *Journal of Disability Policy Studies, 15*(3), 130–134.

Grossman, H. J. (Ed.). (1973). *A Manual on terminology and classification in mental retardation* (Rev. ed.). Washington, DC: American Association on Mental Deficiency.

Grossman, H. J. (Ed.). (1983). *Classification in mental retardation* (Rev. ed.). Washington, DC: American Association on Mental Deficiency.

Guscia, R., Ekberg, S., Harries, J., & Kirby, N. (2006). Measurement of environmental constructs in disability assessment instruments. *Journal of Policy and Practice in Intellectual Disabilities, 3*(3), 173–180.

Hahn, H., & Hegamin, A. P. (2001). Assessing scientific meaning of disability. *Journal of Disability Policy Studies, 12*, 114–121.

Hall, A., Wood, D., Hou, T., & Zhang, J. (2007). Patterns in primary health care utilization among individuals with intellectual and developmental disabilities in Florida. *Intellectual and Developmental Disabilities, 45*(5), 310–322.

Halpern, D. F. (1998). Teaching critical thinking skills for transfer across domains: Disposition skill, structure training, and metacognitive monitoring. *American Psychologist, 53*, 449–455.

Hamill, D., Pearson, N., & Wiederholt, J. (1997). *Comprehensive Test of Nonverbal Intelligence*. Austin, TX: Pro-Ed.

Harré, R., & Lamb, R. (1988). *The encyclopedic dictionary of psychology*. Oxford: Blackwell.

Harris, J. C. (2006). *Intellectual disability: Understanding its development, causes, classification, evaluation and treatment.* New York: Oxford.

Harrison, P. L. (1987). Research with adaptive behavior scales. *Journal of Special Education, 21,* 37–68.

Harrison, P. L., & Oakland, T. (2003). *Adaptive behavior assessment system manual* (2nd ed.). San Antonio, TX: Harcourt Assessment.

Harrison, P. L., & Raineri, G. (2008). Best practices in the assessment of adaptive behavior. In A. Thomas & J. Grimes (Eds.), *Best practices in school psychology* (5th ed., pp. 605–616). Bethesda, MD: NASP Press.

Hart, A. C., Hopkins, C. A., & Ford, B. (Eds.). (2005). *ICD-9-CM professional: International classification of diseases, 9th revision, clinical modification* (6th ed.). Salt Lake City: Ingenix.

Heber, R. (1959). *A manual on terminology and classification in mental retardation: A monograph supplement to the American Journal on Mental Deficiency, 64* (Monograph Suppl.).

Heber, R. (1961). *A manual on terminology and classification on mental retardation* (Rev. ed.). Washington, DC: American Association on Mental Deficiency.

Hernstein, R. J., & Murray, C. (1994). *The bell curve.* New York: Free Press.

Herr, S. S., O'Sullivan, J., & Hogan, C. (2002). A friend in court: The association's role and judicial trends. In R. L. Schalock, P. C. Baker, & M. D. Croser (Eds.), *Embarking on a new century: Mental retardation at the end of the 20th century* (pp. 27–44). Washington, DC: American Association on Mental Retardation.

Hewstone, M. (1990). The "ultimate attribution error"? A review of the literature on intergroup causal attribution. *European Journal of Social Psychology, 20,* 311–335.

Hodapp, R. M., Burack, J. A., & Zigler, E. (1990). *Issues in the developmental approach to mental retardation.* Cambridge, MA: Cambridge University Press.

Holburn, C. S., Jacobson, J. W., Schwartz, A., Flori, M., & Vietze, P. (2004). The Willowbrook Futures Project: A longitudinal analysis of person-centered planning. *American Journal on Mental Retardation, 109,* 63–76.

Holburn, S., Gordon, A., & Vietze, P. M. (2007). *Person-centered planning made easy.* Baltimore: Paul Brookes.

Horn, J. L., & Cattell, R. B. (1966). Refinement and test of the theory of fluid and crystallized general intelligences. *Journal of Educational Psychology, 57,* 253–270.

Horner, R., Dunlap, G., Beasley, J., Fox, L., Lambara, L., Brown, F., et al. (2005). Positive support for behavioral, mental health, communication, and crisis needs. In K. Lakin & A. Turnbull (Eds.), *National goals and research for people with intellectual and developmental disabilities* (pp. 93–108). Washington, DC: American Association on Mental Retardation.

Horner, R. H., Albin, R. W., Sprague, J. R., & Todd, A. W. (2006). Positive behavior support. In M. E. Snell & F. Brown (Eds.), *Instruction of students with severe disabilities* (5th ed., pp. 207–244). Upper Saddle River, NJ: Merrill Publishing.

Horner, R. H., & Carr, E. G. (1997). Behavioral supports of students with severe disabilities: Functional assessment and comprehensive intervention. *Journal of Special Education, 31*(1), 84–104.

Individuals With Disabilities Education Improvement Act of 2004 (IDEIA). Public Law No. 108–446; 20 U.S.C. & 1400 et seq. (§611–614).

Institute of Medicine. (1991). *Disability in America: Towards a national agenda for prevention.* Washington, DC: National Academy Press.

Institute of Medicine. (2007). *The future of disability in America.* Washington, DC: National Academies Press.

Isaacs, B. J., Brown, I., Brown, R. I., Baum, N., Meyerscough, T., Neikrug, S., et al. (2007). The international family quality of life project: Goals and description of a survey tool. *Journal of Policy and Practice in Intellectual Disabilities, 4,* 177–185.

Jacobson, J. W., & Mulick, J. A. (2006). Ten years later: Two AAMR tales of a condition. In H. N. Switzky & S. Greenspan (Eds.), *What is mental retardation: Ideas for an evolving disability in the 21st century* (pp. 187–196). Washington, DC: American Association on Mental Retardation.

Janney, R. E., & Snell, M. E. (2004). *Practices for inclusive schools: Modifying schoolwork* (2nd ed.). Baltimore: Brookes.

Jones, K. L. (Ed.). (2005). *Smith's recognizable patterns of human malformation.* Philadelphia: Elsevier Saunders.

Kahn, R. L., & Juster, F. T. (2002). Well-being: Concepts and measures. *Journal of Social Issues, 58,* 627–644.

Kamphaus, R. W. (1987). Defining the construct of adaptive behavior by the Vineland Adaptive Behavior Scales. *Journal of School Psychology, 25,* 97–100.

Kanaya, T., Scullin, M. H., & Ceci, S. J. (2003). The Flynn effect and U.S. Policies: The impact of rising IQ scores on American society via mental retardation diagnoses. *American Psychologist, 58*(6), 778–790.

Kaufman, A. S. (1994). Practice effects. In R. J. Sternberg (Ed.), *Encyclopedia of human intelligence* (Vol. 2, pp. 828–833). New York: MacMillan.

Keith, K. D., & Bonham, G. S. (2005). The use of quality of life data at the organization and systems level. *Journal of Intellectual Disability Research, 49,* 799–805.

Khemka, I., & Hickson, L. (2006). The role of motivation in the decision making of adolescents with mental retardation. *International Review of Research in Mental Retardation, 31,* 73–115.

Kirchner, N., & Moseley, C. (2007). *Money follows the person: Population, functional, and quality indicators for people with developmental disabilities.* Alexandria: National Association of State Directors of Developmental Disabilities Services.

Krahn, G. L., & Drum, C. E. (2007). Translating policy principles into practice to improve health care access for adults with intellectual disabilities: A research review of the past decade. *Mental Retardation and Developmental Disabilities Research Review, 13*(2), 160–168.

Krahn, G. L., Putnam, M., Drum, C. E., & Powers, L. (2006). Disabilities and health: Toward a national agenda for research. *Journal of Disability Policy Studies, 17*(1), 18–27.

Lakin, K. C., & Stancliffe, R. J. (2005). Expenditures and outcomes: Directions in financing, policy and research. In R. Stancliffe & K. C. Lakin (Eds.), *Costs and outcomes of community services for people with intellectual disabilities* (pp. 313–337). Baltimore: Brookes.

Larson, S. A., Lakin, K. C., & Bruininks, R. H. (1998). *Staff recruitment and retention: Study results and intervention strategies.* Washington, DC: American Association on Mental Retardation.

Lewis, D. R., & Johnson, D. R. (2005). Costs of family care for individuals with developmental disabilities. In R. J. Stancliffe & K. C. Lakin (Eds.), *Costs and outcomes of community services for people with intellectual disabilities* (pp. 63–89). Baltimore: Brookes.

Lord, J., & Hutchison, P. (2003). Individualized support and funding: Building blocks for capacity building and inclusion. *Disability & Society, 18,* 71–86.

Lowe, K., Allen, D., Jones, E., Brophy, S., Moore, K., & Jones, W. (2007). Challenging behaviours: Prevalence and topographies. *Journal of Intellectual Disability Research, 51,* 625–636.

Luckasson, R., Borthwick-Duffy, S., Buntinx, W. H. E., Coulter, D. L., Craig, E. M., Reeve, A., et al. (2002). *Mental retardation: Definition, classification, and systems of supports* (10th ed.). Washington, DC: American Association on Mental Retardation.

Luckasson, R., Coulter, D. L., Polloway, E. A., Reiss, S., Schalock, R. L., Snell, M. E., et al. (1992). *Mental retardation: Definition, classification, and systems of supports* (9th ed.). Washington, DC: American Association on Mental Retardation.

Luckasson, R., & Reeve, A. (2001). Naming, defining, and classifying in mental retardation. *Mental Retardation, 39,* 47–52.

Luckasson, R., & Walker-Hirsch, L. (2007). Consent to sexual activity: Legal and clinical considerations. In L. Walker-Hirsch (Ed.), *The facts of life and more: Sexuality and intimacy for people with intellectual disability* (pp. 179–192). Baltimore: Brookes.

Lukens, J., & Hurrell, M. (1996). A comparison of the Stanford Binet IV and the WISC-III with mildly retarded children. *Psychology in the Schools, 33*, 24–27.

Lynch, E. W., & Hanson, M. J. (1992). *Developing cross-cultural competence: A guide for working with young children and their families.* Baltimore: Brookes.

Mackenbach, J. P., Stirbu, I., Roskam, A. R., Schapp, M. M., Menvielle, G., & Kunst, A. E. (2008). Socioeconomic inequalities in health in 22 European countries. *The New England Journal of Medicine, 358*, 2468–2481.

MacMillan, D. L., Siperstein, G. N., & Gresham, F. M. (1996). A challenge to the viability of mild mental retardation as a diagnostic category. *Exceptional Children, 62*, 356–371.

Maister, D. H. (1997). *True professionalism: The courage to care about your people, your clients, and your career.* New York: Free Press.

Mandal, R. L., LeVelle, J., & Wilson, D. (2006). Community support teams: A collaborative home-based support model. In J. Holderegger & A. R. Poindexter (Eds.), *Providing health care for individuals with intellectual disability and mental health conditions in rural settings: Problems, practice and progress* (pp. 51–64). Kingston, ON: National Association for the Dually Diagnosed.

Mank, D. (2007). Employment. In S. L. Odom, R. H. Horner, M. E. Snell, & J. Blacher (Eds.), *Handbook of developmental disabilities* (pp. 390–409). New York: Guilford Press.

McGrew, K. S., Bruininks, R. H., & Johnson, D. R. (1996). Confirmatory factor analytic investigation of Greenspan's model of personal competence. *American Journal on Mental Retardation, 100*, 533–545.

McLeskey, J., Tyler, N., & Flippin, S. S. (2004). The supply of and demand for special education teachers: A review of research regarding the nature of the chronic shortage of special education teachers. *Journal of Special Education, 38*, 5–21.

Meacham, F. R., Kline, M. M., Stovall, J. A., & Sands, D. I. (1987). Adaptive behavior and low incidence handicaps: Hearing and visual impairments. Special Issue: Adaptive behavior. *Journal of Special Education, 21*, 183–196.

Meijer, M. M., Carpenter, S., & Scholte, F. A. (2004). European manifesto on basic standards of health care for people with intellectual disabilities. *Journal of Policy and Practice in Intellectual Disability, 1*, 10–15.

Mercer, J. (1973). *Labeling the mentally retarded: Clinical and social systems perspectives in ID.* Berkeley: University of California Press.

Merrick, J., Merrick, E., Lunsky, Y., & Kandel, I. (2006). A review of suicidality in persons with intellectual disability. *Israel Journal of Psychiatry and Related Sciences*, *43*, 258–264.

Mills v. District of Columbia Board of Education, 348 F. Supp. 866 (D.D.C. 1972).

Moeschler, J. B., & Shevell, M. (2006). Clinical genetic evaluation of the child with mental retardation or developmental delays. *Pediatrics*, *117*, 2304–2316.

Montreal Declaration. (2004). *Montreal declaration on intellectual disability*. Montreal, Canada: PAHO/WHO Conference.

Myrbakk, E., & von Tetzchner, S. (2008). Screening individuals with intellectual disability for psychiatric disorders: Comparison of four measures. *American Journal on Mental Retardation*, *113*, 54–70.

Naglieri, J., & Das, J. (1997). *Cognitive assessment system: Interpretive handbook*. Itasca, IL: Riverside.

National Center for Health Statistics. (2008). *About the international classification of diseases, tenth revision, clinical modification (ICD-10-CM)*. Available at http://www .cdc.gov/nchs/about/otheract/icd9/abticd10.htm

National Core Indicators. (2003). *National core indicators: 5 years of performance measurement*. Alexandria, VA: National Association on State Directors of Developmental Disabilities Services (NASDDDS) and Human Services Research Institute (HSRI).

National Council on Disability and Social Security Administration. (2000). *Transition and post-school outcomes for youth with disabilities: Closing the gaps to post-secondary education and employment*. Washington, DC: Social Security Administration.

National Research Council. (2002). *Community and quality of life: Data needs for informed decision making*. Washington, DC: National Academy Press.

National Research Council, Committee on Disability Determination for Mental Retardation. (2002). In D. J. Reschly, T. G. Meters, & C.R. Hartel (Eds.), *Mental retardation: Determining eligibility for Social Security benefits*. Washington, DC: National Academy Press.

Neisser, U. (1976). General, academic, and artificial intelligence. In L. B. Resnick (Ed.), *The nature of intelligence* (pp. 135–144). Hillsdale, NJ: Erlbaum.

Neisser, U., Boodo, G., Bouchard, T., Boykin, A., Brody, N., Ceci, S., et al. (1996). Intelligence: Knowns and unknowns. *American Psychologist*, *51*, 77–101.

Nelson, E. C., Batalden, P. B., & Godfrey, M. M. (Eds.). (2007). *Quality by design. A clinical microsystems approach*. New York: Wiley.

Nelson, W., & Dacey, C. (1999). Validity of the Stanford-Binet Intelligence Scale–IV: Its use in young adults with mental retardation. *Mental Retardation*, *37*, 319–325.

Nettelbeck, T., & Wilson, C. (2001). Criminal victimization of persons with mental retardation: The influence of interpersonal competence on risk. *International Review of Research in Mental Retardation, 24,* 137–169.

Nihira, K. (1999). Adaptive behavior: A historical overview (pp 7–14). In R. L. Schalock (Ed.), *Adaptive behavior and its measurement: Implications for the field of mental retardation.* Washington, DC: American Association on Mental Retardation.

Nihira, K., Leland, H., & Lambert, N. (1993). *Adaptive behavior scale–Residential and community* (2nd ed.). Austin, TX: Pro-Ed.

Nirje, B. (1969). The normalization principle and its human management implications. In R. Kugel & W. Wolfensberger (Eds.), *Changing patterns in residential services for the mentally retarded* (pp. 181–195). Washington, DC: President's Committee on Mental Retardation.

Nisbett, R. E. (Ed.). (1993). *Rules for reasoning.* Hillsdale, NJ: Erlbaum.

Noordegraaf, M. (2007). From "pure" to "hybrid" professionalism: Present-day professionalism in ambiguous public domains. *Administration & Society, 39,* 761–784.

Norman, G. (2005). Research in clinical reasoning: Past history and current trends. *Medical Education, 39,* 418–427.

O'Brien, C. L., & O'Brien, J. (2002). The origins of person-centered planning. In S. Holburn & P. Vietze (Eds.), *Person-centered planning: Research, practice, and future directions* (pp. 3–27). Baltimore: Brookes.

Office of the Surgeon General. (2002). *Closing the gap: A national blueprint to improve the health of persons with mental retardation.* Washington, DC: Author.

Oliver, M. (1996). *Understanding disability from theory to practice.* Basingstoke Hampshire, UK: Palgrave Macmillan.

Olmstead v. L. C., 527 U.S. 581, 138 F.3d 893 (1999).

Orkwis, R., & McLane, K. (1998). A curriculum every student can use: Design principles for student access. *ERIC/OSEP Topical Brief.* Reston, VA: Council for Exceptional Children.

Papadakis, M. A., Teherani, A., & Banach, M. A. (2005). Disciplinary action by medical boards and prior behavior in medical schools. *New England Journal of Medicine, 353,* 2673–2682.

Park, J., Hoffman, L., Marquis, J., Turnbull, A. P., Poston, D., Hamman, H., et al. (2003). Toward assessing family outcomes of service delivery: Validation of a family quality of life survey. *Journal of Intellectual Disability Research, 47,* 367–384.

Parish, S., Moss, K., & Richman, E. L. (2008). Perspectives on health care of adults with developmental disabilities. *Intellectual and Developmental Disabilities, 46*, 411–426.

Parker, S., Zuckerman, B., & Augustyn, M. (2005). *Developmental and behavioral pediatrics: A handbook for primary care* (2nd ed.). Philadelphia: Lippincott, Williams & Wilkins.

Patton, J. R., & Keyes, D. (2006). Death penalty issues following *Atkins. Exceptionality, 14*, 237–255.

Pennhurst State School and Hospital v. Halderman (Pennhurst II), 465 U.S. 89 (1984).

Pennsylvania Association for Retarded Children v. Commonwealth of Pennsylvania, 344 F. Supp. 1257, 343 F. Supp. 279 (E.D. Pa. 1972).

Perner, D. E., & Porter, G. L. (2008). Creating inclusive schools: Changing roles and strategies. *Best and promising practices in developmental disabilities* (pp. 236–251). Austin, TX: Pro-Ed.

Perry, J., & Felce, D. (2005). Factors associated with outcome in community group homes. *American Journal on Mental Retardation, 110*, 121–135.

Perske, R. (2005). Strange shift in the case of Daryl Atkins. *Mental Retardation, 43*, 454–455.

Perske, R. (2008). False confessions from 53 persons with intellectual disabilities: The list keeps growing. *Intellectual and Developmental Disabilities, 46*, 468–479.

Pollingue, A. B. (1987). Adaptive behavior and low incidence handicaps: Use of adaptive behavior instruments for persons with physical handicaps. *Journal of Special Education, 21*, 117–125.

Polloway, E. A., Lubin, J., Smith, J. D., & Patton, J. R. (in press). Mild mental retardation/ intellectual disabilities: Legacies and trends in concept and practice. *Education and Training in Developmental Disabilities*.

Powers, L., Dinerstein, R., & Holmes, S. (2005). Self-advocacy, self-determination, social freedom, and opportunity. In K. C. Lakin & A. Turnbull (Eds.), *National goals and research for people with intellectual and developmental disabilities* (pp. 257–287). Washington, DC: American Association on Mental Retardation.

Prater, M. A. (2007). *Teaching strategies for students with mild to moderate disabilities*. Boston: Allyn & Bacon.

President's Committee on Mental Retardation. (1969). *The six-hour retarded child*. Washington, DC: Government Printing Office.

President's Committee on Mental Retardation. (1999). *Report to the President: The forgotten generation*. Washington, DC: U.S. Government Printing Office.

President's Committee for People With Intellectual Disabilities. (2004). *A charge we have to keep: A road map to personal and economic freedom for persons with intellectual disabilities in the 21st century*. Washington, DC: U.S. Department of Health and Human Services.

Prewett, P. N., & Matavich, M. A. (1992). Mean-score differences between the WISC–R and the Stanford-Binet intelligence Scale: Fourth Edition. *Diagnostique, 17*, 195–201.

Prouty, R., Alba, K. M., Scott, N. L., & Lakin, K. C. (2008). Trends and milestones: Where people lived while receiving services and supports from state developmental disabilities programs in 2006. *Intellectual and Developmental Disabilities, 46*, 82–85.

Pulcini, J., & Howard, A. M. (1997). Framework for analyzing health care models serving adults with mental retardation and other developmental disabilities. *Mental Retardation, 35*, 209–217.

Putnam, M. (2005). Conceptualizing disability: Developing a framework for political disability identity. *Journal of Disability Policy Studies, 16*, 188–198.

Quereshi, M., & Seitz, R. (1994). Non-equivalence of WPPSI, WPPSI–R, and WISC–R scores. *Current Psychology, 13*, 210–225.

Redermeier, D. A. (2005). The cognitive psychology of missed diagnoses. *Annuals of Internal Medicine, 142*, 115–120.

Reinders, H. (2008). The transformation of human services. *Journal of Intellectual Disability Research, 52*, 564–571.

Repp, A. C., & Horner, R. H. (1999). *Functional analysis of problem behavior: From effective assessment to effective support*. Belmont, CA: Wadsworth.

Reschly, D. J. (1987). Best practices in adaptive behavior. In A. Thomas & J. Grimes (Eds.), *Best practices in school psychology* (pp. 29–42). Washington, DC: National Association of School Psychologists.

Reschly, D. J., Myers, T. G., & Hartel, C. R. (Eds.). (2002). *Mental retardation: Determining eligibility for social security benefits*. Washington, DC: National Academy Press.

Richardson, S. A., & Koller, H. (1996). *Twenty-two years: Causes and consequences of mental retardation*. Cambridge, MA: Harvard University Press.

Rioux, M. H. (1997). Disability: The place of judgment in a world of fact. *Journal of Intellectual Disability Research, 41*, 102–111.

Robertson, J., Emerson, E., Hatton, C., Elliott, J., McIntosh, B., Swift, P., et al. (2006). Longitudinal analysis of the impact and cost of person-centered planning for people with intellectual disabilities in England. *American Journal on Mental Retardation*, *111*, 400–416.

Rousso, H., & Wehmeyer, M. L. (Eds.). (2001). *Double jeopardy: Addressing gender equity in special education*. Albany: State University of New York Press.

Rutter, M. (2008). *Rutter's child and adolescent psychiatry* (5th ed.). Malden, MA: Blackwell.

Sackett, D. (1996). Evidence-based medicine—What it is and what it isn't. Retrieved July 6, 2009, from http://www.cebm.net/ebm_is_isnt.asp

Salamanca Statement. (1994). *Salamanca statement and framework for action in special needs education*. Salamanca, Spain: University of Salamanca, Department of Psychology.

Sattler, J. (1988). *Assessment of children* (3rd ed.). San Diego: Author.

Schalock, R. L. (2001). *Outcome-based evaluation* (2nd ed.). New York: Kluwer Academic/Plenum.

Schalock, R. L., Bonham, G. S., & Verdugo, M. A. (2008). The conceptualization and measurement of quality of life: Implications for program planning and evaluation in the field of intellectual disabilities. *Evaluation and Program Planning, 31*, 181–190.

Schalock, R. L., Buntinx, W., Borthwick-Duffy, S., Luckasson, R., Snell, M., Tassé, M. J., et al. (2007). *User's guide: Mental retardation definition, classification, and systems of supports*. Washington, DC: American Association on Intellectual and Developmental Disabilities.

Schalock, R. L., Gardner, J. F., & Bradley, V. (2007). *Quality of life: Applications for people with intellectual developmental disabilities*. Washington, DC: American Association on Intellectual and Developmental Disabilities.

Schalock, R. L., & Luckasson, R. (2005). *Clinical judgment*. Washington, DC: American Association on Mental Retardation.

Schalock, R. L., Luckasson, R. A., & Shogren, K. A. (with Borthwick-Duffy, S., Bradley, V., Buntinx, W. H. E., et al.). (2007). The renaming of mental retardation: Understanding the change to the term intellectual disability. *Intellectual and Developmental Disabilities, 45*, 116–124.

Schalock, R. L., Thompson, J. R., & Tassé, M. J. (Eds.). (2008). *Resource allocation and the Supports Intensity Scale: Four papers on issues and approaches*. Washington, DC: American Association on Intellectual and Developmental Disabilities. http://www.aaidd.org

Schalock, R. L., Verdugo, M. A., Jenaro, C., Wang, M., Wehmeyer, M. L., Xu, J., et al. (2005). A cross-cultural study of quality of life indicators. *American Journal on Mental Retardation, 110*, 298–311.

Scheerenberger, R. (1983). *A history of mental retardation: A quarter century of progress.* Baltimore: Brookes.

Schroeder, S. R., Gertz, G., & Velazquez, F. (2002). *Final project report: Usage of the term "mental retardation": Language, image and public education.* Lawrence, KS: University of Kansas, Center on Developmental Disabilities.

Scullin, M. S. (2006). Large state-level fluctuations in mental retardation classifications related to introduction of renormed intelligence test. *American Journal of Mental Retardation, 111*, 322–335.

Senge, P. M. (2006). *The fifth discipline: The art and practice of the learning organization* (Rev. ed.). New York: Doubleday.

Shelden, D. L., & Hutchins, M. P. (2008). Personalized curriculum development. In H. P. Parette & G. Peterson-Karlan (Eds.), *Best and promising practices in developmental disabilities* (pp. 521–542). Austin, TX: Pro-Ed.

Shevell, M., Ashwal, S., Donley, D., Flint, J., Gingold, M., Hirtz, D., et al. (2003). Practice parameter: Evaluation of the child with global developmental delay. *Neurology, 60*, 367–380.

Shogren, K. A., Bradley, V. J., Gomez, S. C., Yeager, M. H., Schalock, R. L., Borthwick-Duffy, S., et al. (2009). Public policy and the enhancement of desired outcomes for persons with intellectual disability. *Intellectual and Developmental Disabilities, 47*(4), 307–319.

Shogren, K. A., Wehmeyer, M. L., Buchanan, C. L., & Lopez, S. J. (2006). The application of positive psychology and self-determination to research in intellectual disability: A content analysis of 30 years of literature. *Research and Practice for Persons with Severe Disabilities, 31*, 338–345.

Simeonsson, R. J., Granlund, M., & Bjorck-Akesson, E. (2006). The concept and classification of mental retardation. In H. N. Switzky & S. Greenspan (Eds.), *What is mental retardation? Ideas for an evolving disability in the 21st century* (Rev. and Updated ed., pp. 247–266). Washington DC: American Association on Mental Retardation.

Sirgy, M. J., Michalos, A. C., Ferriss, A. L., Easterlin, R. A., Patrick, D., & Pavot, W. (2006). The quality of life research movement: Past, present, and future. *Social Indicators Research, 76*, 343–466.

Skiba, R. J., Poloni-Staudinger, L., Gallini, S., Simmons, A. B., & Feggins-Azziz, R. (2006). Disparate access: The disproportionality of African-American students with disabilities across educational environments. *Exceptional Children, 72,* 411–424.

Skiba, R. J., Simmons, A. B., Ritter, S., Gibb, A. C., Rausch, M. K., Cuadrado, J., et al. (2008). Achieving equity in special education: History, status, and current challenges. *Exceptional Children, 74,* 264–288.

Slosson, R. (1983). *Slosson Intelligence Test (SIT) and Oral Reading Test (SORT) for children and adults.* East Aurora, NY: Slosson Educational Publications.

Sluyter, G. V. (Ed.). (2000). *Total quality management in mental health and mental retardation.* Washington, DC: American Association on Mental Retardation.

Smith, P. (2007). Have we made any progress? Including students with intellectual disabilities in regular education classrooms. *Intellectual and Developmental Disabilities, 45,* 297–309.

Snell, M. E. (2007). Advances in instruction. In S. L. Odom, R. H. Horner, M. E. Snell, & J. Blacher (Eds.), *Handbook on developmental disabilities* (pp. 249–268). New York: Guilford Press.

Snell, M. E., & Brown, F. (2006). Designing and implementing instructional programs. In M. E. Snell & F. Brown (Eds.), *Instruction of students with severe disabilities* (6th ed., pp. 111–169). Upper Saddle River, NJ: Macmillan/Merrill.

Snell, M. E., & Janney, R. E. (2005). *Practices for inclusive schools: Collaborative teaming* (2nd ed.). Baltimore: Brookes.

Snell, M. E., & Luckasson, R. A. (with Borthwick-Duffy, S., Bradley, V., Buntinx, W. H. E., Coulter, D. L., et al. (2009). The characteristics and needs of people with intellectual disability who have higher IQ scores. *Intellectual and Developmental Disabilities, 47*(3), 220–233.

Social Security Administration. (2008). *Code of federal regulations* (Title 20, Parts 400 to 499). Retrieved June 10, 2008, from http://www.ssa.gov/OP–Home/cfr20/cfrdoc .htm

Soukup, J. H., Wehmeyer, M. L., Bashinski, S. M., & Bovaird, J. (2007). Classroom variables and access to the general education curriculum of students with intellectual and developmental disabilities. *Exceptional Children, 74,* 101–120.

Sparrow, S. S., Cicchetti, D. V., & Balla, D. A. (2005). *Vineland Adaptive Behavior Scales* (2nd ed.). Circle Pines, MN: American Guidance Services.

Spearman, C. (1927). *The abilities of man: Their nature and measurements.* New York: Macmillan.

Spitalnik, D. M., & White-Scott, S. (2000). Access to health services. In A. J. Tymchuk, K. C. Lakin, & R. Luckasson (Eds.), *The forgotten generation: The status and challenges of adults with mild cognitive limitations* (pp. 203–220). Baltimore: Brookes.

Stancliffe, R. J., & Lakin, K. C. (2007). Independent living. In S. L. Odom, R. H. Horner, M. E. Snell, & J. Blacher (Eds.), *Handbook of developmental disabilities* (pp. 429–448). New York: Guilford Press.

Stancliffe, R. J., Lakin, K. C., Doljanac, R., Byun, S., Taub, S., & Chiri, G. (2007). Loneliness and living arrangements. *Intellectual and Developmental Disabilities, 45,* 380–390.

Starr, J. M., & Marsden, L. (2008). Characterization of user-defined health status in older adults with intellectual disabilities. *Journal of Intellectual Disability Research, 52,* 483–489.

Sternberg, R. J. (1988). *The triarchic mind: A new theory of human intelligence.* New York: Penguin.

Sternberg, R. J., & Detterman, D. (1986). *What is intelligence? Contemporary viewpoints on its nature and definition.* Norwood, NJ: Ablex.

Stowe, M. J., Turnbull, H. R., & Sublet, C. (2006). The Supreme Court, "our town," and disability policy: Boardrooms and bedrooms, courtrooms and cloakrooms. *Mental Retardation, 44,* 83–99.

Sulewski, J. S., Butterworth, J., & Gilmore, D. (2008). Community-based nonwork supports: Findings from the national survey of day and employment programs for people with developmental disabilities. *Intellectual and Developmental Disabilities, 46,* 456–467.

Summers, J. A., Poston, D. J., Turnbull, A. P., Marquis, J., Hoffman, L., Mannan, H., et al. (2005). Conceptualizing and measuring family quality of life. *Journal of Intellectual Disability Research, 49,* 777–783.

Sundet, J., Barlaug, D., & Torjussen, T. (2004). The end of the Flynn effect? A study of secular trends in mean intelligence test scores of Norwegian conscripts during half a century. *Intelligence, 32,* 349–367.

Swayne, L. E., Duncan, W. J., & Ginter, P. M. (2006). *Strategic management of health care organizations* (5th ed.). Oxford: Blackwell.

Swenson, S. (2008). Neoliberalism and human services: Threat and innovation. *Journal of Intellectual Disability Research, 52,* 626–634.

Swenson, J., & Brock, B. (2007). *Theology, disability and the new genetics.* London: T&T Clark.

Switzky, H. N., & Greenspan, S. (2006a). *What is mental retardation: Ideas for an evolving disability.* Washington, DC: American Association on Mental Retardation.

Switzky, H. N., & Greenspan, S. (2006b). Summary and conclusion: Can so many diverse ideas be integrated? In H. N. Switzky & S. Greenspan (Eds.), *What is mental retardation? Ideas for an evolving disability in the 21st century* (pp. 337–354). Washington, DC: American Association on Mental Retardation.

Taggart, L., McLaughlin, D., Quinn, B., & McFarlane, C. (2007). Listening to people with intellectual disabilities who misuse alcohol and drugs. *Health and Social Care Community, 15*, 360–368.

Tassé, M. J., & Craig, E. M. (1999). Critical issues in the cross-cultural assessment of adaptive behavior. In R. L. Schalock (Ed.), *Adaptive behavior and its measurement: Implications for the field of mental retardation* (pp. 161–184). Washington, DC: American Association on Mental Retardation.

Taylor, R. L., Richards, S. B., & Brady, M. P. (2005). *Mental retardation: Historical perspectives, current practices, and future directions.* Boston: Allyn & Bacon.

Teasdale, T., & Owen, D. (2005). A long-term rise and recent decline in intelligence test performance: The Flynn effect in reverse *Personality and Individual Differences, 39*(4), 837–843.

Thompson, J. R., Bradley, V., Buntinx, W. H. E., Schalock, R. L., Shogren, K. A., Snell, M. E., et al. (2009). Conceptualizing supports and the support needs of people with intellectual disability. *Intellectual and Developmental Disabilities, 47*(2), 135–146.

Thompson, J. R., Bryant, B., Campbell, E. M., Craig, E. M., Hughes, C., Rotholz, D. A., et al. (2004a). *Supports Intensity Scale (SIS).* Washington, DC: American Association on Mental Retardation.

Thompson, J. R., Bryant, B., Campbell, E. M., Craig, E. M., Hughes, C., Rotholz, D. A., et al. (2004b). *The Supports Intensity Scale (SIS): User's manual.* Washington, DC: American Association on Mental Retardation.

Thompson, J. R., Hughes, C., Schalock, R. L., Silverman, W., Tassé, M. J., Bryant. B., et al. (2002). Integrating supports in assessment and planning. *Mental Retardation, 40*, 390–405.

Thompson, J. R., McGrew, K. S., & Bruininks, R. H. (1999). Adaptive and maladaptive behavior: Functional and structural characteristics. In R. L. Schalock (Ed.), *Adaptive behavior and its measurement: Implications for the field of mental retardation* (pp. 15–42). Washington, DC: American Association on Mental Retardation.

Thompson, J. R., & Wehmeyer, M. L. (2008). Historical and legal issues in developmental disabilities. In H. P. Parette & G. R. Peterson-Karlan (Eds.), *Research based practices in developmental disabilities* (2nd ed., pp. 13–42). Austin, TX: Pro-Ed.

Thorndike, R., Hagen, E., & Sattler, J. (1986a). *Stanford-Binet Intelligence Scale* (4th ed.). Chicago: Riverside.

Thorndike, R., Hagen, E., & Sattler, J. (1986b). *Technical manual for Stanford-Binet Intelligence Scale* (4th ed.). Chicago: Riverside.

Tredgold, A. F. (1908). *Mental deficiency.* London: Baillere, Tindell & Fox.

Tredgold, A. F. (1937). *A textbook of mental deficiency.* Baltimore: Woods.

Trent, J. W., Jr. (1994). *Inventing the feeble mind: A history of mental retardation in the United States.* Berkeley: University of California Press.

Thurstone, L. (1938). *Primary mental abilities.* Chicago: University of Chicago Press.

Turnbull, A. P., Brown, I., & Turnbull, H. R. (Eds.). (2004). *Families and people with mental retardation and quality of life: International perspectives.* Washington, DC: American Association on Mental Retardation.

Turnbull, A. P., Turnbull, H. R., Soodak, L. C., & Erwin, E. J. (2006). *Families, professionals and exceptionality: Positive outcomes through partnerships and trust.* Columbus, OH: Merrill/Prentice-Hall.

Turnbull, H. R., Beegle, G., & Stowe, M. J. (2001a). The core concepts of disability policy affecting families who have children with disabilities. *Journal of Disability Policy Studies, 12*(3) 133–143.

Turnbull, H. R., Wilcox, B. L., Stowe, M. J., & Umbarger, G. T. (2001b). Matrix of federal statutes and federal and state court decisions reflecting the core concepts of disability policy. *Journal of Disability Policy Studies, 12*(3), 144–176.

Tymchuk, A. J. (2006). *The health & wellness program: A parenting curriculum for families at risk.* Baltimore: Brookes.

Tymchuk, A. J., Lakin, K. C., & Luckasson, R. (Eds.). (2001). *The forgotten generation: The status and challenges of adults with mild cognitive limitations.* Baltimore: Brookes.

U.S. Department of Education. (2007). *27th annual report to Congress on the implementation of the Individuals With Disabilities Education Act.* Washington, DC: Author.

United Nations. (2006). *Convention on the rights of persons with disability.* Retrieved March 28, 2008 from http://www.un.org/disabilities/convention

United Nations. (2007). *From exclusion to equality: Realizing the rights of persons with disabilities: Handbook for parliamentarians on the convention on the rights of persons with disabilities and its optional protocol.* Geneva: Author.

United Nations Educational, Scientific and Cultural Organization (UNESCO). (1994). *The Salamanca statement and framework for action on special needs education.* Author. Retrieved December 8, 2008 from http://www.unesco.org/education/pdf/ SALAMA_E.PDF

Unwin, G. L., & Deb, S. (2008). Use of medication for the management of behavior problems among adults with intellectual disabilities: A clinician's consensus survey. *American Journal on Mental Retardation, 113,* 19–31.

Van Bilzen, M. A. (2007). *Care for the elderly: An exploration of perceived needs, demands, and service use.* Unpublished doctoral thesis. Maastricht: Maastricht University.

Verdugo, M. A., Arias, B., Gómez, L. E., & Schalock, R. L. (2008). *Escala Gencat: Informe sobre la creació d'una escala multidimensional per avaluar la qualitat de vida de les persones usuàries dels serveis socials a Catalunya.* [GENCAT Scale: Final report about the development of a multidimensional scale for assessing the quality of life of human services users in Catalunya]. Departamento de Acción Social y Ciudadanía, Generalitat de Cataluña. Barcelona, Spain: Author.

Verdugo, M. A., Schalock, R. L., Gomez, L. E., & Arias, B. (2007). Developing multi-dimensional quality of life scales focusing on the context: The GENCAT Scale. *Siglo Cero, 38,* 57–72.

Wagner, M., Newman, L., Cameto, R., Garza, N., & Levine, P. (2005). *After high school: A first look at the postschool experiences of youth with disabilities: A report from the National Longitudinal Transition Study–2* (*NTLS–2*). Menlo Park, CA: SRI International.

Walker-Hirsch, L. (Ed.). (2007). *The facts of life and more: Sexuality and intimacy for people with intellectual disabilities.* Baltimore: Brookes.

Walsh, K. K., & Kastner, T. A. (1999). Quality of health care for people with developmental disabilities: The challenge of managed care. *Mental Retardation, 37,* 1–15.

Wang, M. C., & Walberg, H. J. (1988). Four fallacies of segregationism. *Exceptional Children, 55,* 128–137.

Ward, T., Van De Mark, C. A., & Ryndak, D. L. (2006). Balanced literacy classrooms and embedded instruction for students with severe disabilities: Literacy for all in the age of school reform. In D. M. Browder & F. Spooner (Eds.), *Teaching language arts, math, & science to students with significant cognitive disabilities* (pp. 125–170). Baltimore: Brookes.

Wechsler, D. (1991). *Wechsler Intelligence Scale for Children* (3rd ed.). San Antonio, TX: Psychological Corp.

Wechsler, D. (1997). *Wechsler Adult Intelligence Scale* (3rd ed.). San Antonio, TX: Psychological Corp.

Wechsler, D. (2008). *Wechsler Adult Intelligence Scale* (4th ed.). San Antonio: TX: Pearson.

Wechsler, D., Kaplan, E., Fein, D., Kramer, J., Morris, R., Delis, D., et al. (2004). *WISC-IV integrated and interpretative manual.* San Antonio, TX: Psychological Corp.

Wehmeyer, M. L., Buntinx, W. H. E., Coulter, D. L., Lachapelle, Y., Luckasson, R., Verdugo, M. A., et al. (2008). The intellectual disability construct and its relation to human functioning. *Intellectual and Developmental Disabilities, 46,* 311–318.

Wehmeyer, M. L., Lattin, D., Lapp-Rincker, G., & Agran, M. (2003). Access to the general curriculum of middle-school students with mental retardation: An observational study. *Remedial and Special Education, 24,* 262–272.

Wehmeyer, M. L., & Palmer, S. B. (2003). Adult outcomes for students with cognitive disabilities three years after high school: The impact of self-determination. *Education and Training in Developmental Disabilities, 38,* 131–144.

Wehmeyer, M. L., Sands, D. J., Knowlton, H. E., & Kozleski, E. B. (2002). *Teaching students with mental retardation: Providing access to the general curriculum.* Baltimore: Brookes.

Wehmeyer, M. L., Smith, S. J., Palmer, S. B., Davies, D. K., & Stock, S. (2004). Technology use and people with mental retardation. In L. M. Glidden (Ed.), *International review of research in mental retardation* (Vol. 29, pp. 293–337). San Diego, CA: Academic.

Weiten, W. (2004). *Psychology themes and variations.* Belmont, CA: Wadsworth/ Thompson Learning.

Widdershoven, G. A. M. (2001). Dialogue in evaluation: A hermeneutic perspective. *Evaluation, 7,* 253–263.

Wile, D. (1996). Why doers do. *Performance & Instruction, 35,* 30–35.

Williamson, P., McLeaskey, J., Hoppey, D., & Rentz, T. (2006). Educating students with mental retardation in general education classrooms. *Exceptional Children, 72,* 347–361.

Wolfensberger, W. (1972). *The principle of normalization in human services.* Toronto: National Institute on Mental Retardation.

World Health Organization. (1977). *Manual of the international statistical classification of diseases, injuries, and causes of death* (9th ed., Rev.). Geneva: Author.

World Health Organization. (1993). *International statistical classification of diseases and related health problems* (10th ed.). Geneva: Author.

World Health Organization. (1999). *ICD–10: International statistical classification of diseases and related health problems* (10th ed., Vols. 1–3). Geneva: Author.

World Health Organization. (2001). *International classification of functioning, disability, and health (ICF)*. Geneva: Author.

World Health Organization. (2008). *Revision of the international classification of diseases (ICD)*. Available at http://www.who.int/classifications/icd/ICDRevision/en/index.html

World Health Organization Quality of Life Work Group. (1995). The World Health Organization Quality of Life Assessment (WHOQOL): Position paper from the World Health Organization. *Social Science Medicine, 41*, 1403–1409.

Wright, D., & Digby, A. (Eds.). (1996). *From idiocy to mental deficiency*. London: Routledge.

Wyatt v. Stickney, 503 F. 2d 1305 (5th Cir. 1974).

Yamaki, K., & Fujiura, G. T. (2002). Employment and income status of adults with developmental disabilities living in the community. *Mental Retardation, 40*, 132–141.

Zaharia, R., & Moseley, C. (2008). *State strategies for determining eligibility and level of care for ICF/MR and waiver program participants*. New Brunswick, NJ: Rutgers University, Center for State Health Policy.

Zeithaml, V. A., Bitner, M. J., & Gremler, D. D. (2006). *Services marketing: Integrating customer focus across the firm*. New York: McGraw-Hill.

INDEX